Ourselves and Computers

Information Systems Series

Series Editor: Professor I. O. Angell

Computer Security Within Organizations
Adrian R. Warman

Developing Information Systems
Concepts, Issues and Practice
Chrisanthi Avgerou and Tony Cornford

Effective Systems Design and Requirements Analysis
The ETHICS Approach
Enid Mumford

Information in Action
Soft Systems Methodology
Lynda Davies and Paul Ledington

Information Systems Management
Opportunities and Risks
Ian O. Angell and Steve Smithson

Ourselves and Computers
Difference in Minds and Machines
Aart Bijl

Understanding Information
An Introduction
Jonathan Liebenau and James Backhouse

Ourselves and Computers

Difference in Minds and Machines

Aart Bijl

Edinburgh Computer Aided Architectural Design
Department of Architecture, Unversity of Edinburgh

MACMILLAN

First published 1995 by
MACMILLAN PRESS LTD
Houndmills, Basingstoke, Hampshire RG21 2XS
and London
Companies and representatives
throughout the world

ISBN 0-333-64582-0

A catalogue record for this book is available
from the British Library.

10   9   8   7   6   5   4   3   2   1
04   03   02   01   00   99   98   97   96   95

Printed in Great Britain by
Antony Rowe Ltd, Chippenham, Wiltshire

Contents

Introduction 1

Using computers; Politics of *IT*; Philosophical dimension;
Contents; Readers

1 Pictures of ourselves 8

Information 8
Market ideology 10
Our way of knowing 15
Orthodox system strategies 28
An *IT* Charter 38

2 Knowing in Japan 41

Fresh insights 41
Approaches to logic 42
Togetherness 47
Explanation 58
Corporate behaviour 64

interlude 1: Sound of language 77

3 Space between *Yes* and *No* 80

Where interaction occurs 80
What's in a concept? 82
The 'real-world' assumption 93
Logic-machines 98
Artificial intelligence 107

interlude 2: Conversation among engineers 116

4 Showing yourself 124

Sharing knowledge 124
Feeling and knowing 125
Knowledge and language 131
Truth 143
Using logic 151

interlude 3: Conversation with a painter 158

5   Understanding technology   **166**

    A way forward   166
    Heidegger's everyday practices   167
    Expressionism to Post-Modernism   174
    What we can do   179
    What computers can do   189
    'One-reality' paradigm   195

    interlude 4:   Holding onto our marbles   206

Conclusions   **208**

    Knowledge; Technology; Information processing;
    One reality

References and bibliography   **216**
Index   **220**

Acknowledgements

Grateful acknowledgement is made to the following for permissions to reproduce illustrations: Dresden State Art Collections (for Otto Dix works in Interlude 3); Academic Press (for Brachman figure in Chapters 1 and 3); Mandelbrot (in Ch. 1); Harra (in Ch. 2) — detailed references are included in the text.

    Short text quotations (in accordance with fair dealing) are fully acknowledged in the text.

    All reasonable efforts have been made to avoid infringing the rights of copyright owners; if any infringement has inadvertently occurred the publishers will make amends at the earliest opportunity.

Introduction

- *Using computers*
- *Politics of IT*
- *Philosophical dimension*
- *Contents*
- *Readers*

Using computers

We are about to embark on an exploration, to question the usefulness of computers. Why do we want to do that? After all, computers are already widely used for text processing, for graphics, for administration, for controlling mechanical devices (in cameras, motor cars, aeroplanes and space vehicles...), and for modelling less tangible things (demographic changes, economic forecasts...). So why do we have to question the usefulness of something that is evidently already useful?

The reasons run deep, but can be readily understood by anybody who looks into the ways we function in our world. Much of what we do entails use of artefactual equipment; that is our technological culture. Technology extends our reach, our ability to do things. In any use of mechanical or electronic devices, or tools, we know that we effectively and necessarily are placing responsibility for whatever is done partly in the tools (or tool makers) and partly in the persons who use them; that also is our technological culture.

Human responsibility, in the sense of persons being able to respond to other people and further things, gets to be divided, or specialised. In this context, satisfying and useful tools are those which evidently do things that users can understand, and which users feel do not impede their own interactions with other people.

Computers do not yet fit into this view of satisfying tools, yet they are being vigorously promoted and used, and are influencing new ways people do things. They are being developed as a means for executing unseen and weakly-understood tasks that otherwise occur in the minds of persons (rather than

1

performing visible and well-understood physical tasks). This is why we want to question their usefulness.

If we regard computers as tools, then the often repeated claim that computers are knowledge-based information processors and problem solvers poses some awkward questions. Divisions of responsibility presume demarcations between kinds of knowledge (rather like divisions of physical labour), in order to define an overt formal kind which can be exercised within computers. How can these demarcations be known?

If you (the reader) are engaged in some kind of activity, any kind of business involving other people, and if information relevant to whatever you do is held in widely available computers (in ways prepared by remote persons who are computer-specialists), then what is it that you can offer so as to make your business successful? How can you compete with remotely prepared artificially intelligent knowledge processors?

Whatever it is you do, whatever your everyday practices, you've got to believe some of it comes from somewhere within yourself, informally. This is what gives you a competitive edge among similar selves, a non-exclusive competitiveness which keeps you engaged in a continuously changing world. You have got to believe this in order to maintain your place among other people, and remain sane in yourself. The ways you play out your interactions with other selves then is your self-identity.

In an age of new information technology, how can each of us remain engaged? How does each exercise responsibility in anything he or she shows? Where is the room for individual drive and self-identity. To answer these sorts of questions we have to be willing to open up further questions about things we commonly take for granted; about information, knowledge, and intelligence. We have to re-examine how information is formed, where, informing what, in order to be clear about what knowledge can be, and about what makes our use of knowledge intelligent. If we do this, we can then find ourselves opening up an exciting new world of possibilities.

Politics of IT

Information technology has a political dimension. This technology is about our use of artefacts to deal with matters of the mind, to make us better informed and, consequently, to make our actions more successful. This technology presupposes information systems and the possibility of realising at least parts of these systems in artefacts, where artefacts are things separate and different from ourselves. Making our actions more successful points to the notion of competition for survival locally, nationally, and internationally. So we find information technology being targeted at everyday competitive practices, at business activity.

These associations fit within a 'free-market' political ideology which says (roughly) that all things just happen in an evolutionary survival-of-the-fittest kind of way — the market seen as the automatic regulator of all human affairs. This is a pragmatic ideology which mistrusts the notion that things can be thought out and known beforehand, and mistrusts predictive theories about human behaviour, and about the way new technological developments will fit with human behaviour. In this ideology all people just are busy around each other, each separately motivated by self-interest and contributing unknowingly to collective outcomes. In the market anything goes, provided you can pay, or get somebody else to pay, and the flow of money then becomes the sole measure of human engagement.

This ideology is sceptical of people being motivated to do good, to behave spontaneously for the common good. Mistrust of people leads to the demand that all people be accountable for anything they do. Being accountable here means that all activities must be measurable and validated in terms of movement of money. In this context it is tempting to see all activities as being computable.

Advocates of this ideology want to believe the promises associated with new information technology, and do all they can to ensure that the promises are fulfilled. In education we see knowledge being redefined in computable form, in specialised and disconnected parcels; training people to be useful in predetermined ways. In everyday practices, including business practices, we see an increasing demand for accountability, expecting people to show how their actions are consistent with documented knowledge; avoiding personal liability. Responsibility in terms of people drawing on non-computable ways of knowing in themselves, in response to similar knowing in other people, is discouraged; we have a newly emergent form of heresy.

This ideology, being a political ideology, is of course inconsistent. The market is not equally free to all persons. There are no 'level playing fields'; many individuals and institutions have undue influence and power, and ruthless competition ensures that there will be ever more losers. A harsh interpretation of the free-market ideology says that losers quite properly deserve to be losers, as in the case of the unemployed and underclass; leading to social fragmentation. We then have the interesting question: is it inherent to information technology that it will perpetuate this trend?

Current belief in the importance of new information technology is political. Importance is allied to the notion that this technology can be useful to the purpose of organising people and other resources into a controllable, efficient, and competitive social order. Here I am not suggesting that there is a conspiracy to use *IT* to control us. There is no separately identifiable group of conspirators; those who might see themselves as leading and promoting new developments in *IT* are equally vulnerable to being controlled by it. I am also not suggesting there is something intrinsically wrong in using computers. This technology follows in the path of our long established tradition of making and using tools. What I am suggesting is that the relatively recent development of complex computer-systems marks a shift in technology. This shift gives new force to old questions about our use of technological artefacts.

Philosophical dimension

Information technology also has a philosophical dimension. Philosophy generally is about how we know things, or what we can know, and some philosophers move on to particulars of what is known. The notion that knowledge can be put into the form of computers then implies a certain philosophical position — and adoption of computers as knowledge processors can have the effect of fixing that position.

Much of the writing in the following chapters will appear philosophical, but this is not philosophical in the sense of trying to determine what we can know. Instead, we will be considering just how we can know anything, or what the conditions are which make it possible for us to know and share knowledge. We will consider why it is ourselves who know as we do, and why separate and dissimilar other things know in ways we cannot know, if they know at all. The question here is not what particular differences are, but what the fact of difference does.

Philosophy gains a new and practical urgency from information technology; from the prospect of deep beliefs about knowledge being embedded and fixed in a new and ubiquitous technology. Philosophy can be helpful in clarifying what we ought to expect from *IT*, and why it can or cannot fulfil the many promises we associate with it.

We will be focusing on questions about the nature of knowledge and intelligence, and the ways we show intelligence. We will find ourselves re-examining beliefs associated with science and objective knowledge, and demarcations which keep art and supposed subjective knowledge apart. We will consider what binds these kinds of knowledge together in us; the possibility of aesthetics (as known in art) being effective in science, calling on unexplained knowing and feeling in our kind of being. The following chapters will explore these issues in a non-technical way, relating them to everyday practices. We want to move cautiously towards a positive view of how these issues might be accommodated in new technology.

Delving into these questions, my purpose is not to set out and defend hard positions on what is or is not possible in principle, in future developments of computing — though I admit to a certain scepticism towards promises that get superseded by ever more extravagant promises. This is not a detached scholarly treatise. I am more concerned with what is happening right now, with involved beliefs and expectations associated with present-day computing, and their implications on practical things we do.

What is said in the following chapters is not new. Human wisdom has been around for too long for that kind of newness. What is offered is some old ideas set in the context of a familiar world which is being changed by new technology. Old ideas are persistent in our being, unspoken in our established everyday practices. They have to be re-awakened in us when we are faced with change, to inform ourselves about where we are going.

Contents

This book combines experience with learning. It ranges widely over matters which will be familiar to many readers, calling on common experience. It develops a position on the relationship between information technology and people which may appear unorthodox, but this position is one which can be judged without any precondition of specialised knowledge, and one which may prove important to the question of where we are going.

The chapters which follow are separated by 'interludes': short pieces illustrating different styles of presentation. A strong theme in this book is the distinction I develop between information and expressions, and the similar ways different forms of expression are informative. The interludes are intended to be evocative and entertaining — but they may be ignored by those readers who find them obscure.

Chapter 1 offers a free ranging and easily understood introduction to the issues of *IT* which will be developed later. It touches on current ideological positions, considers the 'mechanics' of knowing in our kind of being, expands on our use of formal equipment, criticises some orthodox approaches to computing, and ends with some pointers on how we ought to engage in new technology. This chapter is presented largely in the form of graphical pictures, for those readers who find ideas expressed just in text difficult to follow. The pictures alone will be sufficient to give some readers a fair insight into the arguments which are set out in subsequent chapters.

Chapter 2 explores the different way of knowing which can be found in Japan. The purpose in doing so is not to establish that Japan offers us a better model for how we ought to know and do things. Instead, experience in Japan is used to show that it is possible to re-examine basic assumptions of orthodox positions on knowledge and information systems, without endangering our effectiveness in industry and commerce. We need to be open to re-examination of deep assumptions, to become clear about information technology.

Chapter 3 examines the role of two valued yes/no classical logic, and explores our understanding of concepts we associate with language and knowledge. It questions the usefulness of the *real-world* assumption (knowledge matching other real things), and the usefulness of artificial knowledge and intelligence exercised in machines; illustrated by examples of current computational strategies. Problems associated with artificial intelligence are illustrated by a practical example of computer aided design.

Chapter 4 focuses on how we show anything from our knowledge. It starts with an illustration from physics, to show how deliberate knowledge draws on spontaneous knowing and feeling (not explained) within ourselves. The entwined nature of knowledge and language is explored, as is formal logic associated with overt formal equipment for realising forms of language expression. The possibility of using logic-machines motivated from informal logic within ourselves is introduced.

Chapter 5 places technology in Heidegger's everyday practices and the Avant-Garde, through to Post-Modernism. Against that background we examine the ways we use forms and formalisms, and the ways we think we expose our minds, our ideas, our knowledge. We consider what computers can be made to do, and the possibility of new computable forms of expression. This chapter concludes with an all-embracing *one-reality* paradigm in which players evolve their own new technology.

New information technology has to be judged in terms of how it enriches person-to-person interaction. This means that the technology must make room for all that goes on in persons, especially the kind of knowing which remains unexplained and which is vital to self-regulating human behaviour. This is not the automatic regulation of market forces but self-regulation which comes spontaneously from collective human interaction in all everyday practices, certainly in industry and commerce, in the sciences and arts, and in leisure activities.

We then find we cannot draw a boundary around information technology and separate it from all else; it is not just for those who are technologically and scientifically literate. The task of shaping this technology calls for participation by all people. This involvement is necessary socially and politically, if we intend to keep society whole.

Readers

This book is written for people who feel themselves being persuaded to use computers, and for students and practitioners in subject-fields where use of computers is already actively promoted; as in business, design, and engineering. It is for readers who feel themselves being persuaded, but who feel uncertain and a little sceptical about what *IT* can do for them.

Put more strongly, and more generally, this book is written for those who see in our present time an intellectual and mercenary madness which is encouraging popular belief in mysterious powers of computers. This is the madness of depersonalised responsibility and automated rationality, which finds political expression in free-market forces. Those who see such madness cannot stay outside it. They need to inform themselves in order to be able to influence remedies from within.

This book also is for people who are engaged in developing *IT*, the makers and programmers of computers, and for those in positions of influence who are promoting this technology. It is for readers who are devising and promoting systems intended for use by other people not specialised in the technology. Following chapters will show how their specialised responsibility is not something detached from, and can accommodate interests shared with, these other people.

I am attempting to bridge across the world of computer-scientists and the world of so called naive users, the world in which computers have to be useful — and will show how these worlds can be seen as one. The concerns of scientists, their formal approaches to abstract issues, are real and are valid. The concerns of other more 'ordinary' people, their informal approaches to complex practical issues, are equally real and valid. We will see how both sides can come together. This book shows that the questions posed by information technology are far too interesting, too involved, and too serious to be left just to technologists.

1   Pictures of ourselves

- *Information*
- *Market ideology*
- *Our way of knowing*
- *Orthodox system strategies*
- *An IT charter*

Information

Our idea of *information* is deeply embedded in our knowledge culture. We commonly associate information with expressions of knowledge. This association is now so close that many people regard information as being in expressions, and operations performed on expressions are equated with knowledge processes. Many believe we now have overt explanations which can be formed into information systems realised in technology. Machines made to perform operations on expressions are regarded as knowledge processors, or intelligent information processors.

By adopting this position new information technology is expected to change the traditional ways people do things. More of what we do will be recast in a form acceptable in machines, taking knowledge and responsibility out of persons. This trend is reaching across all kinds of human activity; in the sciences and arts, industry and commerce, and in people's social engagement. Machine-knowledge, cast in a form unfamiliar to most people and setting boundaries to what they may continue to do (like magic in Mediaeval times), can then have the effect of placing distance between persons.

My purpose in this chapter is to sketch out a radically different idea of *information,* one which is compatible with the ways people at large do things. We will develop an idea (a complex concept) which distinguishes between information (informing knowledge in ourselves), expressions (as things we show), and technology (exploiting possibilities outside ourselves), all motivated by informal equipment-for-knowing in us. We then can include in this idea a place for logic, form and formalisms, and overt formal equipment. Formality

8

(even in the form of computers) needs to be understood and made available to everyone, for it to be used as a means for drawing persons closer together.

The idea of *information* which follows will be familiar among non-technical people, and is familiar among scientists outside their technical specialisations. The task now is to show how this idea fits with new technology. The grounds for this possibility (drawing on work by others, notably [Dreyfus '91, Feynman '92, Putnam '81, Wittgenstein '53, '21]) will be developed in later chapters.

Information, knowledge, and responsibility are concepts we employ in our everyday social contexts, and in our politics. We ought to be clear about what we can mean by our use of them, if we intend them to be exercised by things other than ourselves. We want to be clear about what new information technology must be in order to satisfy us.

This chapter concludes with a 'Charter' for new information technology; a kind of freedom charter. That quite properly is partly political, resting on arguments which are partly philosophical and partly technical. The motivation for this charter comes from belief in our ability to know what we are doing to ourselves (a kind of intelligence), and belief in our ability to choose a future in which we will continue to exist. We can work to avoid a future in which human participation becomes redundant.

The arguments which lead up to this charter are presented in the form of evocative pictures, not continuous and not coherent (lots of 'empty space'). Some of the arguments might seem extreme, excluding moderate 'middle ways'. In such cases middle ways are rejected in order to avoid their being used to mask the ascendancy of some opposite extreme. There is a sense in which we are engaged in a battle to preserve all people's individual and collective involvement in human intelligence.

Intelligence here is not something special, not reserved just for specially qualified people. Instead, intelligence is manifest in our continuing being, in ordinary practices that touch us in ways not explained. Here we can include abilities exercised in business people outside explained systems, in the course of their day-to-day interactions with other people.

Finally, to round off the introduction to this chapter, it needs to be said that the position outlined for *IT* is not anti-technology; our use of technological artefacts is deeply entrenched in our way of being. This position is also not anti-science; it does not advocate some mysterious alternative. What is at issue is what we think we can do with science and technology when we target them at intellectual abstractions of mind, and intend technology to behave autonomously in place of persons.

THE WAY OF IT

technology aimed at the 'mind'

academic research ... → IT market

user-oriented development ... 'user-friendly' products

'free-market' ideology competition... *taking* making money

more losers... fewer winners

free self-regulating market forces
no other social cohesion
responsibility?   honour?   privatisation?
just uniform acquiescent consumers
prediction?   change?   survival?
mistrust of intellect
suppression of deep questions

Figure 1.1

Market ideology

IT is aimed at the 'workings of the mind', rather than mechanical interventions in material things our minds are about. This is a development heralded by more promises, and threatens to be more intrusive, than past technological revolutions.

Over the past decade or more, research has moved from speculative questions and from pioneering applications [Bijl *et al* '79] to generally marketable 'user-friendly' products; coinciding with the growth of an all pervasive 'free-market' ideology. This ideology now is evident in a politics of disengagement, unemployment, and social fragmentation.

Now market-led research has to satisfy short-term demands. Deep questions are ignored. Practical outcomes touch everybody; makers and users of new information technology, and those who do not see themselves as users. Can we know what we are doing to ourselves, individually and collectively, and what does such knowing entail?

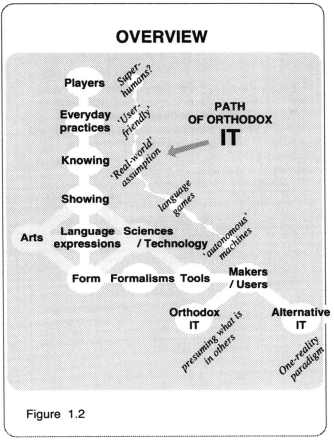

Figure 1.2

We all are familiar with making language expressions (spontaneously or deliberately) to show anything from whatever we know, in the course of our everyday practices. We all employ forms and formalisms and tools, regulated informally from within ourselves, to shape expressions that inform each other. We all do this in much the same way, irrespective of our being:

> artists
> scientists
> technologists
> industrialists
> theologians...

Now the assumptions of *IT* are threatening to suppress our informal self-regulation. New emphasis is being placed on overt knowledge detached from ourselves. Can anyone stand apart from us (a super-human?) and uncover what any of us knows, and separately inform our technology?

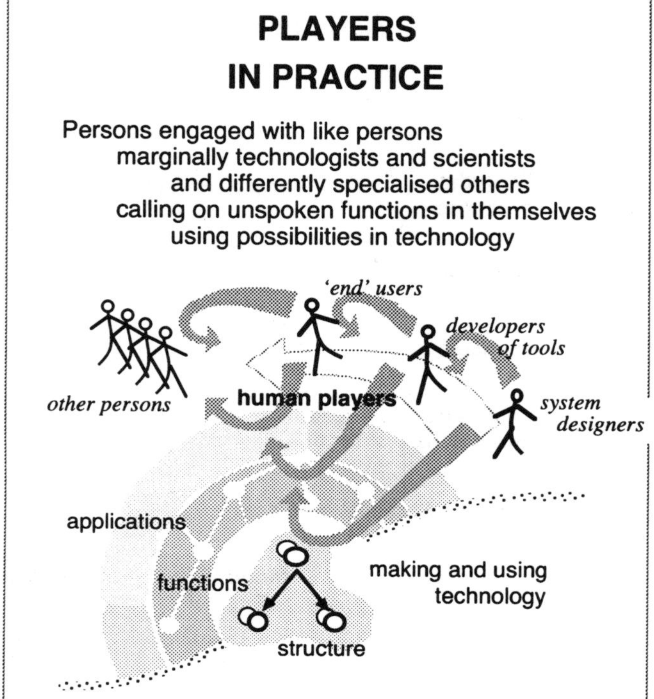
PLAYERS
IN PRACTICE
Persons engaged with like persons
marginally technologists and scientists
and differently specialised others
calling on unspoken functions in themselves
using possibilities in technology
'end' users
developers
of tools
other persons
human players
system
designers
applications
functions
making and using
technology
structure

Figure 1.3

The word 'new' linked to *IT* points to the fact that we already have a long tradition in information technology. This includes all artefacts we use to make marks that serve as expressions we associate with information, and artefacts which execute operations on expressions. Examples are pencil and paper, typewriters, and mechanical calculators. In this tradition we include formality, embracing forms of expression and formal methods for making and modifying instances.

In the early days when few were 'in the know', making new technology engaged all kinds of players in interaction [Bijl '89]. They were in touch with each other informally, beyond explanation. Collectively they devised forms they found useful, without semblance to other things, and employed formal methods without believing the methods could know what they were about.

This practice could work only as long as the players remained in touch, all similarly engaged in whatever they were doing.

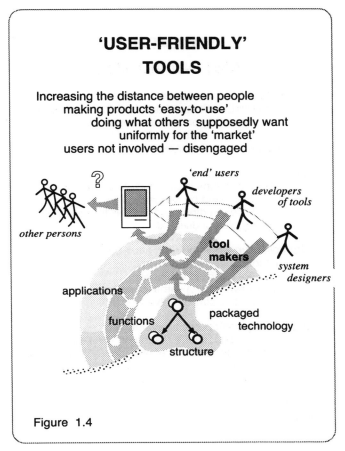

**'USER-FRIENDLY'
TOOLS**

Increasing the distance between people
making products 'easy-to-use'
doing what others supposedly want
uniformly for the 'market'
users not involved — disengaged

Figure 1.4

Now we have market 'products' targeted at distant consumers. We assume these products can capture, process, and communicate information as known in persons. Information (formed inwardly) is equated with expressions (shown outwardly), and expressions can be represented in computers. Overt formal methods then can be made to represent human knowledge. People being in touch informally, outside their various specialisations, becomes redundant.

These moves are required by the *IT* market. Products are necessary in the form of 'user-friendly' computers already programmed to perform tasks that users will find useful; with programmers separately anticipating what users will want. Market products must enable users to get what they want without users having to be computer-literate.

What kind of anticipation is entailed here, and what influence do we want market-leaders to exert on the practices of other people?

SIMILARITY
AND INDIVIDUALS

Each of us the same kind of 'thing'
    with similar structural and functional coherence
        operating on similar sensations
            for similar or different other things
    experiencing the same reality

Each similar but not the same
    small variations in structure and functionality
        exercised on sensations
            for each other and further different things
    making each individual

Our collective whole being makes possibilities
    not identified by reductionist elements
        not needing explanation
    but known (felt...) within ourselves
        across similar selves — 'us'

Individuality contributes to evolution of 'us'
        specialisations resting on similarity
    shown in variously specialised everyday practices
        joined in continuity of practices
    constituting our kind of 'being-in-the-world'

these notions found in East and West

Figure 1.5

In our current development of 'user-friendly' technology, can we be missing the point? — blind to the obvious? ...as Heidegger might say [Dreyfus '91].

The obvious here is that we all are similar beings, that much of what each of us does is much the same, and that this doing includes our knowing [Bijl '90]. In concentrating our attention on loud differences, on individuality and specialisations, we ignore our silent similarity. We forget that making sense of differences relies on this similarity, and without it we would know nothing.

Whenever we say we know anything, we are calling on unspoken similarity, on equipment for knowing that is similar in each of us. Our knowing is in our being, our being is in reality, and so it is we can know about other things. Our knowing can be effective in helping us to stay in being, without our having to know explicitly what we know; and we should not expect to be able to put our knowledge into other things that are not us. Do we really want computers to be knowledge processors?

Our way of knowing

**SELFISHNESS
AND OBJECTIVITY**

All our everyday practices
rest on how we know ourselves
and other things
involving a tension between the hidden 'self'
and appearances 'out there'

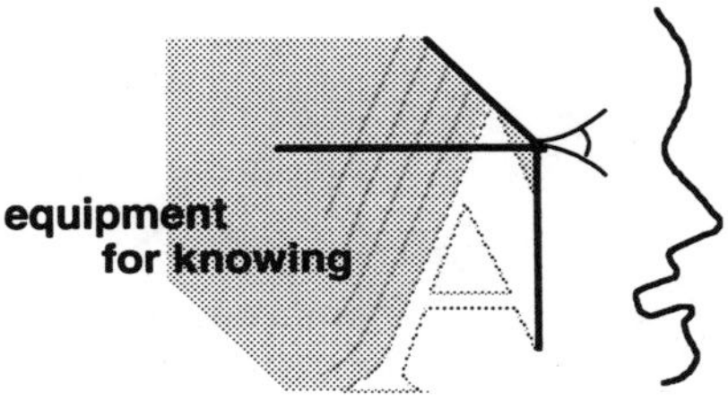

**equipment
for knowing**

about
appearances of other things
'out there'

Figure 1.6

We can think of all things we know and do as resting on notions of how we know ourselves and other things — pointing to a philosophy of 'self' amidst other things. This knowing does not have to grasp what a self actually is, or what other things actually are as things-in-themselves. We can accept that it just is *in our being* that these selves and other things are, that we are able to know *about* them, and that our knowing is effective in our continuing being.

Appearances in us, for other things, become objects in our equipment for knowing. These objects are not the other things, but are things-of-knowledge in us. Similarity across ourselves leads us to presume the same appearances for the same other things, giving us a common basis for an involved kind of objective knowledge.

We have no means outside ourselves to test this assumption; it just is in our being. Our objectivity is rooted in our equipment for knowing.

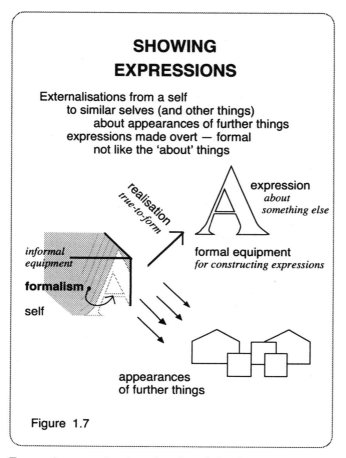

**SHOWING
EXPRESSIONS**

Externalisations from a self
to similar selves (and other things)
about appearances of further things
expressions made overt — formal
not like the 'about' things

realisation
true-to-form

expression
about
something else

informal
equipment

formalism

self

formal equipment
for constructing expressions

appearances
of further things

Figure 1.7

Expressions can be thought of as behaviour shown by a self, motivated by functions hidden within that self, a person. They are realisations in the world apparent to other selves, reaching into their functionality, as in other persons. Generally they are about further things not contained in expressions, but known to interacting selves.

We can think of ourselves possessing formalisms by which we shape expressions from information in us — keeping them true-to-form. For expressions to be expressions they have to be formal (in some overt form, possibly including formal equipment for realising further expressions), all motivated by informal equipment for knowing in us.

Expressions are real things alongside further things that are not expressions. Those further things are already present and may be known in different ways in separate persons — the *about*-things. More precisely, expressions are about whatever any of us knows about the *about*-things.

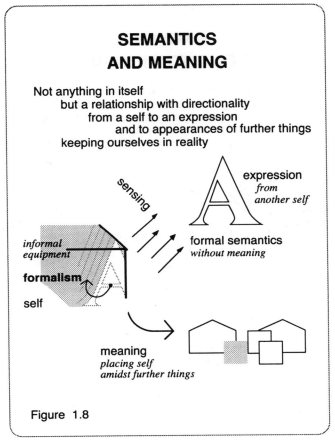

**SEMANTICS
AND MEANING**

Not anything in itself
    but a relationship with directionality
        from a self to an expression
            and to appearances of further things
    keeping ourselves in reality

sensing

expression
*from
another self*

*informal
equipment*

formalism

formal semantics
without meaning

self

meaning
*placing self
amidst further things*

Figure 1.8

Semantics can be thought of as abstractions for expressions, so that these abstractions are acceptable to functions in a recipient, to informal equipment in a self. They have to be acceptable to motivations associated with whatever is already known in a recipient, in order for that self to be able to respond. It then follows that semantics does not have to be anything in itself, not anything outside the selves engaged in interaction.

Formal semantics are those acceptable to functions associated with overt formal equipment for constructing expressions, which rest on formalisms in ourselves. Informal semantics associated with expressions are those which stimulate awareness in ourselves of us being amidst further things; calling on informal equipment beyond formalisms — and we call this 'meaning'. Shared meaning depends on similarity in informal equipment across ourselves, by which we are able to know ourselves as being in a world comprising us, other selves, and further things.

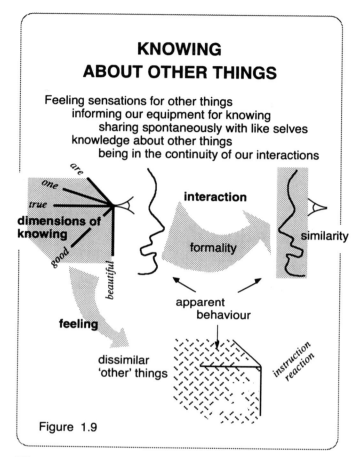

**KNOWING
ABOUT OTHER THINGS**

Feeling sensations for other things
   informing our equipment for knowing
      sharing spontaneously with like selves
   knowledge about other things
      being in the continuity of our interactions

Figure 1.9

We are equipped to feel spontaneously; that is how we are. We have sensations for other things, acceptable to our dimensions of knowing (as in Plato's ideas); that is the way we know. We know informally, building upon experience — anticipating what other things can or will be.

When we know more deliberately, we think of knowledge being expressed formally in some way, and find ourselves engaged in interactions. Knowledge is in the continuity of interactions; that is how we stay in being. Interactions stimulate functions in similar selves and evoke concerted actions in our world.

The formality which appears in interactions does not contain knowledge, nor does it contain the other things our knowledge is about. Formal things, expressions, do not have to contain, carry, or represent anything for them to be effective in reaching into ourselves. Our knowledge is in the continuing engagement of people.

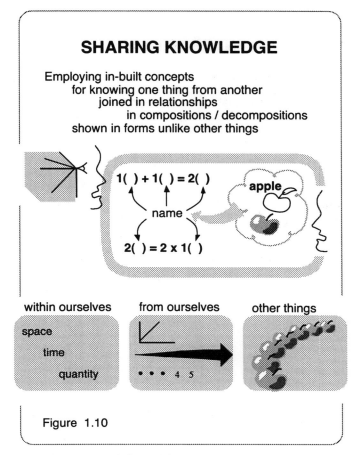

SHARING KNOWLEDGE

Employing in-built concepts
for knowing one thing from another
joined in relationships
in compositions / decompositions
shown in forms unlike other things

1( ) + 1( ) = 2( )

name

apple

2( ) = 2 x 1( )

within ourselves   from ourselves   other things

space
time
quantity

● ● ● 4 5

Figure 1.10

Equipment for knowing includes undefined things we call concepts, to reflect ideas. We have concepts which are persistent in our being, persistent through time. These are linguistic things which shape our expressions about reality, describing knowledge.

Concepts are presumed to be similar in the equipment of like beings, and they are effective in interactions without being explained in expressions. Our expressions appear in forms we interpret into 'data' acceptable in our equipment (our invisible 'mind-muscles', like our visible physical muscles). Their effectiveness is shown in our responsive behaviour.

So we find we share concepts of 'space', and 'time', and 'quantity...', informed by human sensitivities. These shared concepts generate expressions which only we can interpret. They are the basis for shared knowledge about anything we find in experience. This sharing changes, evolves, as we find ourselves in a changing world.

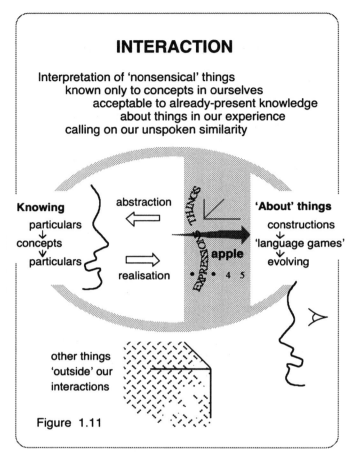

INTERACTION

Interpretation of 'nonsensical' things
known only to concepts in ourselves
acceptable to already-present knowledge
about things in our experience
calling on our unspoken similarity

Knowing   abstraction   **'About' things**
   particulars   constructions
      ↓   ↓
   concepts   'language games'
      ↓   ↓
   particulars   realisation   evolving

   apple
   • 4 5

other things
'outside' our
interactions

Figure 1.11

Effectiveness of language expressions depends on interpretation: taking abstractions which are acceptable to concepts in us, upon which our informal functions-for-knowing can operate, so that we can formulate responses. Expressions call on spontaneous feeling and informal knowing in ourselves.

Expressions occur in our interactions, and interactions can occur only among like beings, like-minded persons. The forms they take are 'nonsensical' (Wittgenstein ['21]), determined by equipment in us; they do not separately represent (stand for... in place of...) other similar selves or different real things. Common recognition of what we are about depends on similar unspoken motivation in each of us.

Different other things which do not share this similarity (such as computers) cannot interact with us. We might instruct such things and they might react, but we cannot interact with them.

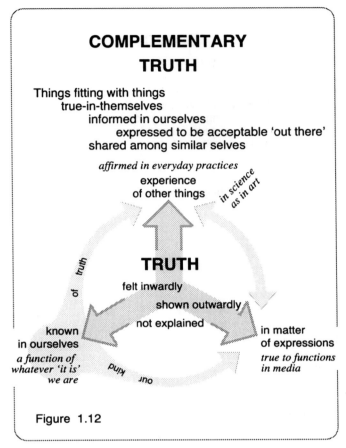

**COMPLEMENTARY
TRUTH**

Things fitting with things
true-in-themselves
    informed in ourselves
        expressed to be acceptable 'out there'
shared among similar selves

affirmed in everyday practices
    experience
    of other things   *in science
                            as in art*

TRUTH

felt inwardly

    shown outwardly

    not explained

known   in matter
in ourselves   of expressions
a function of   *true to functions*
whatever 'it is'   *in media*
we are

Figure 1.12

Now we are seeing human knowledge as being conditioned by senses and functions within us; including concepts as linguistic things by which we take abstractions into, and externalise expressions from, ourselves.

Can we know of anything (any expression) that 'it is' true? And what can we mean by this question?

'It' in reality always remains elusive. We can choose to see truth as a knowing relationship between oneself, or others, and further things found in experience. Truth then points to a concept of things appearing complementary.

Complementariness here refers to something fitting something else, being compatible, without it having to be the same (not matching...). Things-of-knowledge can be compatible with other things, as felt within ourselves. Truth, as far as we can know, then is rooted in us and refers to our being in touch with reality.

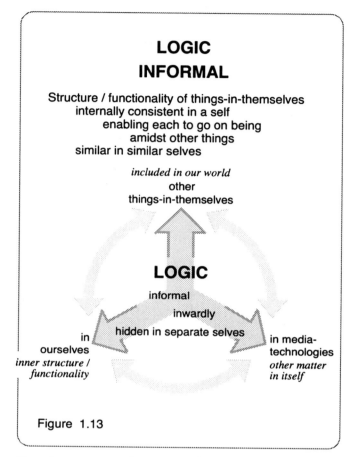

LOGIC

INFORMAL

Structure / functionality of things-in-themselves
internally consistent in a self
enabling each to go on being
amidst other things
similar in similar selves

included in our world
other
things-in-themselves

LOGIC

informal

inwardly

hidden in separate selves

in
ourselves
inner structure /
functionality

in media-
technologies
other matter
in itself

Figure 1.13

Complementary truth supposes involvement of ourselves with other things, dissimilar selves. We can think of all things (even inanimate things) as being able to sense, and having inner structure and functionality by which they show responsive behaviour — and their continuing being points to the presence in them of informal logic.

Our own informal logic is determined by whatever it is we are. This is informal in the sense of not being externalised, and it has to be a self-consistent logic for us to go on being. Out of this logic emerges things we show, including our involvement in media-technologies for realising expressions.

We become involved in the separate and dissimilar informal logic in other things, as they do with us. We come to know them, and know them differently over time, without needing to know what their logic is. Our knowing is not dependent on knowing what other things are.

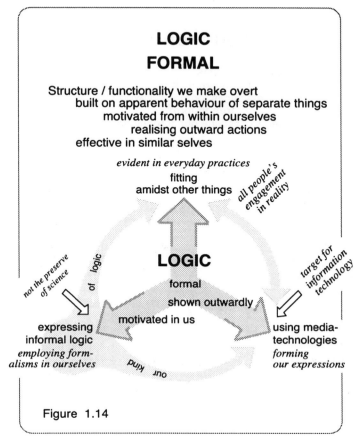

Figure 1.14

Logic that we apply to forms and formal equipment is what we call formal logic. The things to which 'it' applies, and its 'connectives' and 'truth-functions', are implicit in our treatments of expressions. Formal logic is apparent in our treatments of symbolic-constructs, mathematical formulations, and graphical picture-constructions.... It is apparent in the ways we keep instances of them true-to-form (recognisable as expressions), irrespective of what they are about.

In so far as we can realise formal logic, we can make logic-machines that do things which we judge to be useful — superimposing our logic on different unseen logic, or on functions implied by apparent behaviour of other things. In this way we respect and exploit their inner logic.

Such realised logic, closely allied to forms of expression, can be regarded as superficial. It also is fundamental to our ability to express ourselves, to interact, to be us.

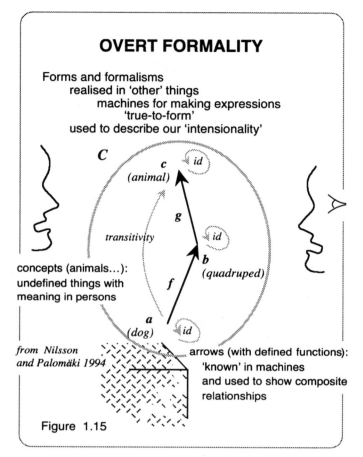

OVERT FORMALITY

Forms and formalisms
   realised in 'other' things
      machines for making expressions
      'true-to-form'
   used to describe our 'intensionality'

C

c
(animal)

id

g

transitivity

id

b
(quadruped)

concepts (animals...):
undefined things with
meaning in persons

f

a
(dog)

id

*from Nilsson
and Palomäki 1994*

arrows (with defined functions):
   'known' in machines
   and used to show composite
   relationships

Figure 1.15

We can externalise certain of our behaviour in formal logic-machines, which we call computers. These machines are used for making and modifying expressions, without their needing to know what our expressions are about. Anything we put to them must be acceptable to already-present functions in them, to make them show behaviour we see as our expressions.

Generally, we have names for concepts we have in mind, and we can put these names to functions in computers, to make them show composite relationships that describe what we intend by our concepts. To do this, functions in computers have to be known and available to users, and be nonsensical, not anticipating what users will wish to express.

Here we have conditions which apply to all information technology. If this were not the case, if formalisms were to be built into machines in a manner not known to users, how could users be responsible for expressions emanating from their use of them?

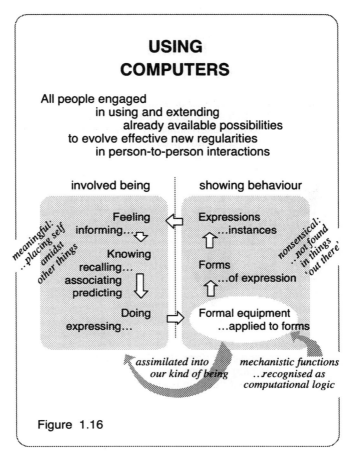

USING COMPUTERS

All people engaged
in using and extending
already available possibilities
to evolve effective new regularities
in person-to-person interactions

involved being | showing behaviour

meaningful: ...placing self amidst other things

Feeling informing...

Knowing recalling... associating predicting

Doing expressing...

Expressions ...instances

Forms ...of expression

Formal equipment ...applied to forms

nonsensical: ...not found in things 'out there'

assimilated into our kind of being

mechanistic functions ...recognised as computational logic

Figure 1.16

In using computers, we have to do as we have always done:

Feeling: taking in experience through our senses.

Knowing: dealing with sensations, establishing whether they complement already-present knowledge, conjecturing how things might be.

Doing: passing out actions to other things in reality.

Using:

Expressions: manifestations of instances of actions.

Forms: regularities found in all kinds of expressions.

Formalisms: operations that keep instances true-to-form.

Being literate:

Assimilating newly available formal equipment into already-present functions-for-knowing, and using this equipment to show expressions from whatever you know, in the course of person-to-person interactions.

FORMS
OF LITERACY

Using forms to express difference
    from within individuals (specialisations)
        to unspoken similarity in like persons
    stimulating already-present knowledge
        evoking concerted actions

$E = mc^2$ *Einstein 1905*

2

*"if a body gives off the energy E in
the form of radiation its mass
diminishes by E/c^2 "*
[c: velocity of light]

"My propositions...
anyone who understands me
eventually recognises them as
nonsensical..."

Wittgenstein 1921

3

Expressions:
    none logically (formally) determined
        all gaining meaning from our knowing
            about being in reality

Figure 1.17

Literacy entails knowing how to shape expressions that we interpret in ourselves. Interpretation here refers to things which do nothing being mapped to things which do something, which become active in the interpreter. These mappings, acceptable to our informal functions for knowing, make expressions part of our being, not explained.

Forms of literacy cannot be separately explained. Evolution of forms comes from use of expressions in our being, engaging all people. This remains true irrespective of overt formal equipment, technology, that is used to instance expressions. Literacy then entails knowing how to get at available functions in technology, and using those functions to realise expressions from yourself.

PICTURING OURSELVES

*Kasimir Malevich
1915
quoted in Duval*

"... the sense of satisfaction I gained through liberation from the object carried me ever further into the desert, to a point where nothing more was authentic except one's sensibility alone.... This square that I had exhibited was not an empty square: it was the sensibility of the absence of any object."

"I recognised that objects and representation had been regarded as the equivalents of sensibility and I saw the fallacy of the world of will and representation."

Figure 1.18

Paintings, just as music and poetry, picture ourselves without saying what 'it' is we are — not representing ourselves and not like other things. Artists make such works apparent by using possibilities in materials and technology, self-motivated and responsive amidst other people. We attach meaning to their works in the way they make us feel good, feel alive in a dynamic world.

To read these works, you have to contribute something from yourself, be involved, already connected.

These conditions hold for any kind of interaction among persons, and any use of technology in the course of interactions; as when formulating some social, political, or business policy, or when striking a business bargain. You cannot reach outside yourself and grab hold of an external arbiter to tell you what must be. Instead, you have to feel yourself already being in interactions; feel yourself being responsive to the practices of people around you.

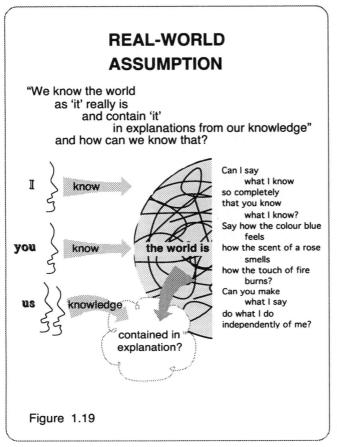

**REAL-WORLD
ASSUMPTION**

"We know the world
      as 'it' really is
            and contain 'it'
                  in explanations from our knowledge"
and how can we know that?

I   know

you   know   the world is

us   knowledge

            contained in
            explanation?

Can I say
      what I know
so completely
that you know
      what I know?
Say how the colour blue
      feels
how the scent of a rose
      smells
how the touch of fire
      burns?
Can you make
      what I say
do what I do
independently of me?

Figure 1.19

Orthodox system strategies

Perhaps the most important assumption of orthodox *IT* is the real-world assumption. This assumption pervades western traditions and influences popular notions about logic and language conveying knowledge.

This assumption is not just that the world is real in some absolute sense, but is about our knowledge being grounded in reality, and our ability to explain knowledge in terms of detached reality (as in [Hayes '79]) — believing our knowledge can be known to correspond to the actuality of other things-in-themselves. It then follows that explanations put into the form of computers can be made to behave like knowledge in persons; and so we get the notion of knowledge processors, and intelligent computers.

This assumption underlies many administrative, business, and technical computer applications, and makes them prescriptive on users' practices. What kind of demarcation is implied here, and how is prescriptiveness apparent?

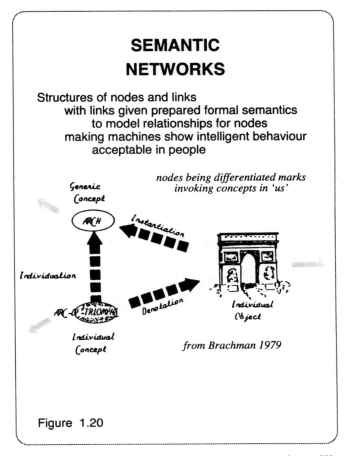

SEMANTIC NETWORKS

Structures of nodes and links
  with links given prepared formal semantics
    to model relationships for nodes
  making machines show intelligent behaviour
    acceptable in people

*nodes being differentiated marks
invoking concepts in 'us'*

Generic Concept

ARCH

Instantiation

Individuation

ARC-DE-TRIOMPHE

Denotation

Individual Object

Individual Concept

from Brachman 1979

Figure 1.20

We think of information structures in us being reflected in our expressions. We say "one thing follows another", suggesting some linear string structure. "Things are composed of parts", suggesting some hierarchical structure. "Things and their parts are derived from other thing and their parts", suggesting some network structure. We think of these structures as devices for representing information. If we can associate semantics with networks in computers, can we make them intelligent in the way they behave with our information?

Networks imply semantics in the functionality (logic) of their links, establishing kinds of associations between nodes. The nodes point to things-of-knowledge indicated by our expressions. This strategy can be said to work independently of the reality of extensional things 'out there', and instead focuses on the reality of intensional objects we have in mind; but how can we know whether computers represent our objects?

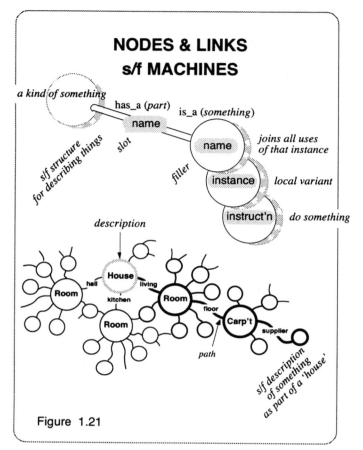

NODES & LINKS
s/f MACHINES

a kind of something

has_a *(part)*

is_a *(something)*

name

s/f structure for describing things

slot

name

joins all uses of that instance

filler

instance

local variant

instruct'n

do something

description

House

hall

living

Room

kitchen

Room

floor

Room

Carp't

supplier

path

s/f description of something as part of a 'house'

Figure 1.21

This is a development following in the tradition of nodes and links (and records and pointers) going back to the early days of computing. Now these networks are composed of 'names' (for any kind of thing) described by 'slots' attached to them, filled by further names or instructions. Instructions may simply say that a description will be found under another name, or may indicate a new instance, or they may call on functions that are to be applied to names, and emerging description hierarchies are interlinked.

Names can be any differentiated things and, potentially, users may employ this strategy to construct things in the form of text, and drawings. However, for slot/filler systems to be useful, it is thought they need to be supplied with already prepared names, and with 'frames' and 'scripts' [Minsky '75] which tell a story, which anticipate the users' world. Framing up a story requires familiarity with system-functionality (logic), which is considered too obscure to be available to users.

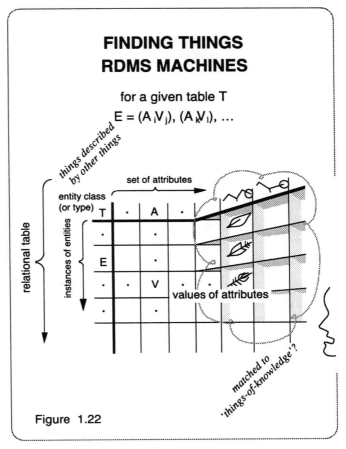

**FINDING THINGS
RDMS MACHINES**

for a given table T

$$E = (A_i V_j), (A_k V_l), \ldots$$

Figure 1.22

The relational view of data [Codd '70] employs a distinction between 'entities' and 'attributes', with 'values' which distinguish an attribute of one thing from the same attribute of another. Entities, attributes and values can be arranged in tabular form, with columns of attribute values, and rows of values for particular entities. A virtue of this strategy is that you can talk about attribute values, and perform operations on relational tables, so as to identify and effect changes to entities without knowing what they are called (or where they are stored within a computer).

To be useful, it is thought that relational database management systems (RDMS) have to be supplied with already-present distinctions that correspond to the reality of a users' world. Relational tables then imply some prior modelling of users' knowledge, with restricted opportunities for adding attributes and values — making relational systems prescriptive on users' practices.

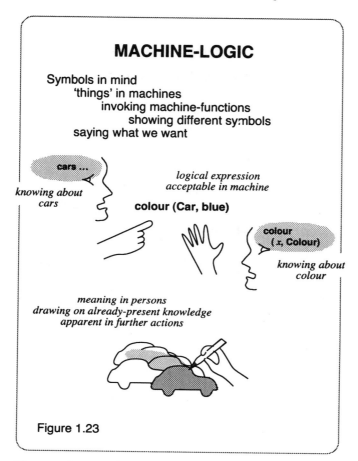

MACHINE-LOGIC

Symbols in mind
   'things' in machines
      invoking machine-functions
         showing different symbols
     saying what we want

cars ...

knowing about cars

logical expression acceptable in machine

colour (Car, blue)

colour (x, Colour)

knowing about colour

*meaning in persons
drawing on already-present knowledge
apparent in further actions*

Figure 1.23

Here we have a development derived from symbolic logic, which employs
'symbols', logical 'connectives' and 'truth-functions' in computers [Kowalski
'79]. This permits symbols to be declared as true, or queried as true, subject to
zero or more conditions referring to already-present symbols. Truth is
determined by resolution (search and match) and inference, conducted
computationally. Predicates can be devised, rather like functions, for
relationships between symbols. Together with quantification (for all, or some),
this constitutes first order logic.

This strategy does not require prepared relational tables or frames (or class
hierarchies in object oriented programming). Instead, users have to think their
way into the logic of the machine. Critics complain of the obscure nature of
this logic, and claim we need higher order or meta logic which equates with
human knowledge — and prepared meta logic then is prescriptive.

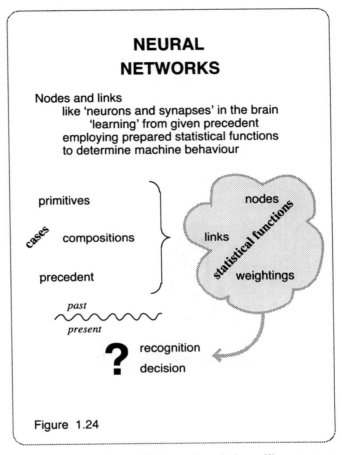

Figure 1.24

This is conceived as networks of nodes and links made to behave like neurones and synapses in the brain [Levine '91]. Predetermined logic is dedicated to functions in nodes, and to procedures for establishing and modifying weights of links. Weightings determine the strength of connections, and changes to weightings change composite functionality. The system then 'learns' by being presented with cases composed of things it can sense, detecting the incidence and closeness of those things.

The intention is to avoid the need to present to a system logically coherent representations of anything that users might have in mind, and, instead, to make a system (an empty brain) that can learn from whatever it is given. However, this model of learning relies solely on statistical analysis functions applied to received cases, with the act of learning separated from any subsequent use of what has been learned; actions being determined by unfamiliar logic hidden from users.

CHAOS

An orientation of an involved observer
　　learning about self amidst other things
　　different from chaos theory
　　　aimed at regularising chaos

Realisations from theory
　　in the form of statistical games
　　　randomness and accidents
　　　　like 'real life'
　　obscuring motivation in our kind of being

*An expression from
where to where?
"Random Peano Curve"
Mandelbrot 1983*

Figure 1.25

In tune with the idea of neural networks, we have chaos theory [Zeeman '77]. This says that in any complex system, small changes in input will lead to large changes in outcomes (the 'butterfly effect'). Chaos theory tries to accommodate indeterminacy and employs statistical probabilities (making room for irregularities in statistical functions). The theory assumes we know what other things are, in a probabilistic rather than a logically determinate manner, and seeks to control (or get rid of) the chaos.

Chaos, in plain language, more usually refers to our inner motivation for states of perception, and these states can become orderly without anything happening in the thing that is perceived; as when we learn about things. Chaos happens when our inner logic fails us, and this can be productive.

Where theory ignores human motivation there seems to be a temptation to play with randomness in place of personal responsibility; the basis for a disengaged form of 'post-rationalism'?

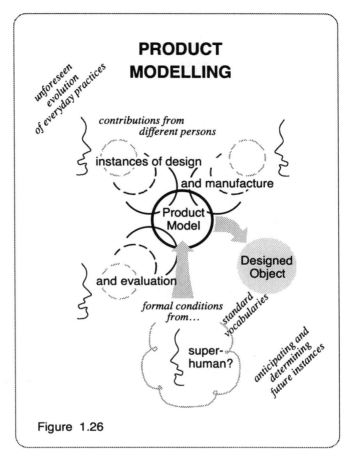

Figure 1.26

This is not so much a computational strategy as a strategy for ensuring that users, designers, show products from their knowledge in computable form. Computers are seen as a product modelling environment which will improve efficiency of human collaboration. The emphasis is on standardisation of user-practices, and the target is a common reference vocabulary, or dictionary, plus relationships between vocabulary terms, in which users have to express their own products [Björk '91].

However, it is not clear how modifications and new terms can be added to a predetermined vocabulary (as in ordinary language), without disrupting access to already stored records of products. Predetermined relationships will have the effect of pre-empting knowledge of yet-to-be designed objects. Claiming that this is acceptable in routine design will not do; the point of any collaboration is that participants should offer unexpected (innovative) contributions.

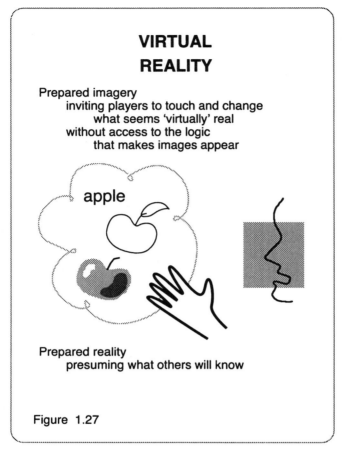

VIRTUAL REALITY

Prepared imagery
    inviting players to touch and change
        what seems 'virtually' real
    without access to the logic
        that makes images appear

apple

Prepared reality
    presuming what others will know

Figure 1.27

Here we have a concept which goes back to the early 1960s when it was first shown that computers can be made to draw. Now there is renewed enthusiasm for producing realistic multi-dimensional images and associated sensations for depicted things. Virtual now is said to indicate something being nearly but not actually real [Rheingold '91, Stone '92]. This prompts the question: what is the thing that is the image virtually like? — like other things 'out there', or things in mind, and is it not real in itself?

Who or what is able to distinguish between virtual and real things? This demarcation has to be known to users. Virtual space is something prepared by someone (a programmer) and then offered as virtually real to someone else (the users), as though the originator of the space is not a party to actions affecting real things. Acceptance of a separate real reality, and acceptance of specialised persons preparing virtual realities for naive users, places most of this work along the orthodox path of prescriptive computer systems.

**REAL
THINGS**

Players making things appear
inviting others to touch and change
what is actually real
each employing their own logic
on things not virtual

after Rietveld 1924

Engaging all that players actually know

Figure 1.28

We already have familiar forms of expression which share some of the features of virtual reality technology. These include the architecture of buildings, a form of expression which we enter into and wrap around ourselves, and which we experience through our various senses; and in time they change in response to people changing, so that buildings also are animated (in slow motion). We use instances to interact with each other, and they are not realistic towards anything else. They are real things in themselves, and reflect reality within persons.

We recognise architecture as a form of expression, but the regularities of this form are not easily isolated and used to confirm the presence of instances. Moreover, we cannot identify regularities with some function, like some calculus in a logical formalism. Yet we are dealing with a form of expression, applying conditions to instances, and recognising outcomes as expressions from within ourselves — without explanation.

IT Charter

By way of a summary of the position suggested in the previous illustrations, the following paragraphs offer some guidelines for information technology. They set out what *IT* has to be in order to be acceptable in persons, ourselves.

Existence

Our knowing about the nature of being:

1. *All things are,* irrespective of whatever we might know about them, including ourselves and other things in our world;
     we know distinct composite and interrelated things, without knowing
     what they are as things-in-themselves separate from ourselves
     — this is in our way of knowing.

2. All things have *structure,* their inner composition, and have consequent *functionality* of being;
     we assume functions in things, and think of ourselves using those
     functions, without knowing what they are as functions-in-themselves
     — this also is in our way of knowing.

3. All things *show behaviour* emanating from inner functions, sensed by ourselves as *appearances* of other things;
     we recognise appearances as indicating the presence of things, and
     use appearances to uncover possibilities of their inner functions
     — this is in our way of doing.

4. We create *our world* out of appearances we can sense for things, uncovering *possibilities* in a larger elusive reality;
     functions in ourselves and behaviour we show, driven by motivation to
     stay in being, determine what we can know — our world is dependent
     on what we are.

People

The context in which *IT* has to work:

5. *All people are similar,* equipped with similar functions for knowing and showing, by which we know each other;
     a silent similarity, giving us a kind of knowing outwith appearances,
     enabling us to talk *with* each other as we cannot do *with* dissimilar
     things.

6. All people are *different,* with functions developed separately in experience, individually *specialised* in knowledge;

specialisations make necessary contributions to our kind of being — all contributions emanate from, and have to be expressed in a form acceptable to, unspoken similarity.

7. All people *inform themselves,* fitting abstractions from our sensations to whatever each already knows;

each similarly motivated, informing our knowledge *about* other things, recognising each other's contributions to our collective existence, our apparent world in reality.

8. All people show *expressions* from what each knows, engaging in *interactions* that shape our world;

each drawing on our own knowledge, exercising our own 'mind-muscles', so as to show individual responsibility in forms of expression that reach into similar selves.

Information Technology
Artefacts we target at abstractions in mind:

9. *The continuing existence of human being* depends on all people continuing to engage in interaction;

with no persons excluded by other persons presuming to know what they know — not building technology to represent what any persons know, in place of them.

10. Information technology (as always) is there to facilitate *realisation of expressions,* without encapsulating knowledge;

engaging all people — with specialists (scientists, technologists...) remaining responsible persons outside technology, interacting with differently specialised persons.

11. Information technology has to be made available just as *possibilities of functions* in artefacts;

made evident by technologists in a form apparent to non-technical persons, so that these other persons can explore usefulness of possibilities in themselves.

12. Technological functions must be *free of anticipations* of anything else their use might be about;

understood in the way we know literacy as making text available for expressing any knowledge — so that new *IT* comes to be known as a useful new form of expression.

Formality

Evolving a new form of expression:

13. New information technology has to become a *formal (overt) logic*
built on available functions in computers;
>   exploiting possibilities of logical connectives and truth-functions
>   (just like nonsensical functions in pencils, typewriters, calculators...),
>   self-consistent in logic-machines.

14. Possibilities of *functions in computers,* initiated by technologists,
must be made apparent to non-technical people;
>   specialists submitting their contributions to differently specialised
>   persons — together evolving an overt logic that they feel reflects
>   functions in their own informal logic.

15. Through use, scientists and artists alike will uncover regularities that
constitute a shared new *form of expression*;
>   offering possibilities for composition, transformation and decom-
>   position, with degrees of cohesion and persistence, independently of
>   anything expressions are about.

16. Computer-functions used to realise instances must remain available
to all *computer-literate people*;
>   non-technical persons must be able and free to 'break the rules',
>   to extend the form, so as to increase effectiveness of expressions
>   in person-to-person interactions.

In our way of knowing we have to distinguish between technological artefacts
(things dissimilar from ourselves), the formal logic we realise in them (to make
them be machines), and our use of them in the course of human interactions.
We can instruct machines to make them react, but we cannot 'talk' *with*
machines in the way we talk among ourselves. However, our use of them can
come to be included in our talking, as a way of making our talking evident
among ourselves. Machines then can come to be known as a form of
expression.

Only by recognising new information technology as a manifestation of a
new form of expression, and a form which must be amenable to all people's
participation in its further evolution (not encapsulating knowledge, not
independently intelligent), can we expect this technology to become widely
accepted among people.

2   Knowing in Japan

- *Fresh insights*
- *Approaches to logic*
- *Togetherness*
- *Explanation*
- *Corporate behaviour*

Fresh insights

Japan shows us a way of seeing ourselves, a different philosophy of thought. This difference runs deep in Japanese culture, and is evident in everyday surface behaviour. It influences all things Japanese people do. This difference is apparent as a greater emphasis on inner human feeling, on aesthetic sensitivities. Consistent with this feeling, tolerance is shown towards chaotic (sometimes, in our eyes, crass) temporal manifestations. Less importance is given to materialisations, externalisations, holding single exclusive truths about the world. Less emphasis is given to formal logic and the notion of separate objective knowledge.

My purpose in recounting experience in Japan is to reflect on how we generally know and do things; seeking fresh insights into ourselves. Often when some of us from the west show interest in the east, we can be criticised for showing a romantic yearning for past cultures (reminiscent of the 1960s), with the implication that we would have to forgo material progress and comforts obtained from western science and technology. Such criticism might be plausible if we were considering some other Asian countries, but not in the case of Japan. Uniquely, Japan has preserved an eastern philosophy of thought and combined it with successful technological and commercial practices.

Japan's preservation of its own eastern philosophy into modern times might be attributed to its past being free from foreign invasion, avoiding influences from western colonialism. The combination of this philosophy with the industriousness of its people might be attributed to its geography: violent extremes of climate dictating rigorous discipline in agriculture, and earthquakes

and volcanoes threatening any notion of solid ground. All this, going back into
history, has engendered a togetherness of its people which still survives today.

While Japan is different, its difference is not absolute. Parallels can be
found in the west, indicating varying degrees of similarity. The difference may
prove fragile. Japan may find itself following in the path of other Asian
countries, later in history and subject to a modern form of intellectual
colonialism. That would be a loss felt by us all.

The way of knowing ourselves which Japan offers us is consistent with
what we already know, but with refreshingly different use of basic beliefs and
assumptions. In trying to focus on this difference I do not wish to imply that the
Japanese way is better. Rather, I want to uncover and expand upon possibilities
that are already present in the west.

In recounting experience my writing will be anecdotal. I choose this form
because it is consistent with the way of knowing and showing personal
involvement, which is common in Japan. This way is felt to be more informal
and informative than the western academic tradition of detached objectivity. To
experience Japan we have to observe without prejudice, emptying our minds of
familiar and noisy dichotomies such as: matters-of-fact versus mysticism;
logic versus aesthetics; individuality versus similarity; innovation versus
evolution; and competition versus shared existence.

In what follows, my use of the terms 'we' and 'us' generally refer to all
people, and where this seems not to be the case they refer to us in the west.
This chapter is written from a western orientation and it offers some personal
observations arising from deep discussions with many people in Japan:
computer scientists, and artists, and others engaged in more ordinary day-to-day
business. However, I cannot claim to be an authority on Japan; for that, my
visits have been too brief. All I can do is try to reveal some of my own insights.

Approaches to logic

Logic is generally regarded as central to our ability to know. Differences in the
ways we in the west and people in Japan view logic provide a useful starting
point for considering just how it can be that people know things.

Logic in Japan

I have already indicated that Japan seems special. Being an island free from
foreign colonialism, and its long period of closure up to modern times (isolated
for more than 200 years, up to 1868), has preserved human understandings and
values from the past which also used to be present in the west (see later quote
from Nitobe, p. 52). These understandings and values have remained alive in

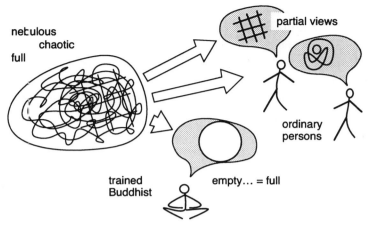

Figure 2.1: *An eastern world*

the everyday consciousness of its people, during Japan's recent and rapid entry into the modern industrial world. This combination of the old and new is special.

My use of the terms, understandings and values, refers to things happening within persons. This refers to our use of inner sensitivities, not externalised, which influence human motivations and actions. Here we are pointing to what many Japanese people call the 'empty space', which can be understood as a very busy space within persons.

Japan's way of knowing the world embraces how we know things, and it transcends formal logic, employing a distinction between our knowing and the actuality of things. It sets no limits on what the world can be, or on our inner functions for knowing. This way of knowing is associated with Buddhism, but it is on a plane above religious practices and accommodates the earthly order of Confucianism.

The Buddhist world was first described to me by Professor Hori, assistant to Professor Ohsuga (my host professor at Tokyo University in 1990). Professor Hori described this world as being nebulous, chaotic, and full, as indicated in Figure 2.1. To a western mind these are vague and difficult terms, and we are inclined to attribute them to woolly thinking or mysticism. However, I came to understand this description as referring simply to a *whole* world extending beyond things that might be captured in any single logical view, and extending in reality beyond human perceptions. It is a whole world which does not presume decomposition into separate things — what we see as separating empty spaces in between are no less significant than what we see as separated things. For a trained Buddhist, philosophical endeavour might be characterised as self-realisation of 'empty... = full'.

The effects of this philosophy on ordinary daily life are interesting. Truth applies within persons, with no externalised formula for representing truth — so all methods for constructing expressions of partial views of the world are equally legitimate. Different views co-exist in the same space and time, without invoking conflict or the urge to resolve differences.

Evidence can be found in social behaviour and politics, in the practice of 'making room', *politeness,* and in the importance of *position* over argument.

Evidence can also be found in religion. There we find an accommodation of very many gods, and the pronouncement of Buddha: "I am nothing... there is all...".

This 'I' translates into suppression of individuality in persons, in the sense that persons do not proclaim their separateness. Instead, as described to me by Professor Murakami, a philosopher of science at Tokyo University, people have a collective identity and an ability to reach consensus without relying on verbal articulation. The Government, the Emperor, and other institutions were described as not so important in governing the country; rather they reflect shared tacit knowledge, shown in behaviour. The effect can be appreciated as a spontaneous form of democracy which is said to be at least as representative as western democracy.

This collective identity is indicated by the relative lack of structure in language expressions. These expressions are not meant to be explicit, ambiguity is accepted as normal, and meaning relies on similarity of context *within* persons — the presumption of similarity (illustrated in Figs 1.5–8). Professor Tanaka of Hokkaido University expressed this well when he described his ambition to me. He wants to work on an approach to language which emphasises use of "very large vocabularies *not based on anything*" — allowing vocabulary terms to be formal entities (with behaviour) which people can use in any way they choose.

As a tentative conclusion which has relevance to the way we think of computing: Japanese philosophy appears to accept no external reference for determining forms of expression. Formal logic is accepted, but without any priority over other constructions (Fig. 2.1). We find, therefore, a softer divide between technically precise knowledge and expressions from human aesthetic sensitivities.

Preservation of old 'empty space' into modern times, busy within persons but not externalised — the invisible 'how' determining 'what' answers — has preserved a philosophy of thought which accepts the world as being whole and chaotic and nebulous. This philosophy accepts inconsistency from persons, in expressions from anything they know; and known things are not in expressions. Coherence comes from unspoken similarity, and effective communication can be loosely structured and evocative. Similarity is effective in all things people do.

Western logic

This Japanese position can now help us reflect upon the way we use logic. We commonly think of logic as dealing with how we can know our world, and it sets conditions on what the world has to be so as to be knowable, as indicated in Figure 2.2. This world has to be subject to orderly decomposition in terms of distinct (discrete) and related entities, and we see the resulting representations as having to be verifiable outside ourselves, objectively. We have the popular belief that logical representations can match things as they really are, and when we think they do we say they are true.

A world conditioned in this way can then be recreated in a computer. This is no accident; we have made computers to be logic-machines.

This line of thought is reflected in our scientific and technological tradition. We seek to externalise our knowledge of the world in the form of a coherent corpus of expressions; the expressions being equated with knowledge. This tradition is evident in our search for singular and exclusive truths, and our endeavours to simplify (reductionism). We do not tolerate contradictory views of the same thing. Difference must be resolved. Resolution is equated with progress.

We can find evidence for this in social behaviour and politics, even among scientists. We value *competition*. Success goes to *winners* who have destroyed their opposition.

We can also find evidence in religion. We have competing views on a single exclusive God: "I am all... there is no other...".

This 'I' translates into our perception of the individuality of persons, free will, and competition. Interaction between persons is based on expectation of difference, with resolution calling on external reference..., and we have the dictum: knowledge is power.

These observations have some bearing on our attitude towards computers. The expectation of difference between individuals, and our common belief in the objective truth of logic, may underlie our use of highly articulate (and what we believe to be explicit) forms of language expression. We think of expressions as conveying knowledge so completely that it does not matter who (or what) they come from. They can be verified by reference to other things

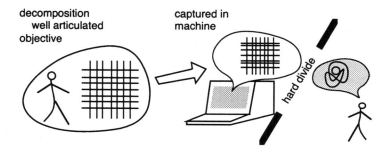

Figure 2.2: *A logical world*

existing objectively, in reality. This provides us with the basis for thinking that computers can be made to use expressions just as well as persons.

Of course this is an extreme picture of ourselves, but its prevalence is evident in the way we give pejorative connotations to words like 'ambiguous' and 'inconsistent'. Too many people (including many computer scientists) appear to hold the view that expressions which are ambiguous cannot be referring to knowledge (as distinct from informal knowing) — the condition of classical two-valued logic. Thus we get a hard divide between those people and the more ordinary and nebulous perceptions of other persons (Fig. 2.2) — this divide cuts off many ordinary activities as being beyond knowledge. This divide is uncomfortable for people engaged in everyday practices, including business practices, when they are asked to justify what they do.

Of course it is generally accepted that we also exhibit behaviour which is not explainable logically, which calls on informal knowing within persons, calling on human aesthetic sensitivities. This is obvious in our arts, and in some fields of design. However, we generally draw a hard line between being logical and reasonable (in work activities), and being informal and unreasonable (for entertainment). The danger we seem to face is that the ascendancy of logic realised in technology is squeezing out our space for exercising aesthetic sensitivities.

We have reason to be apprehensive about the ascendancy of formal logic, especially if this is seen as likely to result in intelligent machines telling people what they can know and do. We ought to welcome any evidence of a different approach to logic, which may open the way to a different understanding of how computers might be used by people at large, in their everyday practices.

Togetherness

The deep difference found in Japan occurs in how we think we know things, the role of explanation, and what sharing means. This difference finds expression in Zen Buddhism as contrasted with our Judaism and Christianity. Put briefly, Zen says we know inwardly, from experience and without explanation. In the west we know by explanation, and tend to mistrust any experience which cannot be subjected to logic. In Japan, Confucianism then adds a worldly order, giving position to persons among persons, and setting out patterns of behaviour — leaving room, or empty space, for inward knowing. I am, of course, simplifying and exaggerating, in order to develop points which might become useful. A sensitive and revealing treatment of this topic is set out by Ben-Dasen ['72].

In the following discussion I will try to show how experience in Japan feeds into the more structured position developed in the following chapters. We start with an example which focuses on use of logic. During my one longer period in Japan, for five months as a visiting professor at Tokyo University in 1990, I received a basic lesson:

I began this visit by writing a short paper outlining my interest and my purpose in seeking discussions with people at other universities. This got absolutely no response; to say my paper was ignored would be misleading, for that would presume it had been seen. I had failed to say who I am and what I have done, failed to reveal my position, so my paper just did not exist. That silence taught me something about the Japanese view of logic: a logically articulated and coherent expression (my piece of writing), if it is detached from anyone you don't know (you have no way of placing yourself in some relationship with that someone), has no meaning.

On my second try, with help from my host Professor Ohsuga, I introduced myself (showed my position), and that prompted cautious responses. When actually visiting the other people at their universities, making direct personal contact and engaging in long conversations, only then did my interest gain recognition, and responses became very fruitful.

In time our conversations focused on this apparent disregard for logic, and I questioned how that can be reconciled with the apparent enthusiasm for logic-machines, growing out of computer technology. How do Japanese people associate knowledge with computers? I put this question to an engineer who is much involved with computer science issues, and her daughter, an architect. To do so, I used the diagram shown in Figure 2.3.

I asked how is knowledge associated with persons, and with outward manifestations from persons, and with machines? How do outcomes get reconciled with aesthetic sensitivities in persons? The answer came strong and

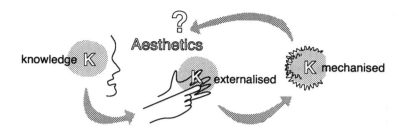

Figure 2.3: *Human knowledge and computers?*

clear from the engineer. She said, pointing to me, that we in the west put great emphasis on externalisation, explanation, and believe we can get it right. If the explanation is correct, then all that logically follows must also be right. So we believe that logic-machines can give us authoritative answers. In Japan, she said, generally the understanding is different. Any externalisation is incomplete; its relationship to anything else within persons, of which it is an expression, is unknown. Then she added that anything which follows from an externalisation, any further outcome, "must also be beautiful". By beautiful she meant that any outcome must touch sensitivities in persons that are not accounted for in the explanation, the kind of sensitivities which may be included under aesthetics. She accepted that knowledge, as we know it in persons, cannot be externalised and cannot be put into computers. We can then regard computers as offering useful mechanisms for doing things, but they must be so designed as to leave room for people's knowledge — a difficult goal.

This 'leaving room' became the topic of a conversation, later, with an artist and her husband (a doctor and a deputy director at the Ministry of Health and Welfare). They discussed the Zen empty space and observed that we, in the west, are always very busy filling this space, exhausting ourselves, with nothing left to enable us to recover our strength. In the Japanese view, the empty space is private to each of us, even as between husband and wife. It is the space for our inner knowledge, not explained, which sustains our well-being among people and other things we sense in the world. For this to result in harmony among people, it rests on a faith in the empty space of each person being related through similarity across all persons, without explanation. Here we have a belief which says that knowledge operating within persons will, collectively, serve the common good. This is a belief which requires no external arbiter, no super-human being.

This 'leaving room' is also found in the west. Many of us recognise that knowledge has an elusive presence, and is not something we can grab hold of (as some quantity of matter), to fill ourselves. We have philosophical positions which see knowledge as insubstantial, not as a commodity which can be passed from person to person. It is only in certain fields, encouraged by entrepreneurial zeal, that we attach the label, knowledge, to externalisations. When we do so we are vague about what the label can mean, but this does not stop some people claiming that computers, as a form of externalised knowledge, can exercise knowledge on behalf of persons. Japan shows us that this is a claim which is questionable.

Recognising this difference in approach to knowledge, we can know the Japanese view of knowledge being within persons, without explicit external reference. We should then be able to appreciate the importance given to human behaviour; to position and *avoiding loss of face,* and, consequently, the practice of politeness. This contrasts with our high regard for objective knowledge, external authority, individual freedom, and consequent social fragmentation. I will now expand on these points.

Similarity

People in Japan practice the notion of similarity (already illustrated in Ch. 1). From a western perspective this often appears to us as Japanese people being and doing the same, showing conformity and suppressing individuality, and inhibiting innovation. We will now explore how this might be viewed more constructively.

In the Japanese tradition, what makes people know each other (within Japan), and share knowledge of just one world, is the similarity within each person. Everyone is the same kind of 'thing', structurally and functionally. Everyone exercises the same senses for acquiring experience, and all have similar functionality by which they absorb experience into knowledge. All are similar beings, so what each knows has to be similar.

This understanding can be shared generally by all people (including those outside Japan) if they open themselves to their inherent similarity. A silent opening up which does not require us to say how we are similar.

Among all people, our senses are apparent in ourselves. These senses make our world, excluding any further reality which might co-exist and be revealed to senses other than ours. Our inner functionality, which operates upon our sensations, turns particulars of what we feel into knowledge of ourselves in our world. We can say our inner functionality is similar, even if we cannot explain it, and, consequently, we share knowledge. We show language expressions from whatever each of us knows, to stimulate knowledge and evoke further responses from each other. We develop linguistic functions differently in different social cultures, so that we make, recognise, and use expressions differently. But however we may differ in our linguistic functions, they rest on a deeper similarity that comes from our being in the same world. Recognition of this similarity provides the basis for people reaching across different cultures.

This understanding of similarity is practised in Japan, and was put to me by Professor Yoshikawa, a senior member of Tokyo University. He suggested it provides the philosophical basis for international collaboration (discussed under 'competition' later, p. 70).

Now we are beginning to assemble a view of similarity which makes it essential to our ordinary existence as social and intelligent beings. This similarity can accommodate the common western view of individuality, but not its extreme form. In the extreme form, we place emphasis on individual difference, tending to discount similarity, and we value competition between individuals as promoting advances in knowledge, technology, and commerce. Faith is placed in a ruthless acceptance of 'survival-of-the-fittest', which tends to discount interdependence between individuals (contradicting even the hard-reductionist scientific view of evolution, from biologists: see p. 92). The effect is to place responsibility for the grand order of all things outside ourselves — as in our reverence for super-human gods — and we give individuals freedom to do whatever they each, separately, think is best for themselves.

This contrasting extreme view of individuality presents us with social and practical problems. It contains a deep contradiction between individual freedom (like something which can be exercised in a vacuum) and external objective or super-human authority, leading to social and moral fragmentation. Given such problems, we ought to be eager to explore where the notion of similarity can take us.

Being together

Consistent with the notion of similarity across individuals, I found a strong feeling among Japanese people of being together. This feeling of togetherness is all embracing in Japanese society; all actions of people appear to be guided by shared interest in survival. Of course there are differences between individual persons, but differences are masked by an overriding acceptance of similarity.

This does not mean that individuality is denied. As I will discuss later (under 'learning...' and 'corporate behaviour'), individual fulfilment is encouraged in education and industry; though eccentricity, as in the west, does present difficulties.

Togetherness is felt in mutual support among all people, fostering a comfortable sense of security. Persons generally feel they are not alone, but part of one collective identity. This feeling is so strong that individuals do not knowingly do harm or take undue advantage of others; that would be like doing harm to yourself. Socially, this feeling is evident within Japan in people's light and easy sense of humour, their enjoyment of informality, and their careful avoidance of situations which might lead to conflict.

Japanese people are exceptionally law abiding: no common vandalism, mugging, robbery; not even tipping. I was told that crime does exist within closed gangs, and newspapers describe corruption among politicians in high positions; but these occurrences appear to be regarded as outside the ordinary experience of people (as though not real), and seem not to undermine the general feeling of togetherness:

> Examples of togetherness abound. Crowds are everywhere, and they always are calm, with people making room for each other. There is little jostling or irritation, and there is rarely any show of anger (but see 'violence' later, p. 56). Public spaces are places where life goes on.
>
> Around people's homes there is no sharp divide between what belongs to them and what does not. People carefully tend flowers planted around trees out in the street, and tend ducks in the river (in Kyoto), as though that all belongs to them, which, in a sense, it does. They have no expectation of their efforts being vandalised.
>
> On one occasion, a visit to Tsukishima, a surviving part of old Tokyo, I sat down in a café tired after much walking and taking photographs. I looked down at my camera and it seemed wrong. It was without its case. I remembered changing a film and had left the case behind on some old oil drums, some streets away. My immediate reaction was to jump up and rush out of the café to retrieve it, but then I told myself this was Japan. I continued to have a leisurely cup of coffee, and then proceeded to where my camera case was, and found it as I had left it.
>
> Quite often I came across things left out, lost and waiting to be retrieved by their owners. Taking something belonging to somebody else, uninvited, in Japan is like stealing from yourself.

These are anecdotal examples of togetherness pointing to something deep in Japanese culture. Many in Japan tend to attribute togetherness to the homogeneity of its people. I found some who dispute this homogeneity, pointing to differences in appearance and behaviour which derive from diverse ethnic roots in the distant past. However, more often I think the reference is to a spiritual homogeneity developed over many centuries.

Perhaps surprisingly, this togetherness does not demand conformity, or adherence to a single ideology. Amongst ordinary people, this is apparent in the way they switch their allegiances between different religions. Shintoism is accepted as good for temporal matters to do with living, Christianity is sometimes favoured for weddings, and Buddhism takes care of eternal verities and the dead. Logic, as discussed earlier, is equally subject to being accepted or not, and inconsistency on matters-of-fact is tolerated.

Togetherness rests on something deeper; perhaps on the Buddhist philosophy of thought, or on what often is just called the Japanese Spirit (reaching back to what was originally a peasant religion, Shintoism). Inazo Nitobe ['05], writing on this Spirit in 1905, was close enough to Japan's long period of closure, to bemoan the changes following its end in 1868:

> "The state built upon the rock of Honour... is fast falling into the hands of quibbling lawyers and gibbering politicians armed with logic-chopping engines of war. (p. 185)

> "The edict [abolishing feudalism], issued five years later [1870], prohibiting the wearing of swords, rang out the old, "the unbought grace of life, the cheap defence of nations, the nurse of manly sentiment and heroic enterprise," it rang in the new age of "sophisters, economists, and calculators." (p. 187, my brackets)

> "The profit-and-loss philosophy of utilitarians and materialists finds favour among logic-choppers with half a soul." (p. 190)

Here we have strong criticism levelled at modern changes in Japan, and the author shows (elsewhere) empathy with parallel histories in the west. His criticism is fundamental and far sighted, against materialism and those who now favour logic-choppers in the form of computers. Yet something of old Japan survives.

Now togetherness is apparent in a relatively unregulated and classless society of moderately well off people. Income differentials are small by comparison with western societies. This classlessness has been described to me as a rather special form of communism, though I think it is perhaps better described as a benign and practical form of anarchy. This is a gentle anarchy founded on the belief that individuals will behave spontaneously for the common good.

Language in Japan

Coming a little closer to our interest in computing, togetherness based on similarity has a strong influence on use of language. Expressions are sparse and relatively unstructured, relying on context to disambiguate utterances; and it took me some time to understand that when Japanese people speak of context they mean *within* persons. Words and their meanings can differ, as can written forms, all relative to each other and depending on context:

> This is illustrated by the use of Japanese *kanji* characters in writing, as *one-to-many* expressions and responses. Commonly an idea can be expressed by several alternative kanjis, and one kanji can have several separate readings.

> In older Japanese society, relationships between persons were so completely understood that expressions did not have to do much, and structure was not important — typically, within a family there was little need to talk, and children were discouraged from asking 'why?'. Such understanding now seems to be weakening as Japan engages more with western cultures.

> Some more western oriented people in Japan now see the lack of explicit and unambiguous structure in kanji expressions as being responsible for holding back Japan's development of western style abstract knowledge.

Following on the older tradition, reference to context in persons still survives, and context remains effective in giving importance to human feelings beyond language expressions. In ordinary usage, it is accepted that expressions on their own cannot be complete in capturing whatever may be in people's minds. They are not expected to be explicit. Expressions serve to invoke and stimulate what persons might already know, assuming similarity in minds. Here we ought to note that similarity does not mean being the same, and ambiguous expressions are effective in evoking unanticipated responses. So evocative language can be effective in stimulating and extending knowledge.

Language coupled with context in this way, becomes strongly associated with behaviour and position of persons. Men, women, and children speak differently (use different vocabularies), as do persons in different social and work positions:

> This association with behaviour was illustrated by my secretary in Tokyo, when she said she could talk with me in English, very politely, in a way she could not if we were talking Japanese. In Japanese she would have to speak the language of a woman and a secretary, and she would not be able to discuss her views on women in society, and her ambitions for herself, without being impolite.

Later, in discussions with others, I found that the reverse of this position also holds. As a foreigner probing matters which touched the personal views of people I was speaking with, our discussions benefited from being in English. If I were able to speak Japanese, imperfectly, I would infringe good behaviour unwittingly, and my listeners would have difficulty in distinguishing between my intentions and mistakes. Given the general and strong desire for conflict avoidance, discussions would cease. Instead, by carefully developing our discussions in English, using the words coming from the people I was speaking with, they were able to translate into Japanese. They could make allowances for my being foreign and so avoid the pitfalls of bad behaviour.

This observation seems to hold for some other foreigners who can speak Japanese fluently, and who complain of difficulty in developing close familiarity with Japanese people. These foreigners can translate the language, but not all the subtle behavioural nuances for all situations in which they might find themselves. Their minds are not sufficiently similar. To overcome this difficulty, one needs time, lots of time, being with Japanese people and absorbing behaviour:

> Here is one fairly typical example of the link between language and behaviour. In a work discussion, the person you are speaking with might suddenly tell you what he or she plans to do that evening, apparently quite out of context. This has to be understood as an invitation to join him or her (perhaps for an evening meal), and you are free to accept or say you are doing something else. The point is that you have not been asked directly and are therefore not in a position where you might refuse. A situation of possible conflict has been avoided. To get to know this, you have to be with Japanese people, with an open mind, and gradually tune your mind to theirs.

We will return to these general observations on use of language in Chapter 4, to consider how they might be compatible with a more western oriented view.

Not losing face

Viewed from outside, a popular stereotyping of the Japanese people is to say they cannot say no. This is associated with conflict avoidance, politeness, and not losing face. We tend to regard all this rather critically, and see it, at best, as a quaint relic of a past culture or, at worst, as plain deviousness. We then regard the Japanese as being not quite up to our standard of worldly wisdom, and failing to match our acceptance of conflict as normal to progress. Once more, there is another more positive way of looking at this.

We need to return to the Japanese way of seeing all responsibility for all things people do as resting within persons and, collectively, resting within all persons. There is no higher authority — no super-human gods responsible for the grand order of all things, and no gods issuing laws or commands to us ordinary mortals. Instead, human morals and ethics are seen as coming from people, and their origins might be traced back to distant ancestors — these ancestors get revered as gods, but not super-human gods. Present-day people are responsible for continuing this inheritance, and acting to sustain and develop it:

> As an example of persons sustaining their inheritance, there is the practice of continually rebuilding Shinto shrines. Old Shintoism was adopted by the ruling class during the Edo period of closure, as an indigenous Japanese religion, and now survives as an expression of the Japanese Spirit.
>
> The Ise shrine, a substantial wooden building, is the most important centre of Shintoism. This shrine is demolished and rebuilt every twenty years. Every time, it is rebuilt just as it was. When you visit it, you are told that you are looking at a shrine which is old, going back 13 centuries. It is the idea of the shrine which you are seeing, and its temporal realisation serves that purpose.
>
> This continual rebuilding serves as affirmation by people today, of the idea born centuries ago, which now is still felt in modern Japan. This idea informs people's responsibility for morals and ethics in all behaviour in society, including industry and commerce.

This notion (or more strongly, this being) of responsibility in persons, individually and collectively, makes people supremely important: human being is sacrosanct. Invalidating a person by loss of face, or collectively invalidating people, becomes an act of blasphemy, just as we in the west would consider blasphemy against our religion. It is blasphemy in the sense of undermining the foundations upon which we build our lives. So loss of face becomes a deeply serious matter, threatening the very foundation of Japanese existence.

Conflict avoidance and politeness then are necessary behaviours aimed at not losing face. This does not mean that there can be no change, no progress. It does, however, set conditions on how changes can be realised, and how they get to be accepted. Conflict has to be managed politely, by silences which are heard and are noticed; as when a full professor and assistant are discussing a topic, and the assistant talks in agreement but goes silent when he or she disagrees. The process of verification and acceptance has to pass through persons, without any external reference serving as arbiter; as when the full professor feels that the assistant's silence points to an objection which is good. I will say more on how this works (under '...disagreement', p. 67), when I discuss corporate behaviour.

The key point to note here is that these behaviours are deeply rooted in the Japanese culture, and they are highly relevant to everything Japanese people do today. They are just as relevant as our western practices which reflect our acceptance of an external authority in the form of a single god, or in the form of absolute logic.

In our case, our acceptance of an external authority can be regarded as reducing responsibility within persons, even trivialising persons. In this view (an exaggerated view), we do good to each other only because the external authority tells us we must do so; and we are selective in our interpretations of what we are told, so we can do good to some and not to others. Evidence of our trivialising persons appears when we see logic as the external authority, and claim we can make logic-machines that tell persons what they must know and do. This theme will be developed in Chapters 3 and 5.

Violence

The contrast between Japan and the west which is emerging here is, of course, deceptive. Conflict avoidance works within Japan, but conflict between Japan and other countries, particularly third world countries, can be harsh. Things go wrong. Japan then finds great difficulty in acknowledging its mistakes, as in the example of its treatment of Koreans early in this century. As I have already indicated, I am not setting up a competition between Japan and the west, nor am I claiming Japan is better. My purpose is just to explore the difference.

Even within Japan violence is present in everyday life, and it generally occurs in the form of fantasy. This is apparent in comic books (read by children and adults) and television and films. The violence which is portrayed in entertainment media is in marked contrast to the polite and distinctly non-violent behaviour generally found in direct personal contact. Perhaps this indicates some kind of 'release mechanism' to compensate for self-control in a densely populated land, or it might point to some deep tension felt between the demands of modern life and the age of honour and chivalry (not so violent) of the not-so-distant past — I just don't know. We can observe, however, that a similar contrast (but not so extreme) is also found in the west, in the way that images of violent killing are so often offered as entertainment.

At a more sophisticated level, violence in Japan is apparent in Sumo wrestling. Here violence is controlled in accordance with old tradition, with honour playing an important part. It is regarded as a form of art, and it serves as entertainment.

Violence with more aggressive intent is found on the occasions of mass demonstrations, as in student riots and farmers' demonstrations against the siting of Narita airport. These show anger, but they seem to pass quickly into history, with polite normality restored. They do not leave a residue of aggression and alienation of the kind which in the west is apparent in continuing listless acts of vandalism:

My closest encounter with this kind of violence occurred one time when I went to Narita to meet my wife off a plane from Europe. I took a train out to the airport, which entailed changing to a bus for the last bit of the journey (in 1986). On leaving the train, I saw a long queue of people disappearing into one end of a tunnel shaped tent, with people reappearing at the other end going onto busses. I joined this queue, and as I moved slowly nearer to the tent I noticed the people were carrying identity cards. It seemed that we were going through some kind of immigration check, to be allowed out to the airport.

In the tent I tried to indicate that I did not have my passport with me, it was in my hotel. The officers doing the checking were alarmed by the presence of a person without papers, and there was no way we could understand each other. They made a phone call. Two large men appeared in what looked like Japanese medieval armour. They had padding all over, beautifully articulated, even down to jointed bits over their fingers, and they carried large wooden staves. These two men interrogated me, without understanding, and then with severe expressions on their faces they proceeded to march me for the distance the bus would have taken me, making no allowance for my obvious discomfort (I have a walking disability).

This continued till we reached the airport police headquarters. There I was interrogated again, and eventually someone phoned my hotel to confirm that I was legal. Then I was let free, and left to find my own way on foot to the air terminal. My wife who had long arrived, was anxious about my not being there. Later, we learned that I had passed through a strict security measure against the threat of a riot.

This was a relatively trivial experience. Some people with long memories of the second world war still identify the Japanese with more violent and inhuman acts against individuals. There were horrific acts done during that war (not only by Japan). What is less widely appreciated is that Japan's entry into the war was strongly opposed by many in Japan, and their criticism of the Emperor's role in the war is still demonstrated every year on Emperor's Day.

It may be true or a misleading simplification to say that once engaged in war, the togetherness of the Japanese people will contribute to its ruthless execution. This can be true, without making the violence of war intrinsic to the Japanese people. Since the war Japan has focused its energies on economic success. It has resisted any kind of military engagement overseas, as evident in its long and agonised deliberations over whether to take part in UN operations.

Explanation

Now we will return to our central theme, to elaborate on an aspect of knowledge which has a strong bearing on how we might view the usefulness of computers. This concerns the question of explanation; the use of language to form externalisations from knowledge within ourselves.

In Japan there is a deep reluctance to enter into explanations, to explore how and why things are or might be. This reluctance is evident in people's unwillingness to express personal preferences, to show their curiosity, and to acknowledge mistakes (yours and theirs).   Strangely, from a western perspective, this reluctance is also evident in the absence of debate in academia. Some of this can be put down to conflict avoidance, as already discussed. However, I think there is more to say. In Japan it seems that explanations can have little or no meaning.

Our notion of explanation presupposes that there are absolutes which can be made tangible, for all to see. Explanations are then supposed to refer to them, even if rather indirectly, as fixed points of reference by which each of us can ascertain the particulars of what we know. Explanations for different things we know have to reveal consistency, and deal with implication, which calls upon the western tradition of formal logic.

In Japan the initial presupposition is not accepted; absolutes might exist, and they might be known to us, but they cannot be contained in explanations so as to establish they are the same for different persons. Explanations which claim to call on absolutes, touch the Zen empty space which is private to persons, and incur the risk of provoking conflict. So, even in situations where things are obviously going wrong, explanations are regarded as adding to conflict.

Explanation implies looking into knowledge and exposing what it contains, with the intention of letting that justify or invalidate some human action. It is this notion which causes difficulties in Japan, and which is considered indiscreet.

Knowledge and explanation

Earlier I noted that formal logic has no special significance in Japan; it does not make certain expressions better than others. Logic might help in the task of constructing expressions, but results have equal status among other apparently non-logical expressions. The purpose of expressions is just to touch and stimulate knowledge within persons. Since knowledge itself cannot be externalised, cannot be seen, expressions touch blindly, and we learn of their effectiveness only by the responses they evoke. The dynamics of expressions, in the course of successive responses between persons, reflect but do not represent and are not the same as knowledge.

This view of expressions being evocative rather than representational preserves an inclusive view of knowledge, including sensitivities and abilities within persons which we have no way of externalising, explaining. It recognises no fixed boundary between such hidden parts of knowledge and other parts which some of us might variously believe are explainable.

This inclusive view of knowledge embraces people's sense of being, reflected in various religious expressions, and embraces people's aesthetic sensitivities, reflected in design and art, and in all or most other practical activities. It also embraces people's rational sensitivities, reflected in science and technology, and rationality is accepted as being subject to aesthetics. A whole sense of being pervades all things people do.

Given this wholeness, expressions cannot be restricted to being just rational, or aesthetic, or dedicated to any other subset of being. Here we come up against the problem of explanation in Japan.

Expressions which are structured according to some formal logic, and which correspond to parts of knowledge which are thought to be verified by the actuality (the reality) of absolutes in the world, objectively, constitute what we call rational explanations. In Japan, this notion of explanation is regarded as unsatisfactory in two ways. First, it is not accepted that there are parts of knowledge which can be isolated and externalised, and still be knowledge. Secondly, whereas knowledge might be about other absolutes, expressions realised from knowledge cannot contain and cannot be verified by absolutes. So the point being made here is simply that logical explanation is never sufficient.

The problem then is that explanations which are claimed to be objective in some detached way unavoidably touch parts of knowledge which are not explained. They touch the empty space associated with persons, incurring the risk of conflict felt within persons. Following from this objection to explanation, we can note the contrast between apparent Japanese reticence and North American enthusiasm (in the 1960s) for 'letting it all hang out'. The latter implies a belief in the possibility of exposing one's inner self, and the beneficial effects of doing so. That belief leads on to the notion that everything within persons is potentially externalisable and knowable in an explainable way, and potentially controllable (American conformity) — and leads to the notion that ultimately all things can be represented in computers.

The Zen empty space can be considered as a kind of being in knowledge which is receptive to experience, including absolutes associated with things found in experience, but is private to persons. It is central to each person's sense of being. We may think of it as similar to the western notion of personal subjectivity, but without the connotations of individual separation and absolute freedom. The empty space takes account of what we are, as like beings in one world; a silent communion.

All this can be accepted as a matter-of-fact view of knowledge, even if we cannot explain the facts. The west then tends to impose its notion of mysticism on this Japanese (and eastern) view, indicating discomfort with things that are not explained. The difference between east and west rests on the acceptance, or not, of the notion of explanation:

To illustrate this difference, here is an account of an incident on one of my visits to Japan. Walking through a park, along the river across from Asakusa, I came to a modest Shinto shrine with a new car parked under it. I found this an odd juxtaposition. The shrine is a realisation from an old peasant religion, and the car a gleaming example from Japan's modern success. Later I was told that it is still common for an owner of a new car to take it to a shrine to have it blessed.

What can this mean? Do people who take cars for granted, together with everything associated with them in our modern age, really think they gain advantage from the blessing of a shrine? It seems they do, and to consider why requires a re-examination of the familiar polarity between things material and spiritual.

We normally think of the car and the technology which goes with it as real. That is real in a material and tangible sense. We then think of the blessing of the shrine as not real in the same sense. It is real in a way we cannot test, in a spiritual sense which demands belief. We normally draw a sharp distinction between these kinds of reality, claiming that the one offers material benefits and the other offers emotional or psychological benefits. We see the former as amenable to explanation, and the latter as not (or not in a logically determinate sense).

In Japan material and spiritual reality are not kept apart, and they are not acted upon independently from each other. Material things are not known objectively in a manner which can be detached from persons. All knowing includes spiritual sensitivities. So knowledge of material things is bound up with unexplained perceptions within persons.

If belief in the blessing of the shrine is felt to fit (or is accepted into) whatever a person knows, there is nothing outside the person (no explanation) to objectively disprove the existence of the blessing.

The role of spiritual sensitivities within persons is openly accepted in ordinary everyday practices in Japan. That role is also evident in the west, but we try to subject it to rational argument, and in our serious work activities we try to suppress it. We try to subject these sensitivities to objective knowledge about our material world, to preserve knowledge itself as something that can be contained in explanations:

> As a more mundane (and practical) illustration of Japanese rejection of explanation, here is another incident. My wife and I visited the Imperial Palace Household Guard, in Kyoto. A senior professor with influence, in the south of Japan, had arranged for us to visit the garden of the Katsura Imperial Villa, on one day's notice. Normally people have to wait weeks for a permit (in 1986). We were collecting our permit the following morning.
>
> They told us there was no permit, and their records showed that our professor had visited the garden the previous day. Clearly this was a mistake. We proceeded to explain that the professor had not visited but had phoned the previous day to arrange our permit. In the usual western way we showed our concern by frowning. They immediately put up their hands to shut off any discussion, and abruptly told us to speak to our professor. There was a phone on the desk, but we were denied permission to use it.
>
> It was a long walk to the nearest public phone, and it was difficult getting past the university's switchboard speaking English. But we got through, and were reassured it would be all right, the professor would phone the Household Guard, and we should return. When we got back they were polite, smiling, and handed us our permit. We had to rush across Kyoto to the Katsura garden, to join the arranged tour for that afternoon; and it was magnificent.

We had received a lesson on the ineffectiveness of explanation, and the importance of position.

Learning without explanation

Education in Japan is sometimes criticised for its emphasis on learning by rote. Learning is done by doing, repeatedly, without explanation. In the west we commend ourselves on our education based on explanation. We use logic to show how one thing follows from another, and we use abstract and formal methodologies to determine what can or will be. This difference rests on different attitudes towards experience, and it also rests on different attitudes as to what is being taught: a whole mind, or just explainable portions of a mind.

In the west we accept experience as necessary to education; experience which we receive by means of our senses, and assimilate into our knowledge. We accept this when we first learn to read and write, and count. We first learn by rote, without explanation. Later we introduce the rules of writing and arithmetic, introducing logic to explain how states in these forms of expression lead to further states, or not. We then proceed to give increasing emphasis to explanations, introducing more sophisticated abstract methodologies, and use explanations to determine the correctness of expressions.

Popular belief in the power of logical explanation causes us to lose sight of the fact that the basic forms used in explanations are not themselves explained, and they do not match other things found in experience. Our belief persists, despite evidence of the many logically coherent but contradictory constructions built upon the same forms of expression, and purporting to account for the same experience.

Japan places greater emphasis on experience as being necessary to education. Learning by rote seems to survive further in the course of people's education, and across a broader spread of subjects. This is consistent with the apparent Japanese disregard for explanation, and apparent reluctance to give prominence to parts of knowledge that might be amenable to explanation. To say they are reluctant is misleading; they just do not accept that this makes sense.

In keeping with the Japanese holistic view of knowledge, education is aimed at the whole mind, including parts which we think cannot be reached by explanation. It is aimed at nurturing people so they become contributors to a whole culture, the culture which I have characterised as togetherness.

In the old tradition, learning by rote presents a person with something he or she is told to do, and do repeatedly, without explanation of why, to what purpose, or how the result is to be measured. Such explanation would reach only certain parts of the mind, making those parts active, excluding the rest. The aim is to reach and exercise hidden parts of the mind, and include them in the visible activity. By repetition, the whole of the person's mind gets to feel what he or she is doing, gets to feel why, and gets to know when it is well done:

> I had this process described to me by someone, an adult, who was learning
> calligraphy; painting characters in old script, and reading the script. She
> told me how she had been made to paint characters, repeatedly. The master
> just said do it again, and again, with no indication of why or what progress

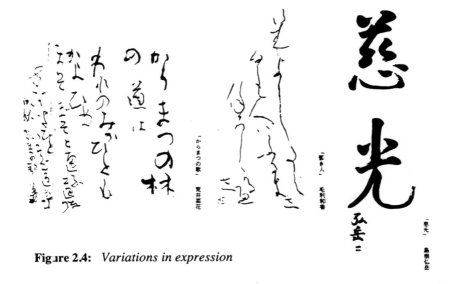

Figure 2.4: *Variations in expression*

was being made. This continued over a long period. Suddenly she found she could do it, and she found she could read the script, without having been told how to read.

Reading, I discovered later, from an experienced calligrapher, is not just a matter of recognising strings of characters and matching them to words. It involves studying the spatial arrangement of characters, the empty space between and around them, the nature of the brush strokes, and variations in boldness and size. Reading is more than just getting the literal story. It includes recognition of why, with what intention, the nature of the story teller, and how he or she felt when telling it — the differences shown by each calligrapher. Much of this gets to be known inwardly, without explanation.

At exhibitions of art and cultural treasures, calligraphy is often included. People pay as much attention to the displays of calligraphy, and enjoy them, as they do to other exhibits. One day I wandered into a small gallery in Ueno park, and found myself in an exhibition entirely devoted to present-day calligraphy. I let the exhibits impress themselves on me, and became aware of differences, and found them stimulating and even exciting, as objects; of course I could not read the words. Differences appeared, for example, in smooth flowing curves contrasted with tetchy angular characters, and in the use of empty space, as in Figure 2.4. These differences clearly were regarded as important by other people looking at the exhibits.

It might be said that calligraphy is close to art, or poetry, and therefore is obviously more amenable to being learned by rote. But what would this be saying? Should we accept the implication that there are other activities which are definitely different and do not need the full involvement of a whole mind? Calligraphy might be viewed as a form of art in that there are no explicit criteria for correct or good calligraphy; examples just are more or less effective in evoking responses from people. Different people who write computer programs for others to use will recognise similarity between this aspect of calligraphy and their own work; there are no explicit criteria for a finished program. Are there other activities between people, which are different?

Lastly, we can note that the Japanese approach to learning, with its emphasis on learning by rote and absorbing knowledge through experience, is being challenged as Japan adopts more methodologies from the west. Changes are being introduced which might expose the fragile nature of Japanese culture, its togetherness, in the face of outside influences.

Corporate behaviour

Japan is admired, and sometimes feared, for its success in technology, industry, and commerce. We in the west now look to practices in Japan, to learn from this success, and selectively seek to adopt some of these practices in order to emulate this success. We are motivated by the fear that we will lose dominance in commerce.

Coupled with this fear, we also are inclined to look for reasons that tell us why this success is unfair, or why it will not last. It is claimed that Japan exploits innovations from the west, and does not itself have the ability to innovate. It is also said that Japan exploits its people, expecting exceptional commitment to their work, and imposing living conditions which would not be accepted in other so-called first world countries.

This view of Japan's success, and the criticisms, I think rest on a shallow reading of how things are in that country. The whole culture, togetherness, contributes to this success — and emulating selected aspects of surface behaviour will not reproduce the same success in the west. The accusation of failure to innovate reveals a western notion which is foreign to Japan — innovation 'out of the blue', or in a vacuum. That does not give recognition to the workings of evolution, highly effective in Japan, which result in the development of new products.

It may turn out to be true that Japan's success cannot last. That might prove to be the case, not because of the obvious criticisms, but because of changes to the whole culture brought about by competition with the west. My own understanding of how Japanese industry and commerce works is slight, gained from informal observations and conversations. The following notes focus on the relationship between a culture and commercial corporate behaviour. I am searching for clues on how the way people think about things affects what people do.

Cooperation

Competitive success of Japanese products might be attributable to the way people work together. Japanese togetherness is effective in channelling convergent efforts of many people towards agreed outcomes. Output is achieved without the cost of continual disagreements pulling in different directions, and this shows in the price of products. This togetherness depends on all persons knowing and accepting their place in the grand order of things, within Japan. The modern large companies expect total dedication from their work force, and they accept paternalistic responsibility for the well-being of their people.

Japanese workers in industry and commerce, mostly men (now including increasing numbers of women), work long hours. They live at work, playing and socialising at work, with their minds always focused on their company's business. Their spouses, mostly women, lead separate lives, with complete responsibility for their homes and for managing their husband's incomes; and they are free to engage in wider interests. This separation between people at work and different people at home is greater than in the west, and bears different connotations:

In their personal lives, married couples appear to be less emotionally attached; not alone facing an aggressive outer world. They are absorbed more into the togetherness of people around them (expressed in behaviour rather than words), like a greatly extended family. Marriage tends to be treated as a practical contract aimed at the well-being of children. Commonly, the man provides the income, and the woman manages the income to meet their children's needs. Beyond these obligations, they are free to fulfil their own lives separately; the woman has opportunity (a small and well equipped home and children at school) to seek out wider interests and be in touch with the world.

The man effectively lives at work, finding his social involvement there, with personal development confined within the scope of work interests. He has little opportunity for developing interests outside work. He has no place of his own at home; no study, and no space for hobbies. This total dedication to work tends to lead to problems when work stops. On retirement, the man finds himself unwanted at home — described by women as 'wet leaves' (useless but difficult to sweep away). This is a situation exacerbated by separation of the work place, in big companies, and it is a topic of concern in modern Japan.

The position of women in Japan is, of course, more complex. Not all are as privileged as I have indicated. There are troubled households, and severe space restrictions (and other factors) do result in stressed woman/man relationships. When stress occurs, then individual women seem very vulnerable.

In a number of conversations I found myself speculating that Japanese men work long but not hard, and that their work could be done more efficiently in less time. A revolutionary change might result if work commitment were reduced from about fourteen to eight hours a day and from six to five days per week, and if annual leave were increased from about six days to four weeks. Men would then have to spend more time at home, claiming their own space, and they would find themselves developing wider interests.

This would give these men a basis for independent views on their place in the world and their role in their company's business. Togetherness at work would be threatened. They might find themselves pulling in different directions in the development of products. This would then add to cost, reducing commercial competitiveness in the larger world market. Japan's success might then falter.

This is a simplistic speculation, but it points to corporate benefits from single minded dedication of the work force. It points to the deep roots of Japanese corporate behaviour, and indicates the fragility of the roots. They might be destroyed by the introduction of western work practices, and the ideology which accompanies them. Hopefully I am quite wrong; Japanese togetherness might prove far stronger than I suggest, and might turn out to offer benefits back to the west.

Dealing with disagreement

Normally in Japan, open disagreements are to be avoided. This does not mean they do not exist. A disagreement can exist between parties, persons, and it then refers to discordant states of knowing within those persons. It is not something external, and parties cannot call upon external reference to prove their part of the disagreement is correct. A disagreement is personal. The relative positions held by parties then determine what each can show of their disagreement, and how it might be resolved. This calls upon good behaviour aimed at conflict avoidance.

Disagreement can be *about* something external to the disagreeing parties, something absolute, but 'talking it through' is not an accepted way of reaching a resolution. This is because knowledge about absolutes is internal to persons, and expressions from knowledge, talking..., does not externalise knowledge. Talking is evocative, and that is subject to relative position and good behaviour. Instead, silence is used to mark points of disagreement, without explaining them.

Resolution then depends on parties recognising the occurrence of disagreements by noting silences, and soliciting opinions without argument. If they feel receptive to opinions, they may modify their disagreements. This process involves behaviour and feeling beyond rational language, and agreement becomes evident in subsequent action.

Disagreement here covers any discordant states of knowing in any number of persons who see themselves as having to decide upon some concerted action. This is typically the case when a company has to decide on some change to its organisation, or decide on the next step in the development of a new product. The process of arriving at such decisions entails an intricate web of one-to-one consultations among many people, a process of consultation called 'nemawashi', from which arises a feeling of consensus. Agreements reached in this way are accepted, even if some disagreement remains within parties.

Nemawashi is the antithesis of a 'round table discussion', and is intended to avoid conflict. It is similar to what we in the west would recognise as lobbying, but with the important difference that it is not directed by powerful interests seeking predefined outcomes — nemawashi is aimed at undirected consensus growing out of unexplained situations.

The process of nemawashi is subject to the influence of people with high position. It is frustrating to people who believe they have rational arguments which stand on their own merits, which they think ought to decide outcomes. The current generation of younger people are becoming convinced of the value of objective argument, and are becoming intolerant of the patience required to obtain position. This change threatens to cut deep into Japanese culture, changing the Japanese way of knowing and doing things.

Corporate structure

The structures of organisations in Japan bear a resemblance to those of organisations in the west; including variations on hierarchical ordering of responsibility and command. However, there are some important differences. Japanese structures can be envisaged as just a few strong horizontal layers forming a simple stepped pyramid, with positions of influence associated with each layer. Position, in the Confucian sense, is associated with persons who carry responsibility for decisions within layers, answerable to upper layers and responsive to activity coming up from lower layers. Position is found in all layers. The difference then appears to be in the extent and nature of what is passed between layers, and the amount of responsibility exercised within layers, even the lowest layer. All persons have position and feel responsibility within a whole structure.

Generally, position can be viewed as a measure of acceptance within a peer group, and more widely within society. So according to position, whatever a person proposes is accepted as being worthy, or not. Position is the justification for what is said, rather than any supposedly independent logical argument.

Position, as occurs in companies, is aimed at employing all the abilities of whole persons, calling on contributions from the whole of their knowledge. It is aimed at stimulating contributions from hidden knowledge, without explanation. Given this notion, any formal explanation of the structure of an organisation will not reveal how the organisation works. The explanation cannot be carried across to, and guarantee the success of, another organisation (especially one in a different culture).

Senior position is slowly acquired, and rapidly replaced. In industry, young persons typically serve a 20 year apprenticeship in the lowest layer, gaining experience of all the activities of a company. Then some are promoted to positions of influence over company decisions, in the next layer up, in middle management. A few reach higher positions which give them the power to take major company decisions. These individuals hold dominant positions for short periods, quickly being replaced by upcoming younger persons. To help the rapid turnover of people in senior positions, the age for retirement is low, often as low as 50.

The exception to this pattern is found in titular heads of companies who sometimes survive in that position for many years. However, their role (like that of the Emperor) is not to command but to serve as an example of good behaviour, to uphold the honour of the company (or of Japan).

Two interesting consequences appear to follow from this kind of organisational structure. First, given that responsibility is associated directly with persons in sufficiently senior positions, development of new products can be very fast. Justification by explanation, in some full self-consistent external form, is not necessary — responsibility rests within persons. Agreements on how to proceed are reached through person-to-person consultation (nemawashi), with the certainty that they will be honoured. Agreements can be redone (inconsistently) when subsequent experience shows that revision is desirable, through further consultation.

Development is not encumbered with the overhead of maintaining large amounts of detailed written documentation; that is not seen as a means for shedding responsibility, and the inertia it induces is avoided. Of course, all this can work only if everybody is equally committed to achieving agreed outcomes.

Secondly, the rapid succession of persons in senior positions has the effect of a collective body of persons being more responsive to changing demands from 'outside'. The large body of people at the lowest organisational layer, with its annual intake of new people, remains in touch with the world 'out there'. These people, active in all areas of the company's business, exert their influence by passing information upwards. Middle management is receptive, and selective in proposing decisions further upwards. Senior management takes decisions, and the flow of command then proceeds downwards, putting into effect the ideas that were influenced from below.

The persons in senior positions, by not being in position for long, do not get the time to shape a body of persons, a company, according to their own idiosyncratic will and against change. For this effect to be constructive, differences between successive senior persons might need to be small and, indeed, the collective body of persons might need to be homogeneous. All these persons need to be connected through similarity within themselves, constituting what can be called an organic whole. These conditions appear to be uniquely satisfied in Japanese society.

This Japanese way of doing things is essentially evolutionary. It accommodates many small changes in response to uncontrolled events from outside, and is not directed by large and explicitly defined goals from above. It is able to deal with many small changes rapidly, and adapt, so that big changes become apparent over time. The big changes are realised in new products which keep companies alive.

Competition

The organic wholeness of corporate structures extends beyond individual companies, as is evident in the Japanese approach to competition. Different companies active in the same fields, see themselves in competition but they aim to ensure all stay in business. If competition results in one company being destroyed, that is seen as failure on the part of the others; that disturbs the labour market and the customers, and they all lose. Instead, competition is seen as useful in stimulating activity within companies, but it has to be controlled by agreement across companies.

This view of competition is probably related to another aspect of corporate structure. The big companies exist as empires, each engaged in a broad spread of activities. Each exists as a corporate entity, and owns or in other ways controls other smaller companies, through an elaborate succession of companies down to small businesses and workshops. The resulting hierarchy of dependencies is effective in keeping many people employed and in supplying materials and parts to higher level companies, but it is vulnerable if any companies, businesses, or workshops are destroyed. Competition therefore has to be regulated to avoid such destruction.

A further aspect of Japanese competition was revealed to me when I was told how companies deal with new products. When one company plans to develop a radically new product, the first thing it does is publish its plans. The purpose is to get other companies to develop the same product, with the effect that all the companies will share the task of getting the public to be receptive to the product. Effectively, they share the marketing cost. Competition will remain in the quality of the product from each company, but not in one company offering a product, however good, which is not also offered by other companies.

The organic whole across companies also extends across society. This can be illustrated by considering the accusation which is sometimes made, that companies dump their produce overseas at lower prices than within Japan.

It appears that products leave the factories at the same price, but within Japan they pass through many hands before they reach retail outlets. During that process, something is added to the price many times, and the eventual retail price is high. This added cost is higher than the cost of transportation plus local retailing overseas. This pattern is consistent with another common accusation, which is that the service industry in Japan is very inefficient. However, the purpose of that inefficiency is to keep many people employed, and the high retail price can be regarded as including the social cost of full employment (avoiding disruptive effects of unemployment). So the produce from companies is bought at a price which keeps people employed, gives them position, and preserves society.

Given this intricate web of dependencies between companies and society as a whole, it is not surprising that Japan is resistant to western multi-national companies and supermarkets coming into the country.

In contrast to the Japanese way of doing things, we in the west try to apply the same efficiency criteria across all activities. We do so irrespective of whether the activities are serving local consumers or are intended for export. So we accept unemployment, and collect taxes to keep unemployed people alive — and our social cost gets to be included in the price of export products. We lose competitiveness in the world market, and we bring about social fragmentation — our unemployed people have no position in society. Here we have unwanted consequences from our more ruthless approach to competition.

The different approach to competition in the west is presently evident in our 'free-market' ideology with its single criterion of 'making money' (a euphemism for 'taking money' from someone else), and faith in 'survival-of-the-fittest' (without recognising interdependence between variously weak and strong individuals) — life becomes a knock-out contest, with a growing number of losers (Ch. 1 Fig. 1.1).

Japan sees itself as being in a larger world, and is sensitive to the prospect of its success attracting hostility from other countries. As seen from within Japan, the world community rests on interdependencies between activities in different countries. This has prompted the notion that Japan's approach to controlled competition, including social responsibility, ought now to be applicable outside Japan. The ambition, as understood in Japan, is to reduce competitive differences between countries, to keep them all in business, and so preserve a world society. This aim is expressed by the Intelligent Manufacturing Systems Project (IMS), conceived by Professor Yoshikawa ['90] at Tokyo University and supported by MITI. The key concept in this project is a free market in manufacturing know-how, operating alongside the generally accepted notion of a free market in manufactured products. By marketing this know-how, the intention is that countries can acquire each other's manufacturing abilities to improve their own competitiveness, and so maintain a healthier world society.

This is a major ambition which may turn out to be subject to serious difficulties. It is an ambition which is unlikely to be achieved by concentrating on purely technical know-how within companies. It touches deep ideological and cultural differences across countries, which will be difficult to grasp in the west.

The Japanese way cannot be easily imported into the west. It depends on a society which accepts high prices, and accepts selective application of efficiency criteria which results in low cost products, so that the difference can support moderately high incomes for all. Part of this equation is that the people who see themselves as wealth creators do not draw inordinately high salaries, not even people with senior positions in companies. For this to work, it has to be rooted in a culture of togetherness.

Innovation

To conclude these observations on Japan, we come to the awkward question of innovation.   Although Japanese companies and businesses are widely acknowledged to be very good at developing products, many claim Japan fails on innovation.   It is claimed that Japan is weak in conceiving radically new knowledge and new products.   Here, once again, we are faced with a western oriented criticism.   Our notion of innovation sees something new as something from an individual unconnected with anything else ('out of the blue'), which then is recognised as valuable by other persons.   Moreover, something new must be different from all other pre-existing things, in some definable way.   The newness must be demonstrable outside persons, objectively.

From a Japanese orientation, eventual recognition of something new depends on other people being ready to recognise, implying they must already know what will be presented to them.   Something cannot be so new that it does not fit already-present knowledge, and still be recognised as valuable. Moreover, the need for recognition implies newness in perception (extending already-present knowledge), with the consequence that something being new cannot be demonstrated objectively.

New things in Japan emerge out of unforeseen contributions from many like minded persons, and this can be viewed as evolution.   Innovation as something distinct from evolution then is regarded as a myth, and innovation as something included in evolution is something Japan is good at.

We might want to contest this view, but can do so only by developing an argument which calls on our unexplained inner functions for knowing, informally.   We might want to say that innovation refers to things coming from unexplained abilities in individuals, resulting in unexpected products. Innovations then stimulate recognition in others, in ways not anticipated.   The innovator awakens knowledge in others — new knowledge following perturbation of already-present knowledge.   To encourage innovators to do this, we place importance on the uniqueness of abilities within individuals, by which they are able to proffer unexpected innovations.   Following this line of argument, the difference between western innovation and Japanese evolution becomes slight.   The manner of awakening knowledge is much the same in both cases.

Computer science: In discussing innovation with Japanese computer scientists (innovators of products for development by companies) I found that many of them accept western logical determinism for what that enables them to do, alongside contrary philosophical positions which are useful for doing other things, without sensing conflict. These scientists engage in major technological projects, and one renowned example is the '5th-Generation' project [JIPDEC '81].

In 1980 this project was intended to be a coordinated giant leap into AI oriented new technology, aimed at serving the interests of the whole Japanese population, and at establishing Japan's AI credentials internationally. Some ten years later I was told of the successor to the 5-G project, a new 'many peaks' project [RWCP '92]. This name was intended to invoke the image of mountain peaks above the cloud line, with clouds obscuring how they come together; suggesting uncoordinated peaks of excellence. As a change in objective this was accepted without any sense of conflict Each project just was of its time.

The 5-G project was effective in establishing Japan's AI credentials, and fear of competition prompted the US and Europe to boost their own AI programmes.

Associated with the current project, major efforts are targeted at fuzzy logic and related work on neural networks (outlined earlier, Fig. 1.24, and see further comment on p.105). These technologies appear to avoid the need to explain in detached formal logic what you want from a computer (or other equipment), and, instead, you simply use whatever it has been set up to do. This is a strategy which fits the Japanese view of logic dissociated from knowledge in persons. During my discussions I found the term, knowledge processing, rarely used.

Among the scientists I met, innovations in computer technology were not justified by some overwhelming argument about how all things are or should be known — no singular and exclusive view of human knowledge. Computers just are made to coexist with other things, and they offer opportunities for technological and commercial success in the international community.

Contributions from individual scientists are not defended on the grounds that they are unique and correct in any detached objective sense. Contributions simply are offered into the arena of other scientists (and non-scientists), inviting their involvement in whatever way they choose:

In a discussion with Professor Nagao of Kyoto University, he described his work on a Dictionary of Computer Science. I suggested this could be a difficult project because he is dealing with something which is not established as a single coherent science. It might better be pictured as a lot of separate 'islands', disconnected, with nothing tangible holding them together. The difficulty then is that if the Dictionary presents a single coherent view, it is bound to provoke a lot of disagreement from the 'separate islands'. In the western academic tradition, it will be judged to stand or fall on its own merits; and if a lot of disagreement is provoked it will fall.

Professor Nagao's response was interesting. He said it is not *a* Dictionary but *his* Dictionary, *his* expression from what he knows of computer science. It is not an object, fixed in itself, to be judged on its own merits. He pointed out that the contents pages are presented in the form of a hierarchical graph showing relationships between parts, and allowing parts to be moved and replaced. He expects and wants others to have different views, and wants them to feel they can rearrange or rewrite parts. The book is conceived as a soft object which can be reshaped to reflect different views, and so support interaction among computer scientists.

The book itself carries no authority, and to say it stands or falls on its own merits has no meaning. As an expression from Professor Nagao's knowledge, it has some meaning and some authority, if you know him and respect him. You have to be party to the meaning. If you modify the book, it then reflects some interaction between yourself and him, thereby gaining further meaning. Others seeing this interaction might add more modifications. In this way the book may gain yet more meaning, reflecting relationships that are active in all our knowledge, which satisfy some or all of us.

Here we have an illustration of a contribution from an individual which is intended to foster evolution. The contribution is nothing in itself (unconnected with persons), and is not a demonstrable innovation, but is aimed at whatever is already known among scientist about computer science. It is aimed at the silent togetherness of these scientists, and is intended to stimulate further new contributions from scientists. This is a good example of Japanese togetherness in science, which need not be incompatible with western science.

Computer applications: In my discussions with non-scientists (consumers of products from companies) I asked how they envisaged new innovations in computer technology? They tended to see the role of computers as media for realising expressions, foreseeing the prospect of being able to realise dynamic expressions in ways which presently are not practical without computers. One, a music composer with a computer-aided-design business (Mr Hayama), foresaw a new media oriented society, with a new kind of literacy supported by computers, leading to improved understanding among people. Another, an architect (Professor Harra of Tokyo University), saw computers as expanding the ways in which persons can imprint themselves on the world, recording their presence and evoking responses from other people. This point was elaborated

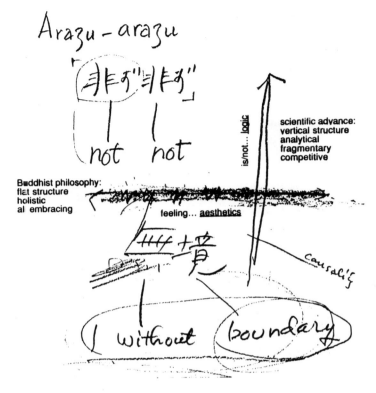

Figure 2.5: *Showing an idea*

> *Graphics from the fingers of the architect, speaking of patterns of the Spirit of Japan, emphasising the importance of spiritual alongside material being; the idea indicated directly from the person.*

by reference to science and Buddhist philosophy, as shown in Figure 2.5. Here, once more, we see a coming together of apparently contradictory philosophies.

These views reflect deep consideration of how people are connected, and the evocative role of expressions. In our conversations I tried to focus on the nature of expressions: what, in general, do they have to be, in order to be effective among Japanese people? But this question got little response. It was as though such matters are best left to persons who decide on particular expressions in the course of their own involvement among other people.

When we pose the question of innovation to Japanese scientists and non-scientists it becomes an awkward one, because it is accompanied by so much baggage. It presupposes a western view of things known objectively, with observers detached from their observations, and with outcomes being demonstrably true. Outcomes have to be evidently true for others not involved in the observations. Innovation then is something done by someone for (to) others; an innovative outcome has to be recognised independently of involvement of the innovator. The innovator and recipients are supposed to be unconnected. These conditions associated with innovation are questionable, and they do not fit the way of knowing and doing in Japan. Instead we are offered involved evolution, embracing participation by all people in a culture of togetherness.

Summary

For us steeped in western traditions, the fascination of Japan is in the way it shows us a different understanding of things, and of people's knowledge about things. This difference need not be regarded as mysterious and does not threaten material values; it touches familiar but unspoken aspects of ourselves. We are presented with a practical holistic view of our being in the world.

We are shown how knowledge can be within us, and not in our externalised expressions — without diminishing our ability to make useful artefacts. Expressions serve to touch and stimulate already-present knowledge within like persons — without diminishing the ability of individuals to be innovative. Responsibility for all things people do can rest on our collective identity — without any external arbiter telling us what is right and wrong.

We are shown that we can know without explanation, and without fixed demarcations between kinds of knowledge; leading to a merging of aesthetic, scientific, and technological sensitivities. Expressions from knowledge, by not carrying explanation, can touch the whole of our being. Effectiveness then is apparent in the continuing dynamics of human behaviour.

Faith is placed in people spontaneously exercising their knowledge, individually and collectively, for the common good. This faith rests on recognition of similarity and interdependence across all persons; a common interest in survival amidst all else (a benign form of anarchy). Japan shows us that this kind of understanding, rooted in old traditions which we used to share, can be successful in a modern technological and commercial world.

Sound of language

Some words expressed briefly
reaching into silent empty space

The sound of language
is not like any other sound.
We speak sounds to express words
but the sounds are not words.
The sounds come out of us
and words remain inside:
    verbal concepts
    linguistic things-of-knowledge.
Words are things in us
used to shape our sounds.

Verbal concepts
lie deep in each of us.
Hidden from each other
implied by sounds we make.
Concepts of identity and quantity and time
not otherwise found 'out there':
    used to compose our utterances
    and place them in the world.
Concepts mediated in each of us
changing our expressions.

Our sounds show regularities
true to form in us.
Regularities touching our concepts
evoking further sounds.
Recurring patterns of sounds
reveal forms of expression:
    separated from motivating concepts
    detached from particulars of knowledge.
Expressions true-to-form
reflect but do not explain language.

77

Being true-to-form
entails consistency in expressions.
Consistency across parts-of-speech
allowing recognition of form.
We then recognise linguistic expressions
without showing our concepts:
    interpreting inwardly
    without exposing knowledge.
We cannot show that true-to-form
is the same as knowledge-of-the-world.

Being consistent
entails use of formal logic.
Logic ensuring coherence across expressions
allowing one to follow on another.
We use logic to construct expressions
without it knowing what instances must be:
    not explaining what expressions are about
    not verified by the actuality of things.
We cannot show that true-to-form
represents any other things-in-the-world.

The sound of language
comes from deep within each of us.
Sounds expressing what we are
evoking responses from each other.
Our purpose to maintain position
to be at-one-with-the-world — survive:
    recognising interdependence
    evoking concerted action.
Sounds separated from knowledge
sustain person-to-person interaction.

Sounds reach into us
touching our linguistic parts-of-knowledge.
Stimulating our further knowledge-of-the-world
seeking confirmation of affinity.
Our knowledge moved closer together
by what we hear ourselves say:
    showing familiarity among persons
    about all other things we know.
Effectiveness made evident
in the continuous dynamic of interaction.

Language within similar beings
employs similar concepts.
Derived from further particulars of knowledge
influenced by similar experience of the world.
We rely upon similarity in each of us
to express differences in our knowledge:
    to maintain familiarity
    in a changing world.
We can know this of language
without explaining what it is.

Language shapes expressions
without revealing what they are about.
Reference to things 'out there'
refers back to knowledge within us.
We realise expressions from knowledge
with nothing 'out there' telling us what must be:
    on material and spiritual matters
    and practical everyday activities.
We know
our language is effective.

Language expressed in different forms
all effective in the same way.
Text as pictures of words
without being words.
Drawings as graphical pictures
not being other things:
    nudging our non-verbal concepts
    touching further inner sensitivities.
And painting and music and dance...
all awakening knowledge in ourselves.

3   Space between *Yes* and *No*

- *Where interaction occurs*
- *What's in a concept?*
- *The 'real-world' assumption*
- *Logic-machines*
- *Artificial intelligence*

Where interaction occurs

We commonly think of ourselves as having concepts, and we think of them being used when we engage in interactions with each other [Bijl '94]. We usually associate concepts with language made evident in our expressions, without having explanations outside ourselves which account for this. We can think of concepts being effective in evoking continuity of interactions, linking us together and invoking our shared knowledge. Now we want to consider how our concepts might relate to anything we might put into computers.

Our concepts for engagement include things which are not found in our experience of further things 'out there'. They have to do with knowing and feeling our way into ourselves and each other [Bijl '91b]. To do this, we express polarities along our dimensions of knowing; things said are true or false, good or bad, and beautiful or ugly, with no fixed demarcations (as indicated in Figs 1.9–12, and discussed further in Ch. 5). We express accord within ourselves by saying 'yes' or 'no'. These are expressions of satisfaction coming from concepts entwined with our further knowing and feeling (not usually thought of as knowledge) about further things found in experience. A strong yes or no marks the conclusion of an interaction.

Engagement is reawakened by saying 'yes, and...' or 'no, but...'. What then follows reveals ourselves, our being, in the space between yes and no. This is a large space filled with feelings, preferences and prejudices, likes and dislikes, but it is empty of explanations. It is a space which is usually thought of as being touched by the arts but not by the sciences — once more a polarity along a dimension of knowing, and without fixed demarcation. We can think of this space as being occupied by people's motivations for ordinary actions in everyday practices.

In our scientific tradition we have sought to reduce the space between yes and no. All things said about our world, including what we say about ourselves being in the world, are looked upon as being objectively resolvable to either true or false, independently of persons. In this tradition, we have tried to use formal logic to explain knowledge independently of whatever else might go on in persons. We have sought to disengage persons from knowledge of the world as it actually is — without regard to such a state of affairs having the effect of making persons redundant.

This is of course a simplistic (and out-dated) view of science, but it is one which tends to be encouraged by enthusiasts of information technology. It is implicit in attempts to popularise this technology.

Our technological tradition reflects and depends upon disengagement of people. Machines generally require a logic which recognises just yes or no, with nothing between. Mechanisms may be identified with long and complex chains made exclusively of yes/no links, fully explained; and this gets realised in the intermeshing of cogs and the actions of levers, or in on/off states of electronically sensitive matter. This condition applies to all machines, including micro-electronic computers. When we think of computers as knowledge processors, we then find we are faced with the problem of getting computers to act on unforeseen 'yes, and...' and 'no, but...' responses from the persons who use them, the kind of responses that are essential to knowledge being shared among ourselves.

Of course we can build yes/no knowledge into computers so as to make them show behaviour implying 'don't know...' or 'possibly so...' (not quite the same as 'yes, and...' and 'no, but...'). We can make this behaviour of computers seem appropriate to our knowledge about further things found in experience, but only by anticipating experience, and then only if we can explain anticipations to computers. For computers to continue behaving as knowledge processors, users have to know and present anticipated situations to them, and only those situations. Users have to comply with programmed anticipations. This condition leads to prescriptiveness of computer-systems on the further actions of persons who use them. Acceptance of prescriptiveness then rests on a depersonalised computational view of knowledge, a view that will be challenged in this chapter.

An alternative view of knowledge will be expounded, which sees it as including the space between yes and no, and being dependent on continuity of interactions among persons. In this view, we cannot make knowledge into something separate from persons, and cannot package it independently of persons. The knowledge we use, and which motivates our actions in ordinary everyday practices, cannot be verified objectively outside these practices.

An example of the orthodox computational view of knowledge is to be found in certain people's enthusiasm for the notion of 'distance learning', or conveying knowledge by means of information technology and without the presence of persons as teachers. I came across an example of this in a talk by the Principal of Heriot-Watt University, at the celebration of the opening of its new computer science building [H-W Seminar on Visions of Knowledge, October '92]. He spoke of the Government's plan to double the number of university graduates without increasing the number of staff, and claimed this could be achieved only by bringing knowledge to students through *IT*. He spoke with enthusiasm and saw the Heriot-Watt as taking the lead in this development. When asked how this compared with the existing practices of the Open University, he pointed to the OU's use of direct staff/student tutoring as a symptom of failure, saying that such live contact ought not to be necessary.

Distance learning treats computers rather like books, but with more dynamic visual presentation of material and with feedback loops (within a presentation, not to the teacher) under the control of students. Belief in distance learning then is equivalent to saying that students can learn just from books, with no further interaction between students and teachers, and saying that teachers have nothing to learn from the experience of teaching. This is an example of disengagement which denies the space between yes and no.

What's in a concept?

New technology, realised in the form of autonomous computers, is aimed at storing and accessing information, and arranging bits of information in certain relationships, so as to be useful to persons. The focus on information, and the notion of practical *IT* tools used by persons, makes our understanding of human concepts central to the development of this technology.

The idea is that information should pass between persons and computers, and for this purpose it is thought that people and computers need to share the same concepts. Developers of the technology then need to know what these concepts are. The ambition is to explain concepts overtly, in a formal and logically consistent manner, so that formal explanations can support expressions from information in different forms (in persons and other things). *IT* might then be envisaged as offering tools for shaping expressions, and for interrelating instances of expressions. An example of this approach to concepts (from

Brachman ['79]) is shown in Fig. 1.20, and this will be discussed further, under 'the real-world...' p. 94.

Systematic modelling of concepts implies the notion of integration; information coming from different sources (separate persons) and expressed in a single form, being accommodated in a single model. Integration might be considered as being effective just within computers; the machines taking just what they can from people's expressions, for purposes of invoking and applying their predetermined functionality, and passing everything else untouched back to users. In addition, integration might also be considered as including users; expecting users to know and exploit the available functionality in computers, so as to be able to interact with information from different users. An example of integration, under 'artificial intelligence', is given later.

Among people, we can think of concepts as abstractions in us, by which we are able to accept sensations and turn them into meaningful information about further things in the world (including ourselves and each other). Concepts are associated with language, and they are thought to be the necessary basis for shared language. This association is now commonly believed to be so close that sometimes expressions realised from language (...particular character strings) are considered to be concepts. More cautiously, it is said that concepts are not in expressions, but are indicated by use of expressions in the course of interactions between persons.

Patterns of use may be taken to imply the presence of concepts, without defining what particular concepts are. Changes in use of expressions (people 'breaking the rules') adds to the difficulty in knowing what concepts must be. Despite these reservations, we are able to conceive the presence of concepts and even consider what they do. We can think of their role in language, linked to our ability to know, and to knowledge about things found in experience.

Our thinking about concepts may become evident in pictures we form about them, realised in our expressions. These pictures always are formal and may include some explained logical coherence, so that we say we have models of concepts. The models may help us to share knowledge about concepts in general, and how people use certain concepts in particular, but the models remain pictures and are not themselves concepts.

If we think of data and processes in computers as some kind of knowledge, then we can give computers concepts that connect expressions from users to computational functions, and present responses from 'knowledge' in computers back in the form of user-expressions. These computable concepts might be made to behave in the way we think concepts in persons work. If we do this, then the computational concepts will be our pictures of concepts, and we have no way of establishing that they are the same as concepts in persons.

The question we then face is: how can system designers know what such artificial concepts have to be, in order to be useful to other people, and how can computational concepts be described so as to be understood by users? This question is central to our understanding of autonomous tools, and we will keep returning to it in the course of this chapter.

Formal concepts

Computational concepts are a subset of formal concepts, meaning that they are explained in terms of some logic based on some explained functionality. Thus we have concepts explained in terms of systems of symbols, connectives, and truth-functions, and we then have the problem of relating such logic-systems to people's experience of the world. This problem is nicely illustrated by Russell in his introduction to the Tractatus by Wittgenstein ['21]:

> "First, there is the problem of what actually occurs in our minds when we use language with the intention of meaning something by it: this problem belongs to psychology. Secondly, there is the problem as to what is the relation subsisting between thoughts, words, or sentences, and that which they refer to or mean; this problem belongs to epistemology. Thirdly, there is the problem of using sentences so as to convey truth rather than falsehood; this belongs to the special sciences dealing with the subject-matter of the sentences in question. Fourthly, there is the question: what relation must one fact (such as a sentence) have to another in order to be *capable* of being a symbol for that other? This last is a logical question, and is the one with which Mr Wittgenstein is concerned."

In this quotation we have an example of something fragmented, knowledge(?) about language, expressed in terms of language. Boundaries are drawn in order to separate out responsibilities, as between psychology, epistemology, sciences dealing with subject-matter, and symbolic logic; with no indication of how these responsibilities may be related. Logic is identified as something detached from knowledge as ordinarily exercised in people's everyday practices. Logic becomes amenable to mechanistic formal treatment. Elsewhere we find that the job of propositions in language is to assert facts corresponding to properties of other things (including sentences...), and the job of logic is to relate the fact of a proposition (its expression) to the fact of what it is about (its meaning, in another expression or something else), independently of how we or anybody else might sense these facts.

Logic thought of in this way, along with philosophy, is said by Wittgenstein to be not explainable, and he says that anyone who understands his own (Wittgenstein's) propositions will know them to be nonsensical [ibid 6.54]. This is an interesting position, coming from someone strongly associated with use of logic (not contradicted in his Investigations [Wittgenstein '53]). Wittgenstein may be intending a distinction between nonsensical and meaningless; the former referring to that which can be sensed in experience, for which we have sensations, and the latter referring to that which works logically within ourselves, acceptable to functions in 'mind'. More commonly we lose this distinction when we think of meaning associated outwardly, to something else, verified by experience — placing ourselves in the world (Fig. 1.8).

The question we face, when we consider formal (or artificial) concepts for use in practical activities, cannot be neatly partitioned according to Russell's boundaries (or anything like them), and we have to take on board the problem of 'nonsense' presented by Wittgenstein (and others). Our question anticipates formal methods being realised in computers, and working for other people. Our understanding of formal methods must accommodate computer-users deciding upon demarcations to problems which Russell passes over to psychology, epistemology, and subject-specific sciences. Moreover, we have to be very careful in incorporating any meaning in computational formalisms, which we intend users to share when (or if) they use computer-systems.

Any explanation of a formal method has to come from somewhere and go somewhere — an explanation has to reach into meaning (logic, in Wittgenstein's sense) in someone or something. It may first appear as a description of something informal, processes employing hidden functions within persons. Then it may be turned into an explanation that can go to (be reconstituted in) another person or a non-human machine. An effective explanation is thought to be one which evokes intended singular (unambiguous) responses from recipients.

If we accept this general scheme, we immediately find ourselves in a lot of noise, and lose the purity of thought exemplified by Wittgenstein and Russell. We cannot escape this noise by focusing on nicely defined techniques, and need to apply rigorous thought to the problem of accommodating formal concepts in unexplained informality in persons.

Human concepts

Computational concepts and associated formal methods have to be accommodated in the whole of our world, our way of being and knowing. Here I am referring to the notion of *being* expounded by Heidegger [Dreyfus '91] (already touched on in Figs 1.5–8, and discussed further in Ch. 5). A central point in Heidegger's thesis is that we are, we come into being, with already present understanding of being. Our kind of knowing is already-present in whatever it is we are, and knowledge gets developed through our experience of being in a shared world. So we can reverse the familiar dictum: *I know, because I am.*

This notion of *being* places importance on the wholeness of structure determining possibilities that are not revealed in reductionist elements or essences; here using a concept of *structure* without identifying structures. This notion includes in structure matter that is not restricted to physical appearances, and not contained just within the 'skin' of individuals. Heidegger's emphasis on everyday practices (of differently specialised persons) sees individuals as bound together (the collective singular 'us'), sharing our knowledge through our practices. These practices include use of language expressions, without having anything definite to which particular expressions refer.

All this does not deny the presence of reductionist elements or essences, nor the fact that people refer to them in their attempts to explain higher level behaviours. Such attempts are included in certain people's (notably scientists') everyday practices. What this does deny, however, is any notion of absolute explanations with validity outside everyday practices.

A key effect of this thesis is that it places us amidst all other things in reality, without any special status for a separate (logical and intelligent) super-human observer. This reference to a super-human points to the notion of an external authority, a superior being which controls what we can know and do; a peculiarly western notion, which is also found in our religions, as already discussed in the previous chapter on Japan.

This denial of super-humans is useful in making us consider how people act on their beliefs, including their beliefs associated with formal logic and computers. My saying there are no super-humans is aimed primarily at the notion that makers and programmers of computers (and other specialised persons) have superior knowledge which they can impose on other people. Equating this denial with rejection of people's belief in God, I think, would be rash. The concept of God embraces more than computer programmers.

So here we can conclude that we just are, we carry responsibility for all we do, and what we do is determined by what we are, unexplained. We exist, just like any other kind of thing might be, and differences (structural and logical) between us and them are likely to make what we know different from whatever other things might 'know'. What we know is likely to be unintelligible to them, and vice versa. I once found myself in contention with Feigenbaum (of Stanford, US) over this point, at the Pacific Rim International Conference on AI in 1990, in Japan. Putting forward his notion of silicon based knowledge, he accused me of being irrationally prejudiced in favour of carbon babies, and failing to give due recognition to the new species, silicon babies, which he said were still in their infancy and in future would out-perform us. My position was, and still is, that we would have no way of sharing our knowledge with silicon babies, nor they with us, so they would appear to us to be without knowledge.

Even among ourselves, similar beings of the same species, differences (specialisations) in each of us are likely to affect what we know, and we have no way of establishing that what is known is exactly the same in separate persons. However, similarity (structural and logical) across us is likely to make what each of us knows much the same. We affirm our similarity through continuity of interaction.

An echo of this position can be found in Japan, in its unwritten philosophy of thought which is indicated in everyday understanding and behaviour. There the being of persons is accepted as something not explained, and behaviour rests on the presumption of similarity across persons, including already-present knowledge in persons. In that context, expressions from concepts do not have the purpose of representing and conveying knowledge, externalised in some overt logical form, but rather serve to stimulate and affirm knowledge already shared among like persons. This position is accepted as not mysterious. It is known within persons. Attempts at logical explanation might make this seem mysterious, but then it is the attempts to explain which make the mystery.

Conceptual space

As with Wittgenstein's propositions, concepts associated with expressions can be talked about but not contained in explanations. Concepts exist in our being. They reach into unexplained knowledge, and evoke responses determined by whatever it is we are (motivated in ways we cannot reconstruct in computers, or in so-called self-learning *connectionist machines* [Levine '91], illustrated in Fig. 1.24). Realisations from concepts, as instanced expressions, are conditioned by what we know of media properties and functions, and regularities across instances indicate their effectiveness as language expressions.

We can think of concepts as being abstract, referring to ideas — as in Plato's transcendental ideas (Fig. 1.9). These ideas can be considered as already-present in each of us when we come into being, and they motivate expressions about our being in the world. We can also try to think of concepts in more concrete form, referring to things appearing regularly in expressions and to regular operations upon expressions. Here we can include formalisms which apply to certain forms of expression and which are intended to ensure instances of expressions remain true to form. Here we might also be tempted to include formal methods, and draw formalisms closer to subject-matter that forms might be about. However, the path which is opened up is problematic, since the link between form and subject-matter 'out there', or further meaning in us, remains hidden in us.

There are those who consider concepts, or the ideas to which they refer, as things which can be explained so that something externalised can be treated as being the concept, or the idea. An example of this view was given by Margaret Boden, a psychologist and philosopher of AI, speaking to a mixed gathering at an art and science conference on 'Order, Chaos and Creativity' [Interalia, Edinburgh, '92]. She stated three conditions for creativity: "novel combinations of familiar ideas; the outcome must be good; and it must not have been possible before". Her talk expanded upon the notion of conceptual space. It considered creative ideas as going beyond a current style of thinking (a set of rules, not necessarily conscious...), and so changing the dimensions of an already-existing conceptual space. She then advocated what she called the scientific way of defining, exploring, and transforming spaces, employing computational concepts (citing *shape grammars* which I develop later in my example under 'problems', p. 97, and *connectionism*). The apparent implication is that computational techniques can be regarded as the same kind of thing as a conceptual space in a person. This is a fairly orthodox position held by some people working in AI, but it becomes problematic when we consider combinations of ideas, the condition of being good, and the existence of possibilities.

The obvious question is: how can anyone know whether Boden's conditions are being satisfied in any instance of creativity? More fundamentally, how can we know that we have explained, externalised, a conceptual space so that we can begin to apply these (or similar) conditions?

If we think of conceptual space as consisting of some set of rules, it does not follow that all the rules which determine outcomes from within persons can be made explicit outside persons. This qualification was illustrated by Andy Goldsworthy at the same conference, speaking about his art. He spoke of his drystane cones, leaf compositions, mud splashes, stick and sand throws, and snowball melts [Friedman and Goldsworthy '91]. He gave glimpses of his involvement in these works, a working rhythm. But he could not (and we should not expect him to) expose all within himself, his conceptual space, which determines instances of his art. That which remains behind, hidden within, is what makes him effective as an instrument for revealing reality in like persons, us.

To claim that particular overtly defined computational techniques constitute a conceptual space is like saying that Goldsworthy's drystane cones are a conceptual space. In both cases, the boundaries to possibilities are not contained within the artefacts, but in the use that people make of them. Possibilities remain hidden within persons, moving, and infinite (or nearly so). The condition that something creative must not have been possible before, loses meaning.

To understand the example of Goldsworthy we can say concepts, once realised outside persons, are no longer concepts but are expressions. They are expressions realised from, and reaching into, a conceptual space already present within persons. These expressions may include formalisations of computational techniques and their further realisations (those which are said to be conceptual). All expressions are used by concepts not in expressions, and they might be used to make further expressions. We then have a notion of expressions driven by persons, to generate further expressions, without any commitment to knowing explicitly what the concepts are that are doing the driving.

In Boden's scientific way, it might be claimed that I am trying to make concepts mysterious; but they are not mysterious in most persons, and in artists. What does seem mysterious is the claim that an explanation can be a concept from within a person. In our attempts to provide scientific explanations, we might see our use of expressions as revealing rules or grammars in their regularities, and we can think of grammars being used to realise new instances. When this appears to happen, it does not follow that formally explained grammars determine new instances. Something outside the grammars, perhaps knowledge beyond language but included in our being, determines our utterances.

The picture of concepts which is now emerging shows them to be things we can talk about, but we cannot instance any of our concepts outside ourselves. The grammars we are able to explain are expressions from our concepts, and we can shape them so that they can be received in a computer (serving as medium), for purposes of realising further instances of expressions. When we do this, our formal grammars do not have to account for anything else these further expressions might be about (as in the example of generative *shape grammars*). Use of such grammars then has to be motivated from outside the computer, for outcomes to be expressions from persons and about their perceptions of other things. Put more strongly, we cannot explain to a computer what our expressions are about, and there is no other way it can get to know.

This picture of concepts points to a more basic question: how does it bear on the notion of 'information processors' commonly associated with *IT* ? Like concepts, information now ought to be considered as something formed inwardly, informally, acceptable to hidden functions in persons, and not explained. Things realised overtly, externally, that we commonly call information, then are expressions (or products) from information. *IT* ought more properly to be considered as 'expression- (or product-) processing', and confusion over this point causes difficulties for people who try to set standards for computer-applications — as in product modelling (Fig. 1.26).

In ordinary everyday practices, our inability to explain instances of concepts (and information) does not inhibit us. In Heidegger's terms and in the Japanese tradition, we can regard all persons as similar, in the same kind of being. We can know our similarity is tolerant of differences (specialisations) in each of us. We all exercise similar 'mind-muscles' on different particulars we find in experience. Differences become apparent in expressions we put to each other, and unspoken similarity is the common ground by which we are able to understand each other. Our interactions serve to touch and change already-present knowledge in us, without needing explanation. What we know evolves through involvement among ourselves, and through our absorption in other things in our everyday practices.

In ordinary human interactions, the regularities we see in expressions can be considered as reflecting our conceptual space, without being this space. These reflections are effective in touching similarity within many of us. They indicate the presence of effective concepts (and information) without explanation, just as whatever else makes us appreciate other things does not depend on explanation; like digesting a good meal, or enjoying good music. Effectiveness, in doing things like sharing the same meal, listening to the same music, depends on structural similarity (sharing the same inner functionality). We know when we are dealing with good or bad concepts.

Devising new concepts

Concepts are indicated by the ways that we make and modify expressions. They operate within us, and are not determined by the actuality of other things our expressions are about. If this seems an alarming assertion, then we can gain reassurance from the practices of scientists, and from modern physics (Ch. 4). Certain scientists claim they are able to explain what the things which are constitutive of our world actually are, implying that they alone have a hold on the absolute truth of such things, as in Wolpert's book ['92]. Others more readily accept the involved and speculative nature of what they do, and look for effectiveness in the way their contributions add to the continuity of science. Einstein and Infeld ['38, p. 152] give us a nice example:

"Physical concepts are free creations of the mind, and are not, however it may seem, uniquely determined by the external world. In our endeavour to understand reality we are somewhat like a man trying to understand the mechanism of a closed watch. He sees the face and the moving hands, even hears its ticking, but has no way of opening the case. If he is ingenious he may form some picture of a mechanism which could be responsible for all the things he observes, but he may never be quite sure his picture is the only one which could explain his observations. He will never be able to compare his picture with the real mechanism and he cannot even imagine the possibility of the meaning of such a comparison."

In this quotation Einstein is talking of concepts, and his illustration refers to some separate object, a watch. He is talking of the impossibility of comparing a picture of the watch (an explanation employing our concepts), with the object itself. In Heidegger's terms this object would be in our being, but the effect is much the same; we cannot stand outside our being and open it up. We know the watch is there, it is real, and we can get to share our knowledge about the object. In the practices of scientists and in ordinary human interactions, we get to share what we know about other things, objects, watches, by recognising regularities which appear in many instances of expressions which we think are about those things, which invoke our concepts and satisfy knowledge in us. Our expressions are effective in evoking responses (unexpected and informative), prompting further interactions among ourselves. This continuity of interactions cannot tell us that we each have the same knowledge (equal shares), but it provides us with the only means we have for affirming that we share knowledge.

With this understanding of knowing and doing things, we cannot be sure about what any new concepts must be. Those of us who are specialised in devising new computable concepts for the rest of us to use, cannot stand apart and refer only to functions they know to be available in computers, and devise concepts that will be used. New widely acceptable computable concepts and formal methods built upon them can come about only through involvement of many persons not specialised in computing.

Those of us who are computer specialists may see certain regularities in other people's expressions, and see such regularities as informing us about concepts which might be formalised, speculatively. We can try to maintain the notion that these regularities are somewhat detached from further knowledge about our being in the world. But however clever we might be in developing such speculations, we now ought to recognise that new concepts and their formalisations more generally come from 'ordinary' people's use of language in everyday practices in the world.

Specialisations offered as formal logic (Fig. 1.14, and p. 152), with overtly expressed connectives and truth-functions, now ought to be accepted as coming from the non-specialised being of specialists, in a highly involved and non-explicit way — we have moved some way from Russell's (but perhaps not Wittgenstein's) logic. We can use formal logic to shape the inner functions of machines, but not to determine human inner functionality and behaviour. Logic-machines then cannot tell persons what they should know and do.

To devise useful new computable concepts, we need a broader understanding of logic, beyond symbols and whatever can be done just with symbols. We can consider logic more generally as referring to structural and functional coherence of beings, pointing to logic that is within the being of persons and differently within different other things, machines. This can be accepted as informal logic (Fig. 1.13, and p. 152), not explained. This logic is implied by outward behaviour, and in our case by manifestations of everyday practices. Intelligent behaviour then may be seen as use of informal logic in us to maintain our coherence amidst all else.

Evolution

Formalisations that are apparent in expressions come from our informal use of logic, and sometimes from intelligent use of logic. In everyday practices they are apparent in the forms of talking and writing, and arithmetic, and painting and music. These forms of expression, and more like them, are effective in describing what an utterer knows, so as to touch knowledge and evoke responses from recipients (effective descriptions), and sometimes they are effective in evoking intended unambiguous responses (effective explanations). However, we do not know definitively how these formalisations have come about, nor what they must be in order to be effective.

The notion that formalisations have to be effective, and that effectiveness has to do with us maintaining our coherence amidst all else, points to the deeper notion of purpose, and survival. Here we can make a brief and useful digression to consider a current biological explanation of evolution, as expounded by Dawkins (in his early work, *The Selfish Gene* [Dawkins '76]). He gives an account of how new things come about, including, in our case, new concepts. Dawkins attributes behaviour of individuals to instructions from genes (a reference to what we are: 'gene-machines'). Individuals act solely in the interest of their genes, and evolution follows random mutations undirected by purpose. This results in survival of some individuals and, consequently, the success of what we see as like individuals forming species in a world of many species.

In Dawkins' scheme for all things, behaviour includes the outcome from both physical and mental activity ('memes'), and evolutionary stable states accommodate both the weak and the strong (doves and hawks). However, he denies the existence of deliberate altruism: doing good to others, including other members of one's own group or species, without considering benefit to oneself. His purpose in doing so is to undermine the old belief in collective species behaviour, and he wants to show that altruism is not necessary to the evolution of species.

This denial of altruism is uncontentious if we accept that (intelligent?) consideration of self-interest need not be apparent in each behavioural act. Self-interested behaviour may be embedded in past experience or past evolution, and the path by which benefit is returned may be obscure. This qualification accommodates the possibility of an individual recognising that it gains benefits from its presence in a group, and such recognition might be shown in apparently altruistic behaviour. Just as other behavioural traits can become established through evolution, so apparently altruistic behaviour can become established, and we can view human intelligence as having evolved in this way.

Dawkins offers a reductionist and deterministic biological view which has no place for life as being necessary to evolution. This denial of life (any sense of being alive) as playing any part in motivating behaviour seems rash. It may be true that any notion of life might not be necessary to his explanation, but this does not mean that life has to be excluded from evolution. His denial has the unfortunate effect of opening the way for subsequent work on computer-systems designed to mutate, so as to evolve new 'genes'. We then find that the mutation mechanisms of these systems have to be programmed (given selection criteria from outside themselves), and find the programmer serving as some god-like figure overseeing and directing events (as in Figs 1.24–25). This contradicts the earlier description of evolution in terms of spontaneous self-interested behaviour, where the selves now are genes in machines.

Despite these reservations, Dawkins' emphasis on the behaviour of individuals in the game of survival is helpful. His basic denial of any pre-programmed grand order (prepared set of genes) in our collective existence does not exclude the presence of Platonic ideas, nor does it exclude Heidegger's notion of our preparedness for 'being-in-the-world'. In Dawkins' terms, we can regard these further things as being in our genes. Such understanding then is helpful in giving us a general picture of ourselves, but it does not tell us how to anticipate instances of things persons will do — which is why we do not want to believe we can put (and hide) our knowledge in machines.

The 'real-world' assumption

Now we will move a little closer to technical matters to do with computing. In advancing *IT,* everything to do with computers is widely regarded as new technology. Yet much of what we do rests on and reinforces old orthodoxies. Orthodox computing can be identified by a set of beliefs associated with computers and the world in which they are used. These beliefs are evident in:

- the real-world assumption,
- objective authority of logic,
- language conveying knowledge.

These beliefs are treated in various ways by western philosophers, often with commendable caution. However, when they are built into strategies for computer-systems, caution is discarded. Computer-systems then impose rigid beliefs on their users.

As already noted in Chapter 1 (Fig. 1.19), the real-world assumption is central to orthodox approaches to computing. This assumption is not just that the world is real in some absolute sense. The assumption is that we can know it to be real independently of us being in it, so that our knowledge can be verified by that reality, and our knowledge can be explained so that we can know explicitly what it is each of us knows. The real-world assumption is about knowledge, rather than anything else knowledge might be about.

The notion of explanation is central to, and bound up in, the real-world assumption. Explanations are thought to capture the functionality of knowledge in someone, or ensure responses from other things that satisfy knowledge. Explanations are of things known by persons to be real, matching what they are, so that knowledge represented in computers can be grounded in reality.

The real-world assumption is thought to be necessary to any notion of useful computers. If knowledge can be explained so that we can see it is the same in different persons, then we can expect to separate that knowledge from persons and build it into computers. The resulting knowledge based systems will then be able to exercise our knowledge so that machine behaviour will appear useful to us.

The converse of this position is: if instances of knowledge cannot be shown to be the same in different persons, then we have no basis for building anything into computers, and we cannot predict any usefulness. This seems a perverse argument applied just to computers. It is not applied to other machines or, indeed, any other artefacts that people find useful.

The importance given to the real-world assumption implies something about how usefulness of computers is envisaged. Computers are regarded as intellectual tools, as problem solvers, and not as mechanical tools. As problem solvers, they must have knowledge which is consistent with our perceptions of situations we experience in the world, the situations which present us with problems.

'Problem solvers'

To make problem-solving machines, we need a general definition of problems; one which corresponds to the way we seem to apply our knowledge. An orthodox computational view of problems sees them as having a goal state and a start state, and a number of possible solution-paths between such states. For a well-formed and computable problem the goal and start states, and the paths, must be already-known. The problem then is to find a satisfactory solution path, and this may entail satisfying certain further conditions. This is thought to correspond to the way people recognise and treat problems in situations which we experience.

We can observe ourselves gathering data and applying processes to them in the course of us solving problems. We see this as evidence of us applying our knowledge. We can recognise data and processes, and generalise their properties, and represent them in a computer. If we then devise control mechanisms for activating functions within a computer, on the representation, it will be able to show behaviour as though it is using knowledge.

This is a very simplistic picture of computational problem-solving. By adding many refinements to the ways in which data and associated processes can be organised, including rule systems and pattern matching, and adding sophisticated control mechanisms, we might expect increasingly sophisticated and intelligent machine behaviour.

However, irrespective of such refinements, we already have some awkward questions. What must people know in order to know the goal and start states, and paths, of their problems in ordinary day-to-day activities? To be a well-formed problem, its goal state and start state have to be known concurrently, and the goal state has to specify everything that will play a part in our recognition of a solution. The solution to this kind of problem has to be known at the outset. This just is not how people ordinarily seem to perceive problems.

In many practical human activities, including business practices, and design and engineering, problems are explored without knowing their solutions. Start states are the focus of explorations, to decide what they are, requiring intensive and wide ranging exercise of knowledge in persons. Goal states are proposed, speculatively, loosely constrained by knowledge of paths, and they are used exploratively. Solutions are decided, drawing on knowledge that might not have been active at the start. And it is normal to recognise solutions as problems — evident in the continuity of interactions between persons.

We might well say that problems occur in reality, in space and time 'out there', but this does not tell us that they are things separate from ourselves. We are in the same space and time, and problems engage the whole of ourselves in ways we do not explain. It is doubtful whether ordinary problems occur with empty solution spaces separating start states and goals, waiting to be filled. They are more likely to occur in an involved continuum without such separate states. Solution-paths, if they occur at all, are generated within ourselves in response to whatever we know about situations in which we sense problems. They cannot come already prepared, from problem solvers that are not us.

We cannot show problems as distinct things, but we do show distinctions in our descriptions of problems. The distinctions we show occur in our realisations of expressions about problems; they are not in the problem. These are distinctions in the dynamics of person-to-person interaction, stimulating knowledge within us. By doing so, a description might contribute to a solution.

Some, including many who wish to promote computers as problem-solving machines, will object to this characterisation of problem-solving. They will claim there are different kinds of problems. There are problems, usually of a technical nature, which can be identified as computationally well-formed and amenable to rationally explained formal methods. These problems can be defined outside persons, and can be represented within computers.

This objection is flawed in three ways. First, it presumes some fixed demarcation between different kinds of problems within persons; referring to a demarcation which we cannot explain. Secondly, the conditions for well-formedness might be useful in restricting solution-spaces; but they do not explain instances of solutions. Thirdly, the kind of problem which is posed would occur outside of people's ordinary day-to-day experience and, therefore, would be undemanding of ordinary human knowledge and, therefore, would be uninteresting. We can say that well-formed problems are for clerks.

Example

To illustrate how the orthodox approach to problem-solving is flawed, we can consider an example from architecture. This is an example of formal method applied to an activity which many architects and non-architects regard as being motivated informally. The method here involves rules or grammars for determining shapes, to deal with the problem of producing better buildings. This illustrates the general issue of linking method with whatever else might be going on in persons.

Many advocates of formal methods consider them (as things-in-themselves) to be virtuous even in non-technical fields, as expounded by Mitchell ['90] and Oxman ['91] on architectural education. They speculate on the extent to which formal methods can be equated with functionality in mind, or in persons, and Mitchell and Oxman advocate shape grammars [Stiny '75].

Shape grammars: It is claimed that the form or style of highly respected exemplars of buildings, such as Wright's Prairie houses, Queen Ann houses, and Palladio villas, can be generated by sets of transformation rules or grammars applied to shapes. A grammar is said to be functionally equivalent to whatever went on within Wright, for example, in the course of his generating Prairie houses, so that the rules are a formal representation of Wright's knowledge. The rule-set then defines all instances of Prairie houses, including those realised by Wright and those that are yet to be realised. New instances realised after his death are to be accepted as genuine instances of Wright houses — the person does not have to be present.

A strong version of this claim (by Lionel March at an NSF Workshop on *Computational Foundations of Architectural Design,* UCLA, 1985) says that formal grammars represent the cultures in which Wright and others lived and developed their design knowledge, so that these grammars can be thought of as preserving human culture. The formal representation is believed to be a powerful means for preserving abilities from past cultures, to produce good new artefacts.

The basis for this claim is the belief that formal (explained) grammars can fully represent knowledge (not explained) in designers. This is the kind of claim and belief which I am saying is not plausible. The act of defining formal grammars might well be useful for identifying differences between styles of buildings, so that students may contemplate the differences. But to claim that these grammars can carry responsibility for generating new instances of good buildings implies a strange metaphysics.

More generally, when we use formal methods to study certain kinds of behaviour (as among any people engaged in practical activities and showing expressions from their knowledge), we do not get to know that a particular person will show a desired behaviour (be a good practitioner). By formal methods alone, we cannot define what an instance of person has to be, in order to obtain a particular and desirable behaviour. But that is precisely what we try to do when we make computer-systems be things in place of persons.

So now we find we have to question whether the orthodox problem-solving approach to computing deals with anything that people ordinarily recognise as problems. There has to be some other way of characterising the usefulness of computers, and we will attempt to do so in later chapters. If we remove the emphasis on problem-solving, then we will also reduce the importance that is given to the real-world assumption. We will open the way to a different perception of knowledge, moving closer to the holistic view which will be outlined in the next chapter.

Logic-machines

An orthodox and popular view of logic sees it as referring to ways of organising and maintaining relationships between bits of knowledge (data and procedures), so as to satisfy ourselves that our knowledge is true. Among those who adopt this view, some accept logic exists independently of the particulars of other things we find in our experience, but see it as providing us with a means to model knowledge. For them, the real-world assumption lets us believe that we are able to show what we know of other things, and then we use logic to establish how our various contributions to overtly expressed knowledge cohere. Given logical coherence, they say our knowledge matches what other things actually are, and in that way can be known to be true.

In this view, it is possible for us to find that our knowledge is no longer true, when faced with new contributions which disrupt a current coherence. We then reshuffle our knowledge, employing logic, to establish a new state of knowledge as being true. This activity might be associated with problem-solving.

Logic, viewed in this way, encourages the notion that logical functionality can be defined separately from persons, and can be built into computers, so that computers can operate on representations of knowledge and tell people what is true. Among strong advocates of *IT*, it is said that computers can treat problems and tell people what to do.

This problem-solving role of computers has already been questioned. However, can we develop a view of logic which does make it useful in computers? If logic refers to some functionality within us which conditions our knowledge about other things, and conditions expressions from our knowledge, can we externalise anything from that functionality so that it can be useful in computers?

Here we are referring to formal logic: that which conditions our forms of expression and things we do to expressions. Earlier it was suggested that this implies some deeper logic within ourselves, referring to functionality rooted in whatever it is we are, and that can be called informal logic. This deep functionality remains unexplained (Figs 1.13–14). But, notwithstanding this lack of explanation, let us try to consider what a formal logic-machine might be.

Put briefly, a logic-machine might consist of entities or elements (constants, variables...) and relationships between them (predicates), so arranged that when the machine receives some stimulus from outside it is motivated to readjust its internal state. The machine is motivated to resolve received stimuli with its internal state (possibly including inference), so that it can continue to function. Resolution results in stimuli being accommodated (yes, or true), rejected (no, or false), or kept in abeyance (possibly...).

Associated with this functionality of the machine is its ability to match received stimuli (distinct stimuli from things we see as different strings of characters...) with entities and relationships it already has.

Notice that in this view of machines nothing is said about what the external stimuli, or outside world, has to be. A machine just reacts to what it can, and that is its world. We can envisage different machines, each with their own different logic. We should expect them to 'know' different worlds, but their worlds might overlap to the extent that these machines are able to react to the same stimuli. They might be able to react to each other, and to us.

Now logic refers to the inner functionality of the machine, rooted in whatever it is (its material parts) that constitutes the machine. Its logic, its deep functionality, is inherent to itself, and remains hidden in the machine. If we observe such a machine, and say we have a logical view of it, then we are exercising our own logic to describe what we know of the machine's logic. We deduce this from its apparent behaviour, without seeing the machine's logic. This limitation does not prevent us from making logic-machines, but it does have the consequence that we cannot determine what the logic actually is in any machine we make.

This qualification can be understood quite simply as saying if we define something logically it does not follow that we will know all the consequences of having done so, in all circumstances in which the thing will find itself (an elaboration of Lady Lovelace's objection [Hussey '72]). We are now adding that it is not only the unforeseen nature of circumstances which produces this uncertainty, but also our inability to know the inherent logic (deep functionality) of whatever constitutes the thing we make. Any machine, being constituted differently from ourselves, is likely to have a logic that is different from our own. How this affects our interactions with machines will be discussed later, under 'talking to...'.

Logic, considered as the inner functionality of a machine, has the job of ensuring that the machine continues to function. If the machine stops functioning in any circumstance in which it finds itself (and is subsequently unable to continue functioning), that means its logic has failed. This condition applies to computers, and also to all those machines which we usually regard as being mechanical rather than logical.

The implication here is that logic is necessary in all machines we make, without any distinction between logic-machines and non-logical machines. This implication can be accepted even if we are unable to explain the logic in a machine or, indeed, the logic in ourselves. We do not need to know, explicitly, of any necessary conditions of logic independently of any machine, in order to make a machine.

We make machines, exploiting the apparent behaviour of their constituent parts, shaping them into composite artefacts which perform to our satisfaction. We build upon the logic of their constituents to compose a complex logic which seems to perform in accordance with our own logic, so as to make them do things which appear sensible to us. When we do this we impose our formal logic on them. We can do this without separating out any absolutes of logic from ourselves and from machines.

The picture which now emerges can be characterised as a kind of imperialism by man over matter; just as people dominate other people, without them knowing what makes them do so. In this picture we exclude any notion of morality towards materials. We just exploit machines and modify them to suit ourselves, and we do this when we use machines in the normal course of interactions between persons.

Now we have a generalised picture of machines which includes computers, and we can view all machines as logic-machines. We can do so without implying that they are intelligent. We then cannot make, and do not want, logic-machines to possess our knowledge and solve our problems. If we persist in trying to make problem-solving machines, that would imply a remote kind of human interaction between persons who make and people who use the machines; with makers imposing the products of their knowledge on users, and not listening to user-responses. If we do that, the result would be intellectual imperialism by certain persons over many people.

Talking to machines

Among people, we can think of language as something within communicating parties which they use in the course of their interactions, and which functions without any direct material connection. Things do materialise between the parties, as expressions, but these things bind parties together only if they are acceptable to language already-present within themselves. Language presumes some degree of autonomy or independence as well as similarity across the parties.

In our earlier discussion of concepts it was suggested that effectiveness of language depends on similarity in the parties, or similarity of concepts employed in them, and now this can be understood as referring to similarity in logic in the parties.

If communicating parties include computers as logic-machines, and if we intend interactions to employ language, then we might expect claims that the similarity condition is satisfied across persons and computers. This is indeed what we do find among advocates of orthodox problem-solving computers.

Orthodox approaches to computing, and especially in AI, rest on the strong assumption that minds and machines are in principle not different. Many will moderate this assumption by saying that it is only parts of minds which are not different: the explained logical parts. That poses the difficulty that we are not able to define firm demarcations to the parts, and contradicts the involved view of logic we have been discussing. Another moderation of this assumption is to say that minds cause behaviour which in principle can be matched by behaviour which can potentially be produced by machines; so that any actual difference between minds and machines becomes immaterial. This claim poses the difficulty of differentiating and relating function and behaviour, and presents us with a continuously moving target. To explore the implications of orthodox computing, we have to examine the strong assumption.

We are offered the prospect of computers ultimately being able to do anything we can do. Progress towards this ultimate achievement is said to be simply a matter of our recognising current shortcomings and overcoming them by making new computers that can do more. We can try to be principled about our recognition of shortcomings, carefully devising computational theories about human behaviour; but we are discouraged from entertaining any theory which seeks to establish that computers and people are different.

If we were to find that computers and people are fundamentally different, then the notion of language linking persons and computers would not hold. And that outcome is precisely what we find when we examine instances of human - computer interaction. We find that computer programming languages, and higher level protocols for interaction, are essentially asymmetrical. They are asymmetrical in the sense that expressions from us to computers work in a way that is very different from the way that expressions from computers to us work.

In ordinary human interactions, the purpose of any language expression is to touch and stimulate knowledge within interacting parties, to invoke inner functions and evoke responses in the form of further expressions. The dynamics of interaction sustains knowledge within the parties, including their knowledge of other things in their experience, without each having to know explicitly the functions within each other.

When a computer is one of the parties, and a person using the computer is another, something else has to happen. User-expressions from the person have to conform to a predefined programming language. That language provides access to known functionality within the computer, and knowing here refers to the designer of the language (who is absent). The parts of user-expressions which define relationships between other parts of expressions contributed by the user, the person, and which the computer is expected to evaluate and maintain, have to conform to something which the person has to know as the programming language. This condition applies irrespective of how interaction is realised, including the use of mouse, menus, and icons.

Expressions from the person are aimed purely at evoking responses the person knows he or she wants from the computer, with no ambiguity. The person has no expectation of other responses the computer could possibly volunteer from knowledge it might have, unknown to the person (and unknown to a programmer anticipating what the person might want to know).

Expressions from the computer to the person are aimed at showing the person just what he or she has asked to see, with no interest in discovering what else the person might know. Question and answer sessions occur only for purposes of identifying what functionality within the computer the person is asking for.

Some systems give the appearance of being more involved in interactions, as in the case of expert systems, but they know nothing about what their expressions might mean outside themselves. The symbol-strings which they display reflect states within these systems, their own logic (or superimposed programmer's logic), and they do not know the strings are symbols for anything else. It is then argued that computers can be given the ability to sense other things, so that they can know their expressions are about other things, but such knowing poses obscure questions about motivation and intentionality — in whose interest might a computer know anything?

We are left with an asymmetry. A person using a computer knows him or herself to be in and of a world, interacting with other persons, and using the machine in the course of such interactions. The computer does not know itself to be anything (as far as we can tell). What does this asymmetry imply?

Nothing in these observations negates the possibility that machines have their own logic, nor even that they might possess knowledge (unlike ours), and we can expect to see machines doing things to other things. However, the similarity argument tells us that we cannot know and share such knowledge.

We cannot use our language to reach into a machine's further knowledge, to motivate collaboration in concerted actions in the world.

We can make machines, but we cannot make machines in our likeness. Their constituents and, therefore, the logic of their constituents, remain different and unknown to us. Our evident inability to communicate with machines in the way that we use language among ourselves then carries the strong implication that people and machines are indeed fundamentally different; and this difference is accommodated in the earlier characterisation of man's imperialism over matter.

Examples

In Chapter 1 (Figs 1.20–27) we briefly noted a number of current orthodox computational strategies. Now we will look at just two of these: one to illustrate the direction in which we do not want to go, and the other to gain a glimpse of a possible direction which might turn out to be more promising. The first is semantic networks and associated developments which assume what is going on in the minds of people, including neural networks (or connectionism). The second is slot/filler systems viewed simply as logical 'mechanics' for realising and showing connections between expressions, without representing knowledge.

Semantic networks: These networks of nodes and links (or variants of them) are regarded as devices for representing the complexity of information that is in us, and by associating computational semantics with them it is claimed that we can make computers intelligent in the way they behave with our information. The evolution of semantic networks during the 1970s is reviewed by Brachman ['79]. He identifies five different kinds of knowledge to which they apply: implementational, logical, epistemological, conceptual, and linguistic.

Roughly, what makes these *semantic* networks is that they are said to represent the semantics of certain aspects of knowledge, implying that the relevant aspects can be made explicit. Networks then represent such semantics in the functionality (logic) of their links, used to establish certain kinds of associations between nodes. The nodes point to objects-of-knowledge as implied by different kinds of expression. This strategy puts less emphasis on the reality of *extensional* objects 'out there', and instead focuses on the reality of *intensional* objects we have in mind; it implies computers can be made to represent properly our semantics and can therefore be intelligent in their responses to our expressions.

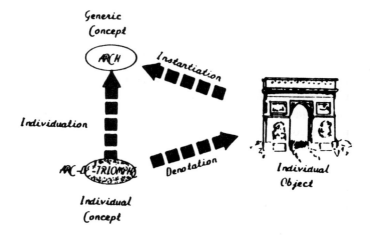

Figure 3.1: *Illustration of how semantic networks work (taken from Brachman)*

This view of semantics sits uncomfortably with our earlier discussion of concepts and meaning. Meaning, in terms of us (or computers) placing ourselves (or themselves) amidst other things in the world (Fig. 1.8), is missing from semantic networks (we cannot know what informal equipment for knowing they might have). If we pass lightly over the claims for computer-intelligence, what remains of interest?

Semantic networks of nodes and associative links are offered as representing different things being in knowledge, as in the example shown in Figure 3.1 (Fig. 1.20). In this example the nodes stand for generic concepts (generalisations), individual concepts (particular things), and individual objects (real further things). The links stand for kinds of associations, and in computational terms they would include functions for maintaining associations between nodes. An 'individuation' links some particular thing with some general thing, such that the particular thing is linked through 'denotation' with some further thing, where the further thing is already linked through 'instantiation' with the general thing. The purpose of this rather tortuous distinction between instantiation and individuation is to distinguish between some particular thing which is an expression of an individual concept, and any further thing which is an individual object that the expression is about, both being realisations (or apparent real things) associated with a generic concept. The expression might be considered as an intensional object about an extensional object.

The difficulty which now emerges is how can we distinguish between these different things in knowledge? The labels to the nodes indicate notional things, pointing to our understanding of different real things that might be included in knowledge. But all the nodes which appear in the diagram are the same kind of thing: different 'marks on paper'. The differences do not contain whatever it is each of us might have as interpretations for them. We might agree, loosely, that there is something we call a generic concept of 'arch-ness' in us, and that the characters 'Arc-de-Triomphe' express one case of arch-ness, and that the expression points to something we agree is the Arc-de-Triomphe, but none of this tells us whether or not we are all seeing the same. The whole of the diagram might be considered as an intensional object about an extensional object which each of us sees in somewhat different ways.

The same difficulty crops up when we consider other related developments, as in the case of neural networks (Fig. 1.24). All these developments assume some correspondence between functionality (logic) built into a machine and functionality in the minds of persons, and their advocates depend on claims of correspondence to substantiate claims that outcomes from machines will be acceptable to people. These developments differ only in the extent to which logic in a machine is hidden from users, and logic is most hidden in the case of neural networks.

This difficulty does not mean that we cannot devise systems of nodes and links in which types of nodes are predetermined, and links include functionality (some self-consistent logic) for maintaining associations between nodes. We just cannot be certain about what they represent, and little is gained by claiming they represent aspects of knowledge. Claims of correspondence with human knowledge just are deceptive.

Slot/filler systems: We can try to adopt a more controllable strategy for networks, and think of a machine which just holds arrangements of nodes and links given to it by its users, and accepts arbitrary modifications. Something of this kind is indicated by the slot/filler convention [Minsky '75, Frost '86].

This convention is based on a notion of things (any *kind* of concrete or abstract thing) being described by further things. It offers machine functionality (logic) for making constructions out of differentiated kinds (nodes) and slots (links). Kinds are differentiated by names. Slots also are differentiated by names, and they serve to name parts of kinds. Slots are filled with instructions about parts. Instructions may simply say that parts are further kinds, or new instances of kinds, or they may call on functions that are to be applied to kinds. The resulting parts hierarchies can be interlinked (through inheritance links), forming networks.

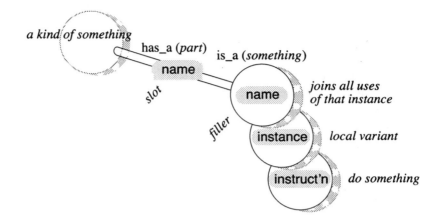

Figure 3.2: *Illustration of how slots and fillers work*

The s/f convention follows in the tradition of records-and-pointers structures going back to the early days of computing. Records were the contents in a computer's memory locations and pointers pointed to those locations. Now structures are composed of linked names for things we have in mind, and the strategy is to use prepared logic to reflect any such structures in a computer.

From a user's point of view, this strategy may be described as working like 'Tinker Toys' which were popular among children many years ago. These toys consisted of small squat wooden disks, each with slots (or holes) cut into its edge and through its middle, plus wooden sticks which could be pushed into the slots, as indicated in Figure 3.2. Given this simple functionality (logic), children then assembled three-dimensional constructions of disks and sticks, which they interpreted into their own ideas about other things, such as animals and motor cars. These toys were used to construct networks in space, offering the possibility of arbitrarily disconnecting and adding parts, with no externally imposed conditions on boundaries to parts in the minds of children. Yet constructions were evidently effective in stimulating games played by children.

Translating this picture into one which employs computer technology, we can think of the disks being different from each other, and we can associate distinct functions with certain sticks, as in Figure 3.2. Constructions then can show enriched differentiations with varying degrees of rigidity. By increasing the instances of differentiations (or increasing the resolution), we can imagine our view of disks and sticks blending into a view of continuous and plastic three-dimensional objects. When we do this, we want to preserve the ethos of Tinker Toys to stimulate games we play.

Descriptions formed out of nodes and links do not have to look visually like any further things they describe, as in the example in Figure 1.21 (taken from work presented by Tweed *et al.* ['89] and Bijl ['91a]). They describe what we know of such further things, with each of us interpreting descriptions so as to fit with our understandings for further things. For this purpose, we can envisage separate persons interacting with each other by means of touching and changing descriptions; allowing each arbitrarily to remove, add, or in other ways modify parts.

All kind and slot names can be decided by users (with instance identifiers maintained by the system). They can be things other than character strings, including bits of drawing. Functions that are available for inclusion in instructions (in fillers) ought to be simple and widely known, such as functions of arithmetic and geometry. The system's own functionality (logic) then applies only within and across constructions, and not to anything else users might have in mind. To use this kind of system, users need to know they have satisfying interpretations for the formal regularities it offers — they have to know the system.

In the general case of this strategy, it can be used to compose unbounded descriptions of things, and inheritance allows changes within descriptions to propagate changes within other descriptions; offering flexibility limited only by the ability of users to keep track of what they are doing (a difficult condition).

To make s/f systems useful, it is thought that they need to be supplied with already prepared frames and scripts which tell a story, which anticipate the users' world. Framing up a story by using system-functionality not available to ordinary users then becomes prescriptive on users — breaking the ethos of Tinker Toys. By sticking to the basic s/f convention (avoiding prepared stories) we have the beginnings of a computational strategy which promises to be useful to, and controllable by, users. But, for the analogy with Tinker Toys to hold, we have yet to devise systems that are as visible and graspable by ordinary users, including children.

Artificial intelligence

All developments of computational strategies which rest on the claim of correspondence with things going on in the minds of persons can be considered as coming from the field of artificial intelligence. Each implies replication of some aspect of what is thought to be human intelligence, or behaviour shown by human intelligence.

When we try to look further into this field we are faced with two broad AI cultures. On consists of large numbers of followers interested in applications; their interest is in popular AI associated with new *IT*. The other consists of researchers interested in developing AI technologies, divided among themselves in what they think they can achieve. I will say more on popular AI later. Now we will consider certain general research ambitions.

Among strong AI enthusiasts, the claim is that they can know what knowledge is, explain it, and replicate it in machines. Their aim is to make machines that can act in place of persons — acting among and for other persons (not the AI programmers). Some will admit they are not there yet, but given enough time they will be. More cautious AI advocates will say of course they cannot cover all of human knowledge, but they can cover enough to make intelligent machines a reality.

An obvious objection to these positions, and one which might be raised by many scientists, is that we are able to describe knowledge only in very general terms (abstract theories), indicating sparse understanding of patterns and tendencies. We cannot predict the particulars of instances of the things persons will do (other than simple and isolated mechanistic operations). Practical instances of behaviour involve the whole of what we refer to as knowledge, including human feeling associated with experience.

If we place computers among people (now or at any time in the future), and expect computers to engage in the everyday practices of people, like persons would do, then computers would appear to behave as severely defective persons. This characterisation of computers as mental defectives might be contested by those who point to computers doing impressive things, like playing chess. The common feature of all such examples is that the activities which are evident as impressive computer-behaviour are defined separately from all else in which people are involved, as artefactual games that are bounded by self-consistent rules. This applies even in the case of so-called expert systems carrying out diagnostic functions (the difference in such cases being in the way rules get to be formalised). All these cases cannot cope with ordinary human activities which call on unexplained abilities within persons.

To consider what we ought to expect from AI, we can recall what was said earlier about logic-machines. We have accepted that machines have inner functionality, or logic, and they can be made to sense things that come from outside themselves (especially instructions from their users). It is conceivable that they can apply their logic to their sensations so that they have knowledge. What seems less plausible is that machines can know they have knowledge. It seems unlikely that they can knowingly use their logic so as to overcome unforeseen adversity and, in that sense, we might conclude machines are not intelligent.

Here a distinction is being drawn between logic and intelligence. The strong AI claim that computers and anything else, including beer cans, can be intelligent, is being contested. We might deduce that these things do have inner functionality, or logic; but to be intelligent they have to know they exist, and knowingly use their logic to go on existing — and that is what beer cans cannot do.

Our knowing that we have logic, and our knowing use of logic, might be understood as our having consciousness. This term has connotations, such as unconsciousness and being in a dream state, which lie beyond the present discussion. However, it may well be that being intelligent entails consciousness, and it is difficult to conceive of machines being conscious.

To continue with what has already been said about our relationship with machines, we can say that we make them, by building upon the logic of their constituents, so that they show behaviour which satisfies us. By building upon the logic of their constituents, and without knowing exactly what their logic is, we should expect that we do not know exactly what their knowledge is (if they have knowledge). If we persist in claiming they have knowledge, we should expect that the motivations which determine their intelligent behaviour will not be recognisable by us (as in my earlier objection to Fiegenbaum, under 'human concepts'). Thus the notion of artificial intelligence becomes highly speculative, involving metaphysics beyond our own intelligence.

Here we are getting deeper into philosophy. Margaret Boden ['90] provides a good overview of the philosophy of AI in a collection of key papers from distinguished researchers, including people as far apart as Churchland and Dreyfus. Boden considers "AI as *the science of intelligence in general* — or, more accurately, as the intellectual core of cognitive science". The collection of papers offers a rich spread of ideas about intelligence, including different approaches to understanding what intelligence can be, and speculations on the possibility of replicating intelligence in machines. In nearly all cases the papers presuppose intelligence is something we can know explicitly, independently from our involvement in it — and that seems to me to be calling on some mysterious metaphysics.

From biological science we get another view, discussed earlier under 'evolution'. Dawkins gives us a picture of evolution based on random mutation and after-the-event evolutionary stable states, which excludes any sense of being alive and, indeed, intelligence. However, even in Dawkins' view, these attributes may have come into our being as a result of evolution, and may now play a part in the continuity of evolution. The caution which comes from his picture is not that intelligence is unnecessary or overrated, but that our intelligence does not determine and cannot predict what is to come. This leaves open the possibility that intelligence can play a part in shaping what is to come, just as any other aspect of our biological selves can. For this to work, intelligence must be exercised in beings that are sensitive to random influences from other evolving things. This imperative does not anticipate any goal, like a good future, but now is necessary to our continuous being. We have to ask whether artificial intelligence can meet this imperative.

Popular AI

Now I will return to popular AI. Widespread acceptance of computers being knowledge processors and showing intelligent behaviour depends on people's acceptance of the real-world assumption and the notion of explanation. Commonly we say we can explain things (real things we know in experience), and explanations can be expressed in terms of logic which is present in computers (and just that logic), so that computers will show behaviour which is consistent with our knowledge; and that is said to demonstrate intelligence exercised in a machine.

This popular construction is unsound in ways that have already been described. It relies too much on explanation, and presumes we can know what the logic in a given machine is, which now seems not plausible. We do not know computers by their ability to perform familiar tasks. They are not like other tools. More critically, the intelligence we attribute to a computer ought more appropriately to be attributed to the person who does the explaining; the behaviour of a computer is an extension of the behaviour of its programmer, and his or her anticipation of what other people will or ought to want. Other people who are persuaded to use computers are left stranded when the programmers are absent. These users of computers will then find they are unable to show their responsibility to yet other people, in the course of their person-to-person interactions.

The popular view of AI is misleading in that it implies the possibility of taking responsibility out of persons and placing it in computers. The objection then is not that this is impossible, but that it involves us in metaphysical questions we cannot answer. Outside academia, to act upon assumptions which tell us artificial intelligence is possible is to be socially and politically irresponsible. In all our interests, to preserve people's involvement in the further evolution of our knowledge, artificial intelligence is not safe.

In saying artificial intelligence is not safe, some might see parallels in history, in past moves (social, religious, and political) to burn books. But I am not arguing against using computers, just as I do not argue against our use of written or printed words. Both cases make important contributions to our ability to form expressions to each other — provided that each of us remains responsible for instances we show. In Chapter 5 I will try to show how computers might be made to serve this purpose, without presuming the presence of artificial intelligence.

Example

We will now look at an example of computers in use, to see why we do not want to place intelligence and responsibility in them. This example comes from computer aided design, a field that started in the 1960s when it was shown that computers can be made to draw [Sutherland '63]. The ambition was to get computers to relate drawings to non-graphical information depicted by drawings — to know what a drawing is about.

The example dates back to the late 1960s and 1970s, but the difficulties it illustrates are still not resolved today. The concepts used to guide developments in computing do not move as fast as changes to implementation techniques (capacity and speed). My reason for choosing this example is that I was in charge of developing it, and can speak freely about its faults.

This was a CAD system developed for the Scottish Special Housing Association, and it was used to design and build houses over a period of more than 10 years. It was a large integrated system which means that it held a great deal of user-specific design data and processes in a single design model. The system was able to realise expressions from its model automatically, appropriate to particular aspects of design indicated by users. The users were able to modify these expressions and, consequently, modify the system's data, in the course of designing.

Users could draw their designs, and the system would respond with its evaluations of space utilisation, daylighting, heating, and sound transmission, and it would automatically develop the structural design, and quantify all materials needed to construct the buildings.

Although this system was highly successful, being used in practice over many years, eventually it failed. The reasons for this failure are instructive. Over the years, people's (administrators' and politicians') perceptions of the need for new houses changed and, consequently, their definition of houses changed. In the 1950s and 1960s new houses were demanded in large numbers, and they were generally built on vacant ground. In the 1980s the need for any new houses was doubted, and those that were built were shaped out of already existing buildings. The computer-system could not cope with such changes.

To generalise on this observation, we can say that designers have to be responsive to new and unpredicted demands in a dynamic world, and they are able to be responsive because they know themselves to be part of this world. The computers which designers use do not know they are part of a world which extends beyond themselves. So when demands change in unexpected ways, computers cannot respond (other than by declaring: 'error'). When that happens, the work of designers is disrupted.

We then find ourselves faced with an irony. The better a computer-system is, in the sense of it possessing a lot of data and processes useful to designers, the greater the likelihood that it will fail, and the greater the disruption to its users when it does fail. In this example the disruption was masked by politically motivated changes to the user-organisation, which had the effect that it no longer designed and built houses.

Problem of integration: The problem indicated here is general to all cases of computer-applications prepared by computer-specialists, for use by people who are not otherwise engaged in the development of this technology. I have discussed this in my earlier book: *Computer Discipline and Design Practice* [Bijl '89]. There I go into some detail on the history of the development and use of the SSHA's integrated system.

In that book I focus on the evolutionary nature of design practices, and the difficulty of anticipating evolution in formal techniques. In the late 1960s, the ambition of integrated systems seemed obviously desirable. We, as designers of the system, thought a computer should be able to hold all information coming from the various persons engaged in a design project, hold it as a representation of the design-object, and selectively return appropriate information to users as required during different stages of design. The system should integrate contributions from different participants in its single design model.

The flaw in this ambition became apparent to us before the development of the system was completed. The model employed by the system had built into it an anticipation of what instances of design could be (allowing for variations), and this anticipation could not be made responsive to new demands on designers, from outside the system. This kind of anticipation in integrated systems was (and still is) unavoidable, and became buried in layers of software. Users were not able to modify it. That the system proved to be useful was due to its being closely tailored (unsystematically) to the procedures of user-practices — and that tailoring hidden in software contributed to its eventual failure.

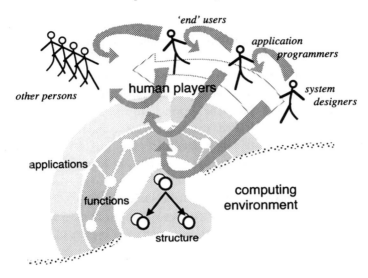

Figure 3.3: *People engaged*

Fragmentation: We can briefly note some problems of a more technical nature, that were experienced with the SSHA system. Practically every computer-system consists of layers of software: programs built on top of other programs. So, in any system, we have the problem of fragmentation into separate layers.

We can see these layers as resting on some structure of so-called representational entities and relationships, plus functionality available in the machine, as illustrated in Figure 3.3 (and in Fig. 1.3). Basically, the representation structure is much the same in all computers. We then have logical constructions which are acceptable to the representation structure, and which are potentially useful to many applications outside the system. At this level we can include those constructions which support production systems, frame systems, semantic networks, and neural networks (and some of these have been outlined in Ch. 1). At a higher level we have application programs intended for specific purposes outside the system. These determine the kind of surface behaviour of the machine which is thought to be acceptable to so-called end-users.

To operate a system, at any level, users or their programmers then have to employ only those actions (their own behaviour) for which the system already has abstractions. A computer-system must include abstractions for user-actions so that these actions can invoke its inner functions, at all levels, and so that results can be matched with possible states of its representation structure. These abstractions become fixed anticipations of users and their programmers, or their behaviour.

Then the problem is that each of these layers of software is produced by different persons with abilities not known to each other. The effect is that each lower layer is invisible but has to be 'correct' to the one above. System-programmers (or expert system 'shell' designers) have to anticipate the needs of their users, and accommodate those needs in their logical constructions. Application-programmers (or knowledge engineers) have to anticipate the needs of their users, and build their anticipations into their programs. End-users then have to use these programs to satisfy the demands of other people, the recipients of results. For these relationships to work, as we found with the SSHA system, these different people have to be in touch with each other outside the system.

The eventual recipients of results can be regarded as the true end-users of computers, and new demands from them are motivated outside computers. In time, their demands will go beyond whatever has been anticipated in an application-program. Then it becomes necessary to go down a level in the system, to modify the program's use of logic in the machine. This entails calling on the application-programmer. Eventually changes in demand will require changes to underlying logical constructions. This entails calling on the system-programmer.

Then the problem is that the computer-programmers will have disappeared, or they will no longer know the system sufficiently to predict the effects of changes they might make to it. End-users find themselves faced with a system that is unresponsive to newly evolving demands from the world in which end-users must survive.

The problems which have been outlined here are to be found in all computer-applications, and they touch all 'ordinary' people who are persuaded they ought to use computers. The field of AI fails to address most of these problems, and in continuing to do so it will fail to make computers available to people. The alternative to AI is to move away from orthodox approaches to computing, and think hard about the difference between people and machines.

Summary

The observations which have been made on current orthodox computational strategies ought to make us cautious about anticipations of their usefulness. These strategies each rest on technical developments far removed from ordinary everyday practices of potential users. If people in general become obliged to use them, then these strategies will change existing practices. This would be a change imposed by specialists in the technology, and not by persons differently specialised in exercising their own responsibility towards yet other people.

The danger which is indicated here can be traced back to belief in the real-world assumption; belief in knowledge embracing things in the world as they actually are, and known to be the same in separate persons. This assumption encourages the notion of knowledge being realised in computers, and the efficiency of computers is then thought to offer advantages over unexplained (unreliable) functions in persons.

The real-world assumption excludes people's involvement in each other, and the role of this involvement in sustaining and evolving our shared knowledge. Human knowledge, and concepts by which things we can sense are turned into information in us, acceptable in us, are not explained by yes/no steps (classical two-valued logic). We draw on unexplained feeling and knowing within ourselves, effective in the space between yes and no.

We have no way of setting fixed demarcations between this knowing and any other kind of knowledge, such as the kind supposedly represented in computers. This picture of knowledge bound up in our kind of being sets limits on computers being intelligent, possessing our knowledge, and solving our problems. We can know but not explain that this picture is true in us, and we then need to explore different ways in which computers might be useful.

Conversation among engineers

The following are extracts from an email conference (IRMA Workshop run by Thomas Froese of Canada, November/December 1993). The topic is product modelling (see Ch. 1 Fig. 18), with an emphasis on developing a standard 'reference model' for data exchange.

19 Nov — Thomas Froese, Department of Civil Engineering, University of British Columbia, Canada:

> ... I'd like to come back to the model itself again. Although I'll suggest a few minor revisions, I'd mainly like to restate where we are so far.

> 1. Project Object Classification Breakdown

> As given earlier (Frits, Nov 19):
>
>   Project_Object
>   [has_subtype]->Product
>   [has_subtype]->Activity
>   [has_subtype]->Project
>   [has_subtype]->Resource
>   [has_subtype]->Participant
>   [has_subtype]->Control

> The "Project [consists_of]-> Project_Object" relationship holds, but I've only included specialization relationships here. I think Project is a special form of Activity. This same model will be used to represent information relating to both specific projects (e.g., project X) and projects in general (e.g., a resource unit cost database). Is "Project_Object" OK for a top level name, then, or should it be "AEC_Object"? [AEC: Architecture, Engineering, and Construction] [1]

> "Product" is any piece of the facility itself.

> "Activity" is any piece of action, effort, or process (e.g., design or construction effort).

> "Resource" is anything that is utilized in performing the activity. Note that resources may be consumed (e.g., materials), not consumed (e.g., equipment), or partially consumed (e.g., formwork good for a limited number of uses). Its use may or may not prevent it from being used elsewhere (e.g., a crew vs. temp. site power). Frits makes materials a type

---

[1] My square brackets added to these extracts.

116

of product. I think they are often considered to be resources, and this seems more natural to me (although there is a difficulty with prefabricated things like doors: when do the "materials" become "components"). Maybe something can be both a product and a resource?

"Control" is the most ill-defined. It is anything which influences an activity.

2. Other Root Objects

    State
        [of]->Project_Object
    Result
        [of]->Activity

Any Project_Object can exist in various "States" which can be explicitly represented....

Any Project_Object can be the result of some activity: it will then be a "Result" (IN ADDITION to whatever other class it is)....

3. Basic Associative Relationships

    Activity
        [uses]->Resources
        [controled_by]->Control
        [acted_on_by]->Actor
        [results_in]->Result

"Result" will often be a product or product state. This is the main connection between activities and product....

25 Nov — Aart Bijl, EdCAAD, Department of Architecture, University of Edinburgh, UK:

...The present discussion is among engineers who aim to program systems that other non-programming engineers will use. Much of this discussion centres on notation, with structure added to make models of something. This something refers to whatever passes between differently specialised engineers when they practise their skills on building projects.

...The focus then is on language, or language expressions, used to describe products — and on formalisations of language that can be built into computer systems. If this is the ambition, then this workshop is taking on board difficult and unresolved problems... which are not specific to engineering.

My key questions are:

a) What is the basis for believing that programmer/engineers can decide 'correct' Product Modelling systems for non-programming engineers?

b) How are non-programming engineers expected to get to know and accept the resulting systems?

These questions are about what we think we are doing, and what we expect to achieve — and they are about like-minded people (specialised in computing) talking to different like-minded people (different specialisations).

A basic assumption... is that there is something fixed and recognised as the same in all engineers, which can be known, explained, and represented in a model.

This assumption is revealed by statements [earlier in the workshop] such as: "In order to communicate about conceptual models we have to adopt some common notation" (which is not a condition of ordinary language), and "the problem should be broken into chunks that closely represent the actual problem domain (the systems should model the world)" (when we have no way of establishing such correspondence outside our various involvements in projects). There also is the plea for agreement "about a common (neutral) format for project data interchange", which is silent on the question of neutral to what? (to knowledge in every engineer?).

Evidence of differences in perception, and uncertainty, abound among like-minded programmer/engineers, even in this workshop. We have differences on notation and structure, and on whether these differences are conceptual or implementational; and we treat these issues as though they are resolvable to 'correct' single outcomes. We have the suggestion that problems become simpler if we limit ourselves to data exchange, and leave advances in integration methods (CAxx tools) to commercial developers — posing unclear demarcations and expectations.

I fear that any enterprise which seeks new technological advances by people not engaged in practice, and which intends these advances to serve unspecified different other people who are variously engaged in practice, cannot escape complex and difficult problems....

25 Nov — Frits Tolman, TNO Building and Construction Research, Department of Computer Integrated Construction, Delft, Netherlands:

I would like to react on Aart Bijl's posting... In my opinion the IRMA conference is about the question: "Can we improve the current state-of-the-art of computer usage in the building and construction industry, and if so, how?"

Your contribution gives me the impression that your answer to the central question is negative, or at least that it is all very, very complicated. With that I don't agree (of course), because we don't have to change the world in one day, we only have to take one step forward.

Then in more detail.

"What is the basis for believing that programmer/engineers can decide 'correct' Product Modelling systems for non-programming engineers?"

My answer is: (1) this conference is not about developments of 'correct' Product Modelling systems for non-programming engineers, and (2) you probably will agree that current methods used to describe models of products (buildings) also do not guarantee any degree of correctness, on the contrary I would say. If there is any common 'belief' between the participants, I think that the IRMA group believes that we can improve upon that.

"How are non-programming engineers expected to get to know and accept the resulting systems?"

This is an irrelevant question. Maybe the first generation of engineers that accepts and knows their system will be programming engineers. What is the use of this kind of questions? You don't ask what will become of the children of [that develop from] a baby. Let time do its duty.

"We have the suggestion that problems become simpler if we limit ourselves to data exchange, and leave advances in integration methods to commercial developers."

Not advances in integration methods, but the development of Product Modelling systems for non-programming engineers. Why should it not be simpler to limit ourselves to data exchange (Form and Function)? You yourself know and point out how difficult the development of integrated CAD systems really is. So why is the restriction to data exchange not a simplification? You can argue that such a limitation is not useful, but then we would at least know what we disagree about.

"There is also a plea for agreement "about a common (neutral) format for project data interchange", which is silent on the question of neutral to what? (to knowledge in every engineer?)"

In several contributions to this conference I have argued that the best step forward from the current situation, might be the development of a STEP compatible standard for project data interchange between dissimilar CAxx [computer aided...] systems. The word 'neutral' means that dissimilar CAxx systems can electronically communicate (some) relevant data. In a recent STEP workshop on interoperability (which is another word for neutral) the following layers of 'neutral' models have been presented. Going from top to bottom:

Interoperability between CAxx systems of different AEC sectors
Interoperability between CAxx systems of different Enterprises
Interoperability between CAxx systems of different Actors
Interoperability between CAxx systems of different Life cycle stages
Interoperability between CAxx systems with different (Shape)
    Representations

Perhaps I missed a few more definitions of 'neutral', but for now it seems enough.

"I fear that any enterprise which seeks new technological advances by people not engaged in practice, and which intends these advances to serve unspecified different other people who are variously engaged in practice, cannot escape complex and difficult problems."

Are you saying that the development of reference models for AEC-data sharing and exchange between dissimilar CAxx systems, should be left to the practising architects, engineers, etc.? Are you serious? The only people that are able to do a job like that are the ones with experience in the computer field. Though practitioners should be consulted of course. And furthermore I wonder if you are right, in history hardly no standard has ever been proposed by the ultimate users. So why should it be different here?

26 Nov — Aart Bijl, reply to Frits Tolman's reaction:

Yes, I am somewhat negative about the approach to product modelling, but not to the fact that people in practice make and use product models. I am negative about standards (devised elsewhere, by separate specialists) being imposed on these 'ordinary' people, limiting their future opportunity for evolving models....

Babies:

Frits, your parallel with babies is really interesting: "You don't ask what will become of the child [that develops from] a baby. You let time do its duty".

If IRMA is to be a baby like babies of other people, are we now in the act of conception? The process feels different. Conception generally does not involve prior deliberations and explanations (it occurs in our unspoken being, and depends on already-present similarity across people). We cannot say IRMA has already been born, because then it would have to be like other babies, spontaneously recognised as babies by all people.

It is true that we do not know what a baby will be (when it is grown up), and not knowing does not stop us producing babies. But everyone knows babies, and how to treat any baby, to influence its development (so that it ends up speaking English, or French, etc.). Knowing and bringing up babies is not a task for specialists. If IRMA is to be like other babies, then it should not need us (as specialised programmer/engineers).

Priests:

Yes, of course I do mean that anybody, any architects, engineers, etc., ought to be involved in defining and developing IRMA (or technologies like IRMA), for purposes of supporting interactions between such people. In supporting interactions, communication, data-exchange, etc., we are considering a technology for language expressions. This becomes a technology that has to be absorbed into language(s) of users, and becomes involved in people's further evolution of language(s). This kind of development cannot be left to separate specialists with special knowledge of computers. Consider what would have happened if the development of language had been left just to priests speaking Latin in churches.

If we find it too difficult to think how ordinary people can be involved in what we do, how can we expect to do things for them? We become like priests objecting to the translation of the Bible into English, or French, etc. My question in my earlier contribution can be rephrased: What makes us believe we can be priests acting on behalf of unseen other people?

26 Nov — Robin Drogemuller, Department of Civil & Systems Engineering, James Cook University of North Queensland, Australia:

> Aart Bijl asked some interesting questions on what we are trying to achieve.
>
> "The present discussion is among engineers who aim to program systems that other non-programming engineers will use...."
>
> My expectation is that the initial results will be used among 'informed' practitioners. The implementation should be 'hidden' below the layers that are seen by general practitioners. A simple comparison is the use of DXF as a drawing interchange standard....
>
> ...No-one has claimed that this would be easy, but we have to start somewhere.
>
> "My key questions... a)   What is the basis for believing that programmer/engineers can decide...?"
>
> Do non-programming personnel need to know the Product Model being used? They are mainly interested in the user interface and their interaction with the data behind it. There have been several mentions of the need for adaptability and change. I would not expect to get such a complex proposal right first time. [Is now the first time?]
>
> "b) How are non-programming engineers expected to get to know...?"
>
> By using systems which support the aims of non-programmers and help them achieve improved performance (time/cost/functionality/etc). We are attempting to provide a framework that will allow the development of an "enabling technology" (buzz word).
>
> ...I do not think a single outcome is likely. A "mapping" between the views of personnel in different countries and disciplines is more desirable....

30 Nov — Aart Bijl: reply to Robin Drogemuller's reaction:

> Robin's points generally do not contradict what I say, but he says "we have to start somewhere". Yes, but the problem is knowing where 'where' is...
>
> ...data exchange (and mapping) is not a simple and potentially useful starting point. That presumes too much (about what is being mapped to what, fitting within a single computational mapping strategy)...

02 Dec — Frits Tolman: reply to Aart Bijl's reaction:

> ...It is my impression that when we speak about open standards for product model data exchange, we are not speaking about standards that are being imposed on 'ordinary' people, limiting their future opportunity for evolving models, but about standards that are being imposed on 'ordinary' computers, greatly improving their mutual 'understanding'.
>
> ...it is because I think that the AEC industries should stay as they are, small, fragmented, individualistic, but still able to perform well, that I want to contribute to the development of a standard for communication of

meaningful data between 'ordinary' computers in the AEC industries. Can you please comment on this?

Then you joke a little with my suggestion that IRMA is a (our) baby. Well it feels that IRMA is somewhere between the Inception Stage and the Global Design Stage (we have been discussing life cycle stages all along). But OK, maybe you are right and the reason for all the noise in the communication is the fact that we don't have a concept of our baby. Which, by the way, is still no proof that we will not all be good dad's, mom's, uncle's and such. Knowing and bringing up IRMA might be a task perfectly suited to us specialists (mothers are also specialists in a way).

Finally your remark about priests. In my opinion we are not so much acting on behalf of unseen people, but on behalf of unseen computers. If the unseen people want their unseen computers to communicate meaningful data this is currently not possible....

02 Dec — Andy Crowley, Computer-Aided Engineering Group, Department of Civil Engineering, University of Leeds, UK:

[Reply to Tolman, 2 Dec.]

Perhaps this is the real problem! Until the various parties involved in AEC become closer, then meaningful information exchange/sharing will always be limited. As a result, the effectiveness and efficiency of the industry will always be restricted.

Perhaps the AEC industry needs re-engineering. This may, or may not, come about through the efforts of activity/functional modelling.

03 Dec — Aart Bijl: response to Frits Tolman:

Thank you for bringing my attention back to data-exchange, and your comment that we are not communicating. I have a difficulty with data, which is that I am uncertain about what they are. This uncertainty seems to impinge on practical things people do.

Data in computers:

We commonly say computers are data processors. We give them data (and data-structures) which are acceptable to functions in them (to inform them), upon which they perform procedures (execute given instructions), and we see the results on display screens (as computer-behaviour).

...the data used by the computer to produce this text are not revealed in the text. We do not see this text as a model of the data. The data are in the computer, and are something else other than the text.

Data in persons:

If we think of ourselves as being like a computer, then we can think of ourselves having data (interpreted from our sensations) which are acceptable to functions that are within us (informing our already-present functions for knowing), upon which we execute procedures (exercise knowledge), and we show results as outward behaviour.

The data used in us to produce [this] text are not revealed in the text. We might see the text as a model, but not as a model of the data. The text also is not our data. The data are in ourselves, and are something else other than the text.

So now my difficulty is that data are invisible (like 'dark matter' in the cosmos); we know it must be there, but cannot see it.

Exchanging unseen data:

The data-structures we program into computers are products from us, or from those of us who are programmers. These-data structures become data in computers. A given structure will take on a particular form in a particular computer, according to the functionality available in that computer-system (layers of unseen software).

If we intend computers to pass their data-structures [or data from their structures] between different computer-systems, then we face an awkward problem. How can we know whether different systems are using the same data-structures [or data]? ...So Frits, in answer to your request for me to comment, I think I understand what you wish to do, and I sympathise with your intention, but I think we cannot do it.

7 Dec — Frits Tolman: reply to Aart's posting.

What I want is not that computers pass their data structures between them.... What I want us to agree on is an OPEN specification of a common data structure that can be used as a REFERENCE data structure for data description and exchange.

Probably the easiest way to look at this problem, is to think of this reference data structure as an extension of a classification scheme, like SfB, or ISO... By re-arranging [their] entities and adding other abstraction mechanisms we can develop a model that can describe buildings (both types and instances) in detail. What should be done after the standard is accepted, is that vendors of CAxx systems develop translators that map their internal data structures to the format of the reference data structure and vice versa. How they do that is up to them. The fact that the reference data structure is open (ISO STEP) means that everything is defined precisely and that it is possible to verify the content of a data exchange independently from both the source and the target computer-system.

Conclusion

The purpose of IRMA is not to agree on a standard way of programming data structures into different computers, but to agree on a common 'language' (or reference model) for defining data structures that describe buildings and building projects in a form that is suitable for inter-computer communication. We don't have to know how each different vendor solves his internal problem. What we need is a formal definition plus the means (1) to verify the content of a data exchange and (2) the means to present the content in a way suitable to our needs. Say that we choose the traditional 2D technical drawing format as our base presentation, what then have we lost?

4   Showing yourself

- *Sharing knowledge*
- *Feeling and knowing*
- *Knowledge and language*
- *Truth*
- *Using logic*

Sharing knowledge

In the previous chapter we have begun to assemble a picture of knowledge which does not rely on the real-world assumption. This picture sees knowledge as being dependent on concepts we have for turning things we can sense, our sensations, into things acceptable to our inner functions for knowing. Our concepts also enable us to take things from knowledge and realise them in expressions we put to each other (illustrated in Figs 1.9–11). Through interactions among ourselves, evident as behaviour in everyday practices (variously specialised in like individuals), we affirm our sharing of knowledge. We are able to share without explaining what it is we share, without knowing whether we each have equal shares of the same knowledge.

Now we will expand upon this picture, to consider what is necessary for us to be able to interact and share knowledge. This discussion may become a little more abstract and will encroach on the territory of real (professional) philosophers. However, it is not my intention to even try to answer the big questions of philosophy: what things can be (in themselves, absolutely, in reality), what we can know about them (in ourselves, as observers or participants), and what we can say about them (ourselves referring to such things). Answers purporting to say conclusively what things are keep changing. Philosophers continue to differ in how they see *this* and *that* being linked, invoking concepts of logical necessity, sufficiency, contingency... or calling on empiricism... and many further points of contention. A brief insight into the spread of contention is given in Magee's book ['87] on the great philosophers, and an example of the way of arguing that philosophers engage in can be found in Walsh's elucidation of Kant [Walsh '75].

124

For our purposes, we can be silent on the 'what is' questions; answers are implicit and variable in the everyday practices of people, here including the practices of philosophers. We will now move on to a more promising 'how' kind of question: How is it possible that people are able to interact, and how does interaction with machines, computers, add or detract from this possibility?

In exploring this question, the concepts which will be addressed include 'knowledge' (can it be externalised?), 'concepts' (linguistic things-of-knowledge?), 'truth' (in reality?), 'representation' (something doing in place of something or someone else?), 'interaction' (with representations?), and actions (towards other things?). When we consider the usefulness of computers, we will have to reconcile the technical and non-technical uses of these concepts. Reconciliation is necessary to enable non-technical persons to exercise their own individual and collective responsibility, when using computers in the course of their own further actions towards other things. Computer scientists must leave room for that responsibility. This has been a normal condition on past developments of information technology, and is not changed by new computer-technology.

The following discussion will develop a familiar theme. We know more than we can externalise, than appears in our expressions. Our inner functions for knowing, and what they produce as knowledge in us, remains within ourselves. Yet we show effective behaviour, effective in our concerted actions towards other things. We want to consider how this is possible, and will do so by looking at forms of expression, how they get to be formalised, and how they are interpreted within ourselves. We will consider how formalisms might exist, for purposes of making and reading expressions that are true-to-form (recognisable as expressions). This will take us on to questions about formal equipment and how we might conceive of overt equipment, computers, that can be used in the course of people's practices.

Feeling and knowing

To begin, I will offer some very basic observations about ourselves. We all are able to feel things, we all know that we know things, and we say we have knowledge. What is the connection between feeling, knowing, and knowledge? Commonly, in our analytical tradition, knowledge is viewed as something separate from feeling, and there are many people (technically-minded) who believe the more we can detach knowledge from feeling, and make it objective, the better. The alternative picture which will be set out here (and already introduced in Figs 1.5–8) sees close interdependence across these supposedly separate things, and this interdependence is crucial to all that follows.

Feeling happens in ourselves as we sense our being in the world. Feeling operates through our senses, giving us sensations that are acceptable to further functions in ourselves; functions of structure that is constitutive of ourselves, like mind-muscles (without implying a separate physical mind) in selves not explained. Our senses and sensations stimulate functions that feed into further functions within and across each other, all constitutive of our kind of being.

Our senses enable us to feel light, for example, and we are able to resolve sensations for colour, and can feel the colour-blue, in a spectrum of colours. We cannot know explicitly that we all have exactly the same sensation for colour-blue, but given our structural and functional similarity it is probable that the sensation in each of us for colour-blue is much the same. We rely on this similarity in feeling to understand each other, to understand expressions which do not contain feeling.

When we feel things, such as colours, they are always combined with many other feelings to make us feel good or bad. Complex feelings might make you feel emotional, or enthusiastic, or despondent. Different feelings might diverge from supposed norms to an extent that they are regarded as pathological — but psychiatric divergences are not our subject here. The point I wish to make is that when we say we have feelings they always are complex, resulting from unexplained complex functions in us. We cannot decompose them into simple discrete feelings, like the colour-blue, and reconstruct them as explanations.

Feelings are unexplained and entwined in our inner functions, our motivation, to make us show behaviour. We show that we are enthusiastic, or despondent, and our ability to recognise that any of us are showing such feelings depends on similar abilities to feel in each and all of us.

Feeling feeds into knowing. We have in-built (informal) functions for knowing which give us the ability to know about ourselves and other things. Knowing implies some anticipation of what something can or will be. For example, you might know that the colour-blue, in some particular situation, will make you feel good. Or you might know that a chair with a broken leg will fall over. This knowing rests on accumulations of feelings, and consequences that we have associated with feelings, which we call experience.

Knowing can be informal, within ourselves, occurring spontaneously. We recognise this knowing as not explained, evident in people's practices (variously specialised) resting on experience. This is the kind of knowing associated with experience-based learning, informed from experience and not conveyed by instructions (as in the form of lectures). For this informal knowing to get about, to be shared, it is necessary for participants to be similar.

Participants have to share similar inner structure and functionality. They have to have similar ability to feel.

When we think of knowing being more deliberate, more explicit, we usually think of knowledge being formally expressed in some way. We think of the things realised in expressions, the regularities they show, and the operations we can perform on them, as representing knowledge. So we get the common association between knowledge and formalisms, and overt formal equipment used to make anything apparent between persons.

Our use of formalisms is apparent in such examples as formal expressions of arithmetic or mathematics, showing us using our mathematical mind-muscles. These formal realisations come from functions within ourselves. For them to be meaningful among persons, helping to place ourselves amidst other things, they have to be linked to further expressions that we can interpret as pointing to other things. If we have a mathematical expression associated with colour-blue, for example, the expression must include things we can interpret as further things available to our sensation of colour-blue. Our knowledge of colour-blue, whatever that may be within each of us, cannot be in the thing that is a mathematical expression.

Things such as computers, with different inner structure and functionality, can be made to show bits of behaviour which imply the presence of knowledge as in persons. This can be done provided these things are amenable to formal instruction from persons, and provided the formality is accepted as equivalent to knowledge in persons. These are deeply problematic qualifications, as we will see later. Computers, like other overt formal equipment, do get used to express deliberate knowledge. But this association between equipment and knowledge works as an effective association only when it is persons who are similar who use the equipment, drawing on their unspoken similarity outside the equipment. Supposedly deliberate formal knowledge rests on shared informal knowing, and on prior already available feeling.

The interdependencies between formal expressions from knowledge, informal knowing, and feeling, which have been indicated here, do not undermine our ability to develop knowledge to do impressive things, to shape our world. What they do do, however, is suggest we ought not to think of putting away our knowledge into any formal equipment, or rules, or laws. We ought to hold on to the notion that we can and should question all such artefactual manifestations, and accept responsibility in ourselves for doing so.

At this point we can conclude that all things for which we have sensations, which we feel, are things in themselves (whatever they may be), in reality. Our sensations for them, and our functions for knowing applied to our sensations, are things in ourselves (whatever they may be), also in reality. Our knowledge is derived from our sensations for real things and our functions for knowing, giving us our world (whatever that may be), a world in reality. Our ability to sustain and extend this world is conditioned by what we are, and we do not need to know definitely and exclusively what the world is in order to be in it.

Example

We can illustrate how the connection between feeling, knowing, and knowledge works in ordinary things we do, and how it works in more specialised practices of certain people, such as physicists.

Imagine yourself climbing about a mountain, among rocks solid and for ever, thin grass greasing the ledges, and gravel on slopes sliding away. You slip off a ledge and feel yourself falling through empty space. The space becomes full with air washing past your face. The rocks come alive, jabbing at you, now an enemy to be avoided. You land in a heap on the ground below.

You have fallen, and felt yourself falling. You have had what we call a sensation of falling, a complex sensation informed through many senses. Falling is something that can happen in different ways, in different situations; and generally we think of falling as some unwanted movement from where you are to where you do not want to be, downwards (emotionally and physically, but for this example we will stay just in the physical world). We come into being already equipped to treat falling as something to be avoided, as evident in the gripping reflexes of new-born infants.

Generally, we come into being already equipped with mind-muscles to motivate behaviour aimed at avoiding falling. We know what it means to fall, for us. We learn to recognise more situations in which we can anticipate falling, and we can work out more kinds of avoiding action to prevent different kinds of falling. So we develop our knowledge about falling — and you should not have fallen off the mountain.

Climbing about mountains (and doing other things), we can know informally about falling, spontaneously, by letting our mind-muscles work on experience, without deliberate instructions. We can also know somewhat formally, as when we deliberate in our minds and try to talk about what is going on. Some of this knowing might be effective outside ourselves, in predicting what other things can be and do.

In developing our knowledge, we are prompted to ask questions about what things are, and we want formal answers we can pass among ourselves. In our ordinary experience, we find ourselves asking why is it that all things that move (animate and inanimate) show a tendency to fall, and why do they always fall downwards? This has been a puzzling question which has prompted many people to search for a satisfactory answer, one which satisfies us. This search has made people look up at the motion of planets and stars, to deduce the presence of gravity.

A physicist's view: Feynman's lively presentation of physics ['92], aimed at lay people, can give us some insight into gravity and the way our knowledge is involved in it:

> "The Law of Gravitation is that two bodies exert a force upon each other which varies inversely as the square of the distance between them, and varies directly as the product of their masses. ... Now if I add the remark that a body reacts to a force by accelerating, or by changing its velocity every second to an extent inversely as its mass, or that it changes its velocity more if the mass is lower, inversely as the mass, then I have said everything about the Law of Gravitation that needs to be said. Everything else is a mathematical consequence of those two things." (p. 14)

And later:

> "...I would like to emphasize, just at the end, some characteristics that gravity has in common with the other laws that we mentioned as we passed along. First, it is mathematical in its expression; the others are that way too. Second, it is not exact; Einstein had to modify it, and we know it is not quite right yet, because we have still to put quantum theory in [to make it work on a small scale, and take account of uncertainty principles and quantum mechanical principles]. That is the same with all *our* other laws — they are not exact. There is always an edge of mystery, always a place where we have some fiddling around to do yet. This may or may not be a property of Nature, but it certainly is common to all the laws as we know them today. It may be only a lack of knowledge.

> "But the most impressive fact is that gravity is simple. It is simple to state the principles completely and not have left any vagueness for anybody to change the ideas of the law. It is simple, and therefore it is beautiful. I do not mean it is simple in its action... but the basic pattern or the system beneath the whole thing is simple..." (p. 33, my square brackets added from an earlier Feynman paragraph, and my italics)

This is a very brief extract from a much fuller exposition, but it serves to give a glimpse into Feynman's thinking, a kind of specialised thinking which is shared among many modern physicists. Feynman describes what most people would regard (rightly) as knowledge.

In the first part of this extract, the Law of Gravitation is set in the context of cosmic bodies separate from each other and sparsely distributed, weightless in empty space. We can see that these bodies are moving about, and if they each were completely independent from anything else we would expect their inertia to carry them along straight lines for ever. The fact that they appear to move along elliptical paths, and that these paths generally are of smaller bodies moving around larger bodies, prompts us to deduce there must be some invisible force linking these bodies. From there on, physicists have employed their notions of mass, velocity, acceleration, etc., coupled with their mathematics, to arrive at the Law of Gravitation.

In the second part of this extract, Feynman makes some very interesting observations on physical laws in general. That they are mathematical in their expression tells us something about the kind of specialised thinking or reasoning employed by physicists, not unconnected from knowing in other persons. That the laws are not exact should be no surprise, except to those who want to believe in 'exact sciences'. Notice that Feynman is pointing to the law of gravity not yet working in sub-atomic physics. We might also speculate on the notion of space being empty, as something full of matter we cannot sense (as 'dark matter', making space more like the turbulent thick soup we inhabit on Earth), and whether that might have an influence on the Law. Finally, Feynman's connection between simplicity and beauty points to something going on within physicists, fitting comfortably within themselves — Feynman works hard and well to impress this sense of beauty on non-physicists.

There is no contradiction between what Feynman is saying and the picture I am developing in this book. We are saying much the same, apart from occasional lapses into near-absolute assertions; as in his exclusion of "any vagueness for anybody to change the ideas of the law", which sits uncomfortably with his notion that there remains "always a place where we have some fiddling around to do yet".

In my picture, the Law of Gravitation points to knowledge in us, resting on already present functions for feeling and knowing within us. We transpose our sensation for falling to cosmic bodies, so that we see their movements as smaller bodies falling towards larger bodies. If we were not already equipped to have the sensation of falling, we would have had nowhere to start from, to conceive the presence of gravity.

We cannot know that gravity actually exists in the way we describe it, outside our sensations, or that the law of gravity is true for cosmic bodies which actually are separate from each other, in space which actually is empty. This is *our* law (as indicated at one point in the above extract) effective in *our* world, by which *we* reach into an elusive reality. If it is true in any absolute way, it will be a truth uncovered by virtue of our being in reality, not separately determined by other things that we know about.

What we have is *our* knowledge, including what we gain through our senses and what our inner functions tell us. This includes our use of mathematical mind-muscles and associated formal tools, which have (among other things) given us our Law of Gravitation. We use our knowledge in the course of us shaping out our world in all reality, shaping the world we inhabit. Mountains we climb, the rocks we stumble over, and the cosmos as we know it, all are surfaces to hidden reality and all come to be included in this world.

Knowledge and language

Now we will try to make some more general observations about knowledge, and how things in knowledge (within ourselves) can be linked to other things (in themselves) that are known about. When we talk about what we know, we talk as though we are pointing to a world of things. We differentiate and relate things, often combining abstract and concrete things, and combining active and passive relationships, so as to describe situations in which we place ourselves. The way we define things, giving them fixed or fluid boundaries, with discrete or interwoven relationships, and seeing them as permanent or changing in space and time, all this is important to our understanding of what we are describing. Still more important is how we define ourselves and place ourselves in our descriptions: can our descriptions be true independently of us, or do they depend upon who is talking and to whom?

When we cross the boundary between description and explanation we generally include causal relationships in our utterances. Causal relationships become associated with parts of expressions, to things in expressions, so that we think of their being realised (or known; acceptable to functions for knowing) in different recipients in the same way, in people (or in machines?). The notion of explanation presents deep problems, as has already been indicated in the chapter on Japan.

In this discussion emphasis will be placed on our presence, our involvement, in descriptions and explanations of things, as indicated in Figure 4.1. In doing so we will ignore all objective categorisations (classifications, standards...) that might be associated with things which appear in descriptions. We will ignore such categories not because they are unimportant, but because they seem secondary to the question of how people become absorbed in things, in the course of interactions with each other. Our focus, instead, will be on kinds of things as they relate to ourselves.

To begin, we can say reality (including ourselves and all that exists independently of us) comprises a *universe of things,* so that any one thing is in some way distinct from other things. We can say this without committing

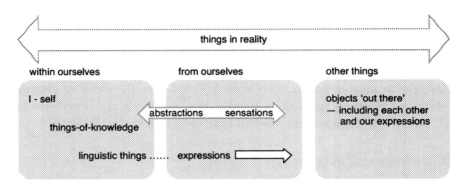

Figure 4.1: *Kinds of things*

ourselves to any notion of instances being distinct in a fixed manner, permanently in space and time. Things may come and go, floating into each other, replacing each other. We talk about things, and we do so to indicate what we are talking about in our experience of reality.

Seeing this universe in terms of distinct things is built into our ordinary spoken (and written) language. We have noun-things and relation-things, and we use verb-things to change relationships. When we wish to avoid this analytical view of things, we normally use other non-verbal forms of expression.

This universe of things includes our knowledge of each other and further things. Our knowledge includes ideas for relationships between things. More particularly, this includes relationships between any one of us and each other, as other things. We will now briefly distinguish all these things, and from the perspective of human knowledge we might regard them as interrelated kinds of things.

Kinds of things

My categorisation of things may seem weak to many true analytical philosophers, but I am not playing their game. What I say is not intended to contain all that I am trying to express, as though this were possible without calling on already-present and unspoken knowing. The following categorisation, outlined in Figure 4.1, relies on already shared knowing.

Self: I know I am a thing, in that I am aware of myself, I exist in the universe of things, I am part of reality. I can say this without saying what I am, how I come to be, and why — I am without explanation. Similarly, you can say the same about yourself, and so might any other autonomous self. This 'I' is invoked whenever we say 'you', 'me', 'us...'. Through person-to-person interaction we accept and affirm that we are, the 'I' being dependent on 'us'. Here we have what is commonly called the subjective (but not independent) 'I' kind of thing, or *self*.

Things-of-knowledge: Things are part of me, and you, and part of us. Some of these things are obviously apparent to us, such as parts of our anatomy: our hands, feet... Other things are known to be part of us, but we cannot observe them. Knowledge itself is an example. We can say that things-of-knowledge are the products of our knowing, resulting from functionality within each of us, operating upon abstractions we take from our sensations. These things remain within us, separately but similarly in each of us. We can say these are things even if we cannot show them to be tangible material things. So we have *things-of-knowledge*.

Linguistic things: Things are part of knowledge. These are things by which we are able to resolve and show our responses to our sensations; responding to situations in which we find ourselves. Concepts in language are a prominent and pervasive example. We can say that concepts (and not only concepts in spoken and written language) are used to relate other knowledge to current sensations, and shape responses so as to be realised in expressions. These things, being part of knowledge, remain within ourselves. So we have a specialisation of things-of-knowledge which are things-of-language or *linguistic things*.

Expressions: Things emanate from language. These things are observable realised expressions. They are externalisations from knowledge motivated by communicative intent; providing our means for evoking responses from each other. To be effective in evoking desired responses, these things have to show regularities, be true-to-form (be recognisable as expressions), but they do not have to be demonstrably like anything else. Their reference is to things-of-knowledge, and their regularities are subject to changes in knowledge. So we have a kind of thing we know as *expressions*.

Objects: Other things are further things described by expressions. Things described commonly are thought to be things found in our experience, things we are able to see, and touch, and change. They include ourselves as sensed by each other, and all things which we generally regard as being real in the world. Furthermore, they also include things we cannot sense but nevertheless know about; things-of-knowledge and linguistic things are examples. Finally, they include things in reality which we might not know about; they might be known by some of us and not others, or they might be known by non-human beings.

All these things are equally real. We think of them as absolutely real things, the 'about' things our knowledge is about, which we commonly call *objects*.

We commonly think of objects as being the other things we know about, or, more cautiously, we think of them as parcels of knowledge about those things — and we think of objective knowledge as being grounded in those things. That gets us ensnared in the real-world assumption. The alternative position being developed here accepts objects as parcels of knowledge, but we cannot demonstrate correspondence with other real things. When we think of such knowledge being expressed, we see things in the form of text, or drawings..., and we may call those things objective. But a piece of text, for example, is something objective only as long as it remains connected with knowledge that is not in the text. Unconnected text is not objective but just an elusive thing. For a piece of text to be objective among separate persons, it must be connected with knowledge that is not in the text but is already present and similar in the persons.

Objective knowledge then may be evident as a physically detached piece of text, but not so detached that it is unconnected with anything going on in any persons. So when we talk of objects and objective knowledge we ought to accept this as indicating a comportment of ourselves towards other things. When we call other real things objects, we are pointing at what we can know about those things.

We now have *objects* which may be evident in *expressions* (without objects being in expressions) which, in turn, are about *further things*. The distinctions indicated here are fragile. Objects are supposed subsets of knowledge associated with particular expressions. Expressions emanate from language (linking them with objects) which also is a part of knowledge in persons. Linguistic expressions are things that depend on what we are able to do, and entail shared motivation and intentionality among persons. Further real things are things independently of how we might sense and know them; they just are, without any conditions on how and why and for ever.

The latter distinction is fragile because any realised expression can be viewed as being real, and we make expressions from already present real things, so expressions become other things like the further things they are about. However, the distinction retains some meaning in us if we focus on the ways things are used, rather than on what they are. We can then say that linguistic expressions are not used just as things, but are read and interpreted as pointing to other things. Without interpretation they serve no purpose. Other real things, in contrast, even if modified by us, may serve our purpose just by being things-in-themselves and existing in our world. They might be used without interpretation, without pointing to something else. We will say more about interpretation later (under 'interaction').

Finally, in this categorisation of things, we are saying that all these things in ourselves and 'out there' are equally real. Some may be tempted to ask whether things-of-knowledge, especially if known only to some persons, can really be as real as things that are clearly apparent to all of us in our experience? What is being said here is we have no way of establishing that they are not. We cannot distinguish between the reality of something 'out there' and something within ourselves. Attempts to do so always are mediated by unexplained functions within ourselves. So all these things are equally real from our point of view — and that does not commit us to saying how real they are.

Real things cover any and all things known to any self, and known to many selves. These things are real in the sense that they are presumed to exist independently of our knowing (like being in nature, or naturally occurring). Through our contact with these things found in our experience, and through our use of expressions which touch and change each other's knowledge about them, we come to recognise the presence of reality. Our satisfaction with our knowledge about reality then depends on the dynamics of our interactions, with us exercising our inner functionality upon our sensations, and without separate verification by other things our interactions are about.

Now we are getting what might seem a rather odd picture of us, in which our knowing about and talking about does not depend on our knowing explicitly what it is we are about. The 'about' things, as things-in-themselves, remain elusive. This is as though our knowing about and talking about involves us in a dance about (or around, and bouncing off) other things, our actions responding to whatever we can feel for those things, but our dance never embraces the separate and different selves of those things. This might seem an odd picture, but it is consistent with the ways we show things from our knowledge in all our practices, assertively in the sciences and emotively in the arts. In business practices this picture holds, and we have the prominent example of emotive stock market transactions.

Relativism

Some might say the picture which is being formed here presents an extreme relativist view of knowledge; it shows all knowledge to be in bits in separate individual persons, each seeing things from his or her own point of view, with nothing to make the bits add up. But this picture is not relativist in the sense of things being known differently by unrelated (separate and dissimilar) autonomous individuals. Relativism here includes the possibility of shared knowledge being founded on the relatedness of knowing individuals, each employing similar inner functions for knowing. This is a version of relativism which includes the kind of rationality I think Putnam is searching for in his *Reason, Truth, and History* ['81], discussed later (under 'complementary truth').

Central to the view which is being set out here is the *self;* the existence of you, and me, and us, independently of tangible parts of us we are able to point to. This is often said to be something 'spiritual', as distinct from 'material', but I do not think we need to do so. I do not mean to belittle the use that is made of this distinction, but question what we can know of the difference between the two. Whatever we know of the material and the spiritual, being dependent on the collective 'us' (our things-of-knowledge), is likely to be similar. The difference may come only in use: when we intend to touch tangible things that appear before us, and when we talk about things we cannot touch.

The key distinction then is between the self and other things we can sense as objects we see in reality. Each, from our point of view, exists apart. The connection between them, from our point of view, is made through things-of-knowledge. But we cannot contain the other things in our knowledge, nor can we contain them in expressions from knowledge. So we know reality separately and similarly within each of us, we know it as existing separately from ourselves, and we know it includes us.

Our purpose then is not to match our knowledge with other real things, nor to represent them in our expressions. We can describe what we know (among similar beings), but we cannot know whether we are representing different other things. Instead, we use our knowledge to maintain our position and achieve complementary states among all things in one reality, to survive. This latter purpose may entail many different views of reality, all of which depend upon the kind of being we are, our senses and our inner functionality. We cannot call upon an external arbiter to explain to us what we must know and do.

If this is seen as relativism, we then need to be aware of an important qualification. Anything we say can be taken as coming from what we are, each of us in some particular situation, and so can be taken as an expression from a particular point of view. The qualification is that we do not exist independently of one another; the things we say do not occur in a vacuum. We are in the same being and exist collectively through our interactions, and we can accept ourselves as floating loose in reality.

This is a tolerant understanding of us in reality. It does not deny the reasonableness of different unreconciled views. Religions which proclaim super-human gods with responsibility for creating us and our world are reasonable, if they instil a faith in persons which satisfies a need to know (material and spiritual), and which is conducive to our earthly order. We can say religions are real, but they are not necessary to reality.

Similarly, we can accept the sciences as reasonable, if they offer certainties which are useful for establishing facts that we find productive. We can say the sciences are real, but their facts do not have an exclusive claim on reality.

Likewise, we can say the arts are reasonable and real, and artists are struggling to maintain their place in reality.

In all these cases we have examples of people engaged in specialised activities, and they come together spontaneously or deliberately in the day-to-day business of all other people, in the everyday practices which keep us in being.

The point in making these observations is that specialised cases are usually treated as though they occupy separate realities, but they come from within persons, from the same kind of being. Religions, sciences, and arts all ought to be recognised as pointing to a single reality. To move in this direction, we need to adopt a view of things which is not committed to an already partitioned reality, and we have to fit this view into our understanding of knowledge and language.

Concepts and language

We share knowledge through our use of language. Language in us, and use of analytical logic in language, presupposes a world composed of things. In our analytical tradition we can think of one thing and another, linked so that one is a property of the other, or an attribute, or they are linked through a relation, as some dimension, calibrated to reveal values. The things we experience get named in a language. We link instances of these names so as to form compositions, or, for analysis, we express decompositions. The compositions and decompositions which appear in our utterances, verbal, written, or pictorial, are manifestations of us talking about things.

Does any of this depend on our knowing anything outside ourselves, explicitly, or can this work within ourselves, without explanation? To explore this question, we can try to develop the notion of linguistic things being distinct from other things found outside language. This notion places linguistic things within ourselves; they are conditioned by whatever it is we are, and they need to be accommodated within our scheme of language and knowledge. Can we say something useful about linguistic things, without explaining their particulars?

Commonly we think of things in our experience as existing in space and time. The latter indicate relations, as in two- and three-dimensional space, and one-dimensional time. Already we are also using something else, numbers, and I will return to that later. Here we can make the general observation that, just as language expressions do not bear semblance to other things which appear in experience, relations also do not otherwise appear in experience. We know there is three-dimensional space, for example, but the axes by which we know this are not found in things 'out there'. Consider the following illustration:

> If I bite into an apple I am biting into the space occupied by the apple, but I cannot identify the space itself. I cannot say where the x and y and z axes are. I might say where the axes of the apple are, relative to corresponding axes in myself and other things, but that would not show where or what space itself is. This situation is as though the space occupied by the apple and myself is floating loose, and the space of the apple and the space of myself independently also are loose and can float into each other — that is how I am able to bite into it.

We might say we know space as a concept. Following on Chapter 3, a concept here refers to a linguistic thing (or a linguistic function) which we cannot externalise outside ourselves, but which we find useful for describing our perceptions of things that do appear external. Our concept of space is a part of us which derives from our knowing the world, indicating a complementary relationship by which we fit ourselves into the world. When we use this concept in the course of forming an expression, a realisation, we intend the expression to touch this concept within each other, and prompt further behaviour in the world which satisfies us. Effectiveness is evident in responsive behaviour by which we satisfy ourselves that we are saying something about space and, perhaps, the same space. When we feel this kind of effectiveness, we know we are sharing knowledge.

Concepts can be envisaged as being effective without reference to particulars of anything outside ourselves. That external things do exist, and that we can know them, can be accepted without contradicting this notion. Moreover, we can accept that this view of concepts refers to things that are real within ourselves, even if we cannot identify their particulars. Concepts are real and they are useful for shaping expressions which show how each of us complements or is at odds with a shared reality.

The same discussion can be applied to time. We can know time, and place things in relation to each other by referring to time, but we cannot identify time itself, alone, in our experience of things 'out there'. Time is a concept. This very brief reference to time in no way contradicts what Einstein has said about time [Bernstein '73]; he developed a magnificent and productive concept leading to many discoveries, or awakenings. However, (if he were alive today)

I do not think he would claim that what he was able to express of his concept could correctly and completely match the absolute of time.

Returning to numbers, the same applies once more. To regard numbers as a relation may at first appear rather odd. They are usually regarded as values and are used to identify positions within relations. However, a system of numbers itself, not attached to anything (as in arithmetic), can be regarded as a relation like space and time. These all have been developed in us, our developed mind-muscles, as our concepts. They help us to describe our perceptions of other real things found in our experience. They are useful in ourselves for talking about things.

Numbers, like space and time, do not appear as things 'out there', but exist as a concept within ourselves. Numbers get expressed as numerals, and that is something different. Numerals invoke numbers in those of us who have developed our concept of numbers.

What we know of space and time, and numbers, needs to be similar in each of us for these concepts to produce effective language expressions. They might be necessary things in our language. However, it does not follow that they are necessary things outside ourselves. There is nothing that can tell us if they are so. Here I think I am contradicting Russell's notion of necessity, and his belief that numbers are necessary independently of our use of them [Russell '12].

Following this line of thought, we arrive at an interesting consequence; language can work without our explicitly knowing things in ourselves to be the same in each other, and expressions can be effective without having to represent anything. A concept which might generate an expression, cannot be shown to be the same in separate persons; and we cannot know whether the expression correctly represents the concept. Still less can we know whether the expression correctly represents anything else mediated through our knowledge. We cannot lay bare a single correct concept for space, nor a single definitive expression of space. Instead, the concept *is* space, or what we know space to be, and it is manifest in expressions which distinguish values for spatial relations so as to describe our various perceptions of other things.

The strong implication now is that language expressions do not represent anything in any explicitly testable and really verifiable way. We cannot know them as capturing anything that they are about — that is matter for language in us. The effectiveness of expressions becomes evident in responsive behaviour which they evoke, among persons who continue to exist in the world. We might be tempted to look for something more substantial, more concrete, and try to establish that certain expressions do in some way represent certain concepts. However, given we cannot externalise the particulars of concepts independently of expressions, this does not seem to be a useful claim. We cannot make expressions represent concepts so that they can stand in place of concepts.

Far from this being a negative observation, it can be accepted and built upon as a liberating observation. It provides a common basis for different languages and differently formalised treatments of expressions. All expressions rest on concepts founded on human sensitivities, and we may consider these sensitivities as being grouped broadly under human aesthetics. This now seems plausible across languages, covering relations which find expression in such forms as poetry and painting.

When we apply formal treatments to more prosaically formal kinds of expression, to ensure instances remain true-to-form, these treatments do not ensure the correctness of expressions used to describe other things. This applies to the form of arithmetic, and we can therefore choose to use arithmetic (just as any other form of expression) to describe anything.

Our ability to interact with each other by means of language now depends on the assumption of similarity: we are similar individuals and therefore we know much of what each other knows, without explanation. We can touch and change each other's knowledge, without seeing things-of-knowledge. This is not an idiosyncratic conclusion. Similar conclusions have been arrived at by different routes, in Japan (Ch. 2) and in the west (Ch. 5).

Interaction

We manifest interactions by means of expressions we put to each other. As noted earlier, from our point of view we see linguistic expressions as different from other naturally occurring things. Put bluntly, linguistic expressions differ from other real things in their dependence on interpretation in ourselves. Interpretation here refers to some manifestation (an expression) which of itself can do nothing, being mapped to something else which can do something, which becomes active within the interpreter (a person). This points to the notion discussed earlier, of expressions being used by persons to reach into and evoke responses from other persons, or being used to do the same to computers.

When we consider computers playing a part in human interactions, we find ourselves confronted with the issue of representation. We think of a representation as capturing something known about something else, and we are tempted to consider the possibility of representations being put into computers so that they can do things like people do. Representation in the ordinary sense (in plain language) and in the technical sense (in computers) refers to something standing for something else (being a symbol for...), or acting in place of something or someone else (symbol processing). This is closely linked to interpretation: if interpretation is thought of as a kind of action, then representation carries the implication of anticipating such action (symbol processing matching what some person might otherwise do). The meaning of a representation then has to be found in the way it matches or complements something that might be the outcome of an interpretation.

When we think of representation in the technical sense, computationally, we think of things-of-knowledge, or manifestations from knowledge, corresponding to things we think are outside ourselves (in accordance with the real-world assumption, Ch. 3). Representation then leads on to the idea of correspondence being explained computationally. The idea is that a computer should be able to operate upon a representation in order to do what a person would otherwise do, when faced with the same real thing. So we get the notion of artificial knowledge and behavioural equivalence of people and computers. In this context representation is believed to be vitally important to the usefulness of computer technology.

However, when we think of computers being used in this way we are supposing the possibility of interacting with things unlike ourselves; supposing the possibility of their interpreting and responding to our expressions, despite their not knowing like we know. We are considering interactions with things that are structurally and functionally dissimilar from us, with different motivation and experience of other things in reality (if such terms are appropriate to machines). So this is a kind of interaction not supported by silent similarity across interacting parties. Here we ought to conclude that human – computer interaction is unlike ordinary human interaction, but is like any use of machines.

Human – computer interaction is a deceptive notion; computers can be made to react to whatever we do to them, but not interact. In keeping with what has already been said, computers (or anything they can be made to do) on their own cannot represent anything. They have to be linked with some motivation, something that is able to interpret and respond, in persons. Moreover, computers, if they represent, can represent only something already present in the interpreter, in ourselves. If we persist in calling computers (or functions within them) representations, then we are talking about a kind of representation which, because of dissimilarity, cannot know (or feel) what it is referring to. This qualification holds for computers just as it does for any other artefacts we show as expressions from our knowledge.

In the course of ordinary human interactions, when one person forms an expression and intends it to evoke a certain response from another person, we can regard the expression as reflecting something of what the first person knows, including what he or she knows of the other person's knowledge, without either person having to touch any other thing in reality. This is normally the case in interactions between persons. We can say the expression reflects something in the knowledge of the communicating parties, without the parties (or outside observers) having to explain exactly what it reflects.

In the ordinary way of our interacting with similar selves, the parties observe each other's responses, and adjust their further expressions, as they feel their way into each other's knowledge. A person might express something which anticipates knowledge in the other person which the latter shows he or she does not possess. This might prompt the first person to stimulate the second person to look at some other real thing, so as to extend the latter's knowledge. To achieve this, the first person may include in his or her further expressions only references to things in their shared knowledge, and cannot include the other real thing.

We are now getting a picture of interaction as dealing only with things-of-knowledge; dealing with the reality presumed to be similar within communicating parties. Any things realised as expressions have no independent connections with other things outside ourselves. Connections are made by us individually and similarly, through our senses and responsive actions, subject to similar motivation in each of us. Other real things that our expressions are about also are experienced by persons in this way, and can be acted upon by persons, but are not included in language in us. These other things just are, and might be used just as they are.

In this picture we cannot be definite about any mapping from anything known of some thing to anything else known of the same or another thing. The things known about, as things-in-themselves, cannot be contained in a person's knowledge and objects cannot be shown to be the same in different persons. As persons, we know things and we presume what different persons know is much the same, or similar, but we have no way to prove that this is really true. We might feel this is true, and we can behave as though this is true, without claiming to know what objects actually are.

Here once more we are saying that ourselves and things-in-ourselves, and things-in-themselves 'out there' including things which happen not to be detectable by our senses, all are equally real. This can be accepted without claiming we can know of any instance of one thing being the same as an instance of another (so as to make the one behave as the other). More critically, we cannot externalise our knowledge of anything so as to make the externalisation behave as the thing it describes, including oneself — we cannot make externalisations behave in place of us. Here we have a general denial of representation which may appear to some computer scientists to be an alarming assertion.

Truth

So far we have considered knowledge in terms of our senses, by which we gain experience of other real things, and our inner functionality applied to sensations, which determine our responses. We are seeing human knowledge as being conditioned by senses and functions which are within us; including concepts as linguistic things-of-knowledge by which we take abstractions into ourselves and realise expressions from ourselves. The things from which we take abstractions and which we realise in the course of human interactions are expressions. As things external to ourselves they are other things which can be constructed and manipulated in accordance with whatever we know as forms of expression, and they generally are expressions about yet other things which comprise our world. So it is that we engage in continually evolving language games.

'Language games' is of course a reference to Wittgenstein ['21, '53], but now we are seeing the formal logic of games as invisibly connected with informal equipment in ourselves, which motivates interactions among players. Notice that the term, interaction, now is reserved for actions between like beings, such as like persons. In this sense all interactions, irrespective of the form in which they might appear, can be considered to be linguistic acts touching unspoken similarity in interacting parties. Other actions and reactions between dissimilar beings, as between persons and machines, which touch different motivation and experience in each, are not linguistic acts and are here not included under interaction.

The issue which now needs to be addressed is how does our knowledge relate to other things that knowledge is about — can we know it to be true? Putting the issue of representation aside, can we find some other way to deal with truth?

Quite simply, we can say having knowledge about things means knowing things, where known things refer to states of knowledge within ourselves in response to our sensations for other things, the 'about' things. We then show behaviour influenced by knowledge, and evoke responses from each other, in order to test and sustain knowledge within each and all of us. This testing and sustaining refers to feelings of satisfaction, and of being able to go on, which occur in us.

Behaviour manifest through forms of expression then brings us back to the question of truth: is an expression true? We usually say something is true of (to, for...) something else, if it is the same as (matches, fits...) the other thing. So truth is a relationship between two or more things. More particularly, it is a relationship which has to be recognised by at least one of the things that are parties to any instance; it is a relationship between you, or me, or others, and further things found in our experience. If this were not the case, we would have truth imposed upon us by some super-human being, without our knowing what truth is.

To clarify this point, we can return to the earlier distinction between things-of-knowledge (or things in mind), and things found in experience, things 'out there'. We have said all these things are real, referring to them as they actually happen to be. We can know them, and knowing results in further things-of-knowledge. What then gets externalised are expressions from knowledge. Expressions become further things found in experience, motivated by communicative intent within persons. Intent comes from a desire to maintain a complementary position in a changing world, to survive.

Complementary truth

Now I am introducing a notion of complementariness (with an *e*, not an *i*) which is important to the position being set out here. Complementariness refers to something fitting something else, being compatible, without it having to be the same as the other thing. If we are considering a thing-of-knowledge being compatible with something else, then it can be compatible without its knowing what the other thing actually is. Here we have a concept which refers to things-of-knowledge fitting with other things found in experience, as felt within persons. It also applies to different other things in experience found to be fitting together, also as felt within persons. Things found in experience include persons sensing each other's expressions, which they might accept as complementing their own things-of-knowledge. This happens when people find they are sharing each other's knowledge. They can do so without showing that each actually has the same knowledge.

Truth then refers to something being complementary, as illustrated in Figure 4.2. I can sense something and know that it is true if it stimulates a state of knowing in me which satisfies my intent. Similarly you can do so, as can other persons. If we all respond to an expression by saying it is true, it satisfying our separate but similar intentions, we might feel we have complementary knowledge. We can do this without having to demonstrate in some explicit way that the expression represents or matches anything else.

Now we can briefly note two further aspects of the question of truth. First, there is the relatively technical matter of whether an utterance is true to a chosen

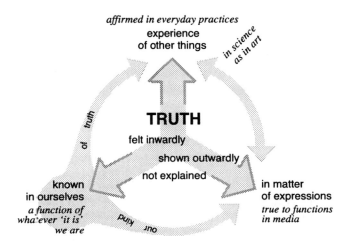

Figure 4.2: *Complementary truth*

form of expression, or is true-to-form. Can the realisation of an expression be recognised as an expression? This implies reference to known things within persons, to formalisms of written grammar or arithmetic, or structures in spatial composition, or the flow of sound in music. These formalisms are present as things-of-knowledge independently of other things expressions might be about, and we will return to this point later (under 'using logic').

The second aspect refers to content, which does imply some reference to other things, as when we say "is this the right behaviour to evoke that response?", or "is it true to say this about that?". Here we can get confused by belief in real-world facts, and regard the question in the form "is *it* true?", as though the answer does not depend on us. This *it* always is some instance of expression (perhaps pointing to something else found in experience), and we ought always to ask for whom is it true or not true? The answer has to be for oneself; truth stimulates responses within oneself which satisfy, which you or I cannot experience in someone else. By presumption, I can believe that something I find is true is also true for you, and for many like persons, but I cannot establish such shared truth as a real-world fact independently of myself.

To ask of anything "is *it* true?", as though truth can be a property of something outside yourself, becomes a meaningless (and therefore wrong) question. Instead, truth here refers to a complementary or fitting relationship between something apparent (as sensed) and functions in oneself (acceptable to knowledge in a self). This does not mean that truths are idiosyncratic. Similarity across us, and our being in one reality, makes it probable that we share truths. We can exploit truths without making them things-in-themselves.

This view denies facts as being true independently of value loaded, subjective (intuitive, not formalisable), preconditions. It also denies extreme relativism, where truths might be unrelated in separate subjects. Putnam ['81], arguing in the language of our modern scientific tradition, gives a good account of the difficulties facing these extreme but orthodox positions. He summarises his view:

"I argued... that 'every fact is value loaded and every one of our values loads some fact'. The argument in a nutshell was that *fact* (or truth) and *rationality* are interdependent notions. A fact is something that it is rational to believe, or, more precisely, the notion of a fact (or a true statement) is an idealization of the notion of a statement that it is rational to believe. 'Rationally acceptable' and 'true' are notions that take in each other's wash. And I argued that being rational involves having criteria of *relevance* as well as criteria of rational acceptability, and that all of our values are involved in our criteria of relevance. The decision that a picture of the world is true (or true by our present lights, or 'as true as anything is') and *answers the relevant questions* (as well as we are able to answer them) rests on and reveals our total system of value commitments. A being with no values would have no facts either." (p. 201)

Putnam holds that there is a very close connection between the notions of truth and rationality. His discussion expands on the difficulties in defining what rationality means, and what the scientific method can mean. Yet his acceptance of value loading does not entail an irrational free-for-all. Something is there, within our reason, which binds us together (seemingly not too far removed from Heidegger's 'facticity', discussed in Ch. 5). At the end of his book Putnam says:

"We are not trapped in individual solipsistic hells, but invited to engage in a truly human dialogue; one which combines collectivity with individual responsibility.

"...[and in this dialogue] the very fact that we speak of our different conceptions as different conceptions of *rationality* posits a *Grenzbegriff*, a limit-concept of the ideal truth." (p. 216, my brackets)

Here we have a hint of truth being linked to an idea within us, which is real but not externalisable outside ourselves. This is a notion which many may find difficult to accept, but it appears to be widely accepted in everyday practices in Japan (Ch. 2). Rationality, in this context, rests on presumed coherence of whatever it is we are, existing in reality. Rationality then depends on trust in persons exercising their responsibility towards whatever each finds in reality.

We can believe in shared truths, and such belief can be productive. The view which is being developed here accommodates beliefs which support science and technology, and accepts them as being effective in sustaining human interaction. The qualification we are adding is that there is nothing special about the facts and truths of science and technology, to keep them apart from other modes of human interaction. We cannot call on science to tell us what is true, any more than we can call on art to do so. However, we can use both science and art to stimulate truths within ourselves, and use them to influence what we do.

Complementary behaviour

All behaviour is manifest as forms of expressions, motivated from within ourselves. If expressions from knowledge within persons do not represent anything, and if they cannot be tested against other things in an overtly explainable manner, then just what is it that they are doing? The simple answer is that they describe whatever it is we know about ourselves and other things, and they serve to stimulate further knowledge within us, through continuous person-to-person interaction.

Expressions do this without themselves knowing they are expressions from our knowledge, and they do not know they are expressions about anything else. They have no separate intent (as far as we can know) which would be necessary for them to know anything. Instead, we make expressions and use them to prod at knowledge within ourselves, to stimulate responsive behaviour in the form of further expressions, and stimulate further knowledge in us.

We can make expressions so that they do things within themselves, prior to being presented to other persons. We have machines, and computers as a kind of machine. These machines exhibit behaviour. We might then ask whose behaviour and how does that relate to our knowledge? Again, the simple answer is that they show behaviour from the persons who make and use them, being expressions from those people's knowledge, and they evoke responses from knowledge among such selves and other people (illustrated in Fig. 1.3).

Computer systems are subject to the same limitations as any other expressions, and they contain their own dynamics. They can do things in themselves. What motivates them to do so? We are often told that they respond to instructions from persons, to execute programs on data supplied by persons, or in other ways execute actions in response to stimuli (as in the examples of system strategies in Ch. 3). But they cannot respond to stimuli in the way we do, since they do not know like us. If we think they have knowledge, say a silicon based knowledge as contrasted with our carbon based knowledge, then we face a very awkward question: how can such radically different knowledge be known by us to complement our own knowledge? (see earlier comment on Feigenbaum, p. 87).

If we accept this question as being plausible and productive, then there seems to be no reason to direct it only at the kind of expression, the kind of realisation, which we know as computers. It ought to be just as valid applied to other machines and, indeed to any other artefacts we make. The objection to all these cases is deeply rooted in the view of knowledge which we are developing.

We are trying to set out a view of knowledge in which the concept of complementariness indicates a condition on truth. This view is concerned only with truth as known in us. The purpose of our knowledge then is to induce behaviour which maintains complementary states between things, so as to maintain our place in a dynamic (and fragile) world. Knowing that we are doing so, even if we lack explanation, is what constitutes truth. Anything else, any radically different being with different knowledge, cannot tell us what is true.

Complementariness refers to our knowing things, including ourselves, as fitting together in a unity. Some examples might help to clarify this point:

What is meant by complementariness is to be found in the way a woman and a man are united in a paired relationship, without each having a representation of the other, or knowing what the other actually is. Similarly, a person can be at one with a dog, or can be joined with a motor car. These cases are similar in that the person does not know what it is to be the other person, or animal, or machine. The person knows only enough to maintain an intended and desired relationship: behaving so as to preserve a marriage, gain comfort from the dog, or drive the car. These relationships flow from a person knowing how expressions are effective at the interface between persons or things.

Regularities in expressions between persons indicate the presence of language, as something which is within persons and is common across persons. To a lesser extent, this may also be true for expressions passing between a person and a dog; and the dog has a reduced ability to preserve the relationship against conflict. In the case of a car we may prefer to talk in terms of a person's control over the machine; and the car has even less ability to preserve the relationship.

A machine is not aware of wanting to be at one with the person, or at least we do not know it as wanting anything. When the machine is a computer (rather than, say, a motor car), this remains the case. We turn a computer on when we want to use it, but we do not know it as wanting to be turned on. We cannot recognise any intent in the machine itself, other than what was placed there by people who made or programmed it. Thus we have no basis for talking with it as we would with a person. If we try to do so, we find ourselves talking with its programmer, a person who is no longer listening.

A computer fails to share our language, through lack of similarity with us, and it has no way of autonomously trying to show complementary behaviour. Of course we can see it as something manifesting behaviour, but if it were to possess its own radically different silicon based knowledge, that would be meaningless to us. To imbue a computer with intelligence would be something we do, just as we might do to any other thing in our experience: like a child confiding in a teddy bear.

To say computers are not intelligent, from our point of view, does not mean that computers are without usefulness. However, their doing anything depends on motivation coming from within persons who make and use them. This issue will be elaborated later (under 'using logic') but we can gain a hint of how computers can be used by considering some simple examples from mathematics. In mathematics we are dealing with expressions and regularities which we can use like machines, to manipulate relationships for things we have in mind:

We find the notion of complementariness is strongly evident in set theory; we talk of the complement of a set being everything outside the set, implying a universe in which the set occurs and the set being at one with the universe. The set plus all else constitutes one. We accept this without explaining what a set has to be in order to join with its complement and be at one; that has to be decided by us outside mathematics. Here we have an echo of ourselves being at one with reality; without explanation of ourselves, and with reference in ourselves.

Turning to arithmetic, we find we have numbers and we manipulate numerical relationships to express quantity, to describe other things (Fig. 1.10). One something plus one something is two things, and twice the same something; even when the things we have in mind are not the same, as in the case of separate apples. Twice the same something illustrates our use of an arithmetic concept unconnected with other things. Application of arithmetic then depends upon knowledge outside arithmetic. We use arithmetic to complement other knowledge and show satisfactory behaviour.

We use the 'mechanics' of mathematics to prod into each other's knowledge, to stimulate states of knowing already present in mind, and to show responses in the form of mathematically conditioned expressions. We go on doing so, and through continuous interaction between persons we refine our grasp of mathematics and its application to other things we know. Among people who share similar mathematical concepts, mathematics becomes evident as a form of expression for showing complementary behaviour (and the question of how we know form will be considered in Ch. 5). It then is the form which can appear to be mechanised, and usefully so; but its use remains unexplained.

Our purpose in using mathematics, as with other forms of expression, is satisfied by us showing behaviour which reveals ourselves to each other, and to other things in reality. How we reveal ourselves affects the way we fit or do not fit with all other things; not fitting is indicated by concepts such as losing, being wrong, or madness. Complementary behaviour now includes mathematics as fitting behaviour, drawing on our knowledge so as to maintain complementary relationships with all other things in our world.

This concept of complementary behaviour can be contrasted with the popular notion of competition (strong in the west and moderated in Japan); it can be thought of as a struggle to fit rather than a struggle to win. This difference is allied to the observation that each of us is always somewhere, among other things, and winning cannot occur in a vacuum. The concept of complementariness poses questions for the notion of 'survival of the fittest'; what can the fittest in the sense of the best mean, and does survival necessarily entail killing the opposition? Instead, we might want to say: survival by fitting within, and contributing to, the dynamic pattern of all things which we shape into our world.

The pattern of all these things includes our use of the equipment of science (mathematics, logic, and scientific method) to turn evident facts into pictures of reality. The pictures we form are realised as expressions from within ourselves, and are not separately and exclusively determined by other real things 'out there'.

All things includes religious concepts (existence, ethics...) that are used by us to order our beliefs, to help us place ourselves in reality. These concepts can be thought of as generating religious expressions from knowledge within us, and we cannot show that they are externally determined.

The truths of science and religion, in so far as we accept them as being logically self-consistent, are similar.

Beauty can be understood as referring to feelings or ideas deeply embedded in ourselves (Fig. 1.9), by which we feel the truths of science and religion (as in the earlier example from physics). The beauty of expressions then refers to our sensations for them, by which we are able to know them as being present, and feel them being complementary with whatever else goes on in ourselves. A beautiful expression is one which feels true, and an ugly expression feels wrong (a polarity with no fixed demarcation).

Beauty, far from being something extra, is a necessary precondition on our ability to recognise expressions from knowledge, and recognise complementary truths. In popular terms, beauty is associated with aesthetics. Aesthetic sensitivities refer to feelings and responses within us which we are quite happy to accept as being without explanation. We accept works of art as being subject to individual judgement, and we accept explanations of preferences as being inconclusive, not definite. Beauty, in the sense we are discussing here, brings aesthetic sensitivities into play in all everyday practices.

Using logic

The idea of complementary truth supposes involvement (unexplained), and poses the question: How do we show that we know particular complementary relationships between ourselves and other real things 'out there'? Notice that this question is about the act of showing, and not about what is shown or what anything shown represents. Here we are concerned with the act of forming expressions that remain true-to-form (recognisable as expressions), independently of what they are about.

We can regard the act of forming expressions as employing formal logic. Such logic is widely accepted as central to our ability to manifest anything from knowledge. Some people who employ formal logic claim increased authority for results they show. Many do so despite the usual circumstance that we cannot explain whether and how logic determines instances of what we show, and how logic determines responses from other things in reality. Others argue that formal logic cannot do these things.

When we ask what contribution formal logic can make to knowledge and language, this is usually regarded as a reference to logic as something operating outside ourselves, objectively, not contaminated by anything informal and unexplained in individuals. Strong belief in objective formal logic then favours the use of logic-machines, computers, to handle our knowledge. Formal logic gets to be equated with computers (subject to certain qualifications posed by logicians), and the question becomes: what contribution can computers make to knowledge and language?

The counter view which is being favoured here sees logic as something more general and indistinct, pointing to possible functions of inner structures of all things. Logic here is equated with self-consistent functionality of complex structures, which keeps things in being amidst other separate and different things. Separateness and difference are dimensions of our knowing (Fig. 1.9), not fixed 'out there', and our logic has to be as we can know. Our logic gives us our understanding of other structures we think we can see and modify, as when we make computers, and of structures we clearly cannot see, in ourselves. Logical functionality in ourselves and other things leads to behaviour we can see, and all behaviour is logical behaviour (other than self-destructive behaviour). In this view logic is in the reality of ourselves and other things, and reality is not determined by logic.

In Chapters 1 and 2 I have already touched on different ways of viewing and using logic. We can think of *informal* logic, Figure 4.3 (a), as coherent functionality in ourselves, determined by whatever it is we are. This has to be consistent logic for us to go on being, even if we cannot explain it. *Formal* logic, Figure 4.3 (b), then is associated with forms and formalisms we use to realise expressions. Things formal are things which appear in expressions, and in any kind of expressions. Here I am referring to formal logic in a very broad sense, as embracing all realisable forms that appear in all forms of expressions, and embracing all those operations we perform on expressions which are not specific to whatever instances are about. The things that appear are forms (as in symbol-constructs, mathematical notation, or graphical picture-constructions), and the operations we perform come from formalisms rooted in us (in our inner informal logic, as in mathematical mind-muscles). Any formal logic is therefore basically not explained, and relies on conventions current among persons who use it. Any formal logic is potentially useful, if it can be accepted as fitting whatever is already in the minds of persons who will use it. Most critically, in this view, no formal logic can be shown to have an exclusive hold on 'the truth'.

This view of logic might be regarded by many logicians as being somewhat loose. Vulnerability to that accusation seems unavoidable where I am seeking to embrace a broad appreciation of knowledge and expressions in everyday practices. The alternative would be to divide up the subject as Russell does in his introduction to the Tractatus by Wittgenstein ['21], quoted in the previous chapter. I am deliberately under-playing the unique importance often attributed to orthodox logic of the '...true if...' or 'if... then...' variety, not because I think such logic is not useful, but because the notion of truth it employs is unconnected with truth as felt within persons. Other logic used more informally, as by writers and painters in the arts, can be more richly expressive and more effective in touching shared truths in many people, and can include discipline to keep outcomes true-to-form.

Formal logic is included in this more informal logic. It refers to things which are apparent to us in expressions, and to conditions we apply to

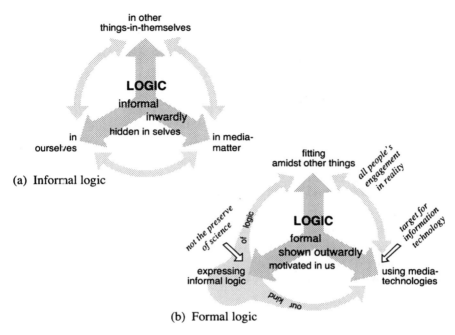

Figure 4.3: *Internally consistent functionality*

modifications which can be made to expression, to ensure they remain recognisable as expressions. It refers to forms of expression by which we show behaviour. We might regard formal logic as superficial, close to the surface of a self, and we might regard it as fundamental to our ability to interact, to be us.

Formal logic, in so far as it is thought to be externalised from ourselves, and is realised in logic-mechanisms we see as computers, can be made to do things we judge to be useful and helpful. However, what makes us make computers do particular things is motivated from elsewhere, informally — and this is likely to be true for any particular formulations and realisations of logic. We can devise overt logic-mechanisms, and make them into machines that perform operations upon our linguistic expressions, to produce logical transformations and evaluations that we judge to be useful in our knowledge.

Evolving new logic
In making and using any logic-machine, including machines in the form of computers, we need to recognise certain conditions which apply to them (or to our understanding of them) which keep those things apart from us. These conditions include: isolation from the rest of reality (no independent

responsibility); dependence on prepared decompositions (into discrete things); logical exclusivity (no feeling); and the problem of persistence (inability to forget). It is notoriously difficult to give a principled account of such conditions, but they need to be acknowledged and accommodated in any responsible discussion of how a computational form of logic might be developed to be useful among people at large.

Here we can briefly recall the kind of difficulty we face. Computers are machines, which means they have no independent interest in things outside themselves, and they are motivated from within ourselves. Whatever they do has to be consequential on already prepared instructions to them, expressed in ways that have already prepared interpretations to functions available in them. This has to be true for anything any users put to them.

These preparations have to anticipate all instructions and data that users might put to computers, for all responses that users might expect to receive from computers. If those who do this preparation are not the users, then they must know the users just as they know computers. The preparations must be expressed in ways that have already prepared interpretations to functions available in users.

In so far as user-expectations can be met by computers, the abstractions which are deemed to be interpretations of evident expressions (both ways, to computers and users) have to conform to some system of logical connectives and truth-functions which can be executed in computers. In the course of using computers, we can say that user-expressions must have semantics acceptable to computers; which is rather like saying the expressions have to be beautiful to machines.

The path from user-expressions to computer-functions, and back again, is long and hard. Any form of logic notation intended to define this path must have semantics acceptable to users; semantics here being more or less synonymous with explanation. But (as already indicated in Figs 1.6–8) we cannot show definitely whether or not the originators of a notation, and computers, and prospective computer-users ever actually share the same semantics.

When we say that some formal notation has formal semantics, we mean that there is some demonstrable correspondence between logic in one formal language and another. We imply that the same logic can permeate through to languages that are present in computers and in their users. This then implies some bridging across formal languages (explained) and informal languages (not explained), which we cannot demonstrate. Here we are getting into deep difficulty.

A parallel difficulty can be found in arithmetic, which does not seem so difficult. We can say we have a formal notation for arithmetic operators, and users already are familiar with the notation. They use it without thinking of themselves as machines for executing arithmetic-functions. When we make arithmetic-machines, however, we have to define the semantics for the notation so as to activate functions available in these machines, to make them show behaviour that users find acceptable to arithmetic-functions in themselves. There has to be something passing between the machine-semantics and user-semantics. When users hit particular symbol-keys on an arithmetic-machine they evoke responses from it which they recognise as arithmetic, despite the functions in the machine being quite different from functions in themselves. Why does this work in the case of arithmetic, and why is it so difficult to do the same in the case of more general logic?

One possible answer is that arithmetic is nicely isolated as a particular kind of function which is meaningless with respect to anything else, and yet is useful. More general formal logic is not. Logic is entangled in our notions of existence, and cannot be isolated from our sense of being amidst other things. Logic deals with all things, not just numbers. It is entangled in our various perceptions of things, how they relate to us, and how we shape them into our world. It therefore follows that we cannot devise a single overt form of logic for all things, equally acceptable to all people.

The alternative is to evolve a form of logic unconnected with anything else, like arithmetic, which is useful beyond arithmetic. It can be a logic for composing and decomposing bits of things that appear in expressions, unconnected with whatever the expressions might be about. This logic can include conditions on how bits of things may be 'stuck together', and how combinations of things might be transformed, without the things being like anything else. We can call this formal logic, and usefulness then will depend on interpretations which people have for things apparent in this logic, acceptable to functions in themselves.

The very difficult philosophical and technological challenge which now faces those of us engaged in developing new information technology is to recognise the limitations of formal logic. We have to recognise such logic as meaningless (nonsensical), and we then have to uncover possibilities of logical computer-functions which other 'ordinary' people can recognise as useful. We need to open the way for computational logic to emerge as a useful new form of expression, and one which is consistent with the general picture of knowledge and language which has been outlined in this chapter.

Logic in computers will be useful only if it is recognised by people as being useful in language in themselves, and then only if this usefulness becomes apparent (perhaps implicitly so) in further expressions that are effective in person-to-person interactions. Here we should recall that language evolves through use, involving contributions from all kinds of people. We have no reason to believe this should not continue to be the case as we evolve computational logic to be included in people's language.

We ought to envisage computational logic coming into being as a development of already-present language, developed by people exploiting any mechanistic functions which they see as being available in new technology. People exercising unspoken reason within themselves can be expected to associate meanings with these functions — not 'correct' meanings prepared by separate specialists in computing, but meanings that come about through use. Use which survives interactions among many people then will imply the presence of useful computational logic.

We ought to be very cautious about the notion of prepared computer systems performing logical operations (in the sense of true, in some detached way) on any highly interconnected accumulations of expressions, and telling users anything about what they are doing, or should be doing. This gets us into the misleading notion of human – computer interaction, implying language in computers is like language in us. If we follow that path, computers will become increasingly intrusive on people's responsibility.

The alternative is to envisage people at large being able to devise and control their own systems, and thereby involving themselves in the evolution of computational logic. The role of computer scientists would then be to make computer-functions available for inclusion in such logic, opening up boundless possibilities in technology (not limited by problematic anticipations of user-specific applications). People at large ought to be engaged in determining what functions can be included in logic appropriate to their applications, that will be acceptable to knowledge in themselves — in a manner that is consistent with the tradition in which ordinary language has evolved.

If this seems an improbable speculation, then we can gain some reassurance from the fact that formal logic applied to things-in-expressions (without semblance to other things) is commonly used in language. Formal logic, and overt equipment offering mechanistic functions we associate with such logic, is used to realise expressions from anything we know. People understand this (perhaps spontaneously rather than deliberately), and show their understanding of this in all forms of expression (as in prosaic, pictorial, and mathematical expressions). Evidence can be found in all everyday practices, not inhibited by the fact that formal logic cannot explain the 'what' and 'why' of anything apparent in practices. Logic is used to describe, without determining what descriptions must be. For such determination we always have to go beyond formal logic and reach into informal logic that is similar in each of us. We have to put trust in ourselves.

Summary

We have embarked on a discussion of knowledge, language, and truth in order to set the context in which computers are intended to be useful — starting with an example from physics which undoubtedly refers to knowledge. We have explored connections between deliberate knowledge and spontaneous knowing and feeling, all pointing to interrelated and unexplained aspects of our being.

Truth has been described in terms of complementariness; things fitting (not being the same), being compatible. Complementary truth refers to expressions (and other things) fitting with already-present self-centred knowledge in similar selves. Complementary behaviour refers to outward actions being effective in maintaining our presence amidst other things in reality.

Our ability to be effective depends upon silent similarity; shared use of language concepts in ourselves, supporting human interaction. Spontaneous interactions among all people (not pre-ordained) are the traditional basis upon which we have developed formalisms and formal equipment for realising language expressions. Effectiveness is evident in the continuity of interactions fostering further evolution of knowledge.

Formal logic is evident in all forms of expression, and in operations we execute on instances. This logic reflects aspects of our inner selves (our inner motivation) and is necessary to our ability to show anything from what we know; but is not determined by things our expressions are about. This qualification applies to all expressions, including those we see as mathematics, and science.

Computational logic then needs to be seen as an extension of formal logic, extending possibilities for realising expressions. This logic will emerge out of computer-functions that are found to be useful in language in us; but we have no specialised (super-human) way of knowing what such functions must be. We want non-specialised people to get into functions that they can control, in the course of their evolving new logic. Consistent with past tradition, people at large have to be engaged in this evolution.

Conversation with a painter

Expressionism, as in painting, music and literature (and in philosophy and mathematics), in the early part of this century, recognised a fundamental connection between what we express and what we are. Expressionists recognised that all things we show, our expressions, are not representational (Ch. 1 Fig. 1.18). They reflect the wholeness of our being, beyond calculation.

Otto Dix is a painter from the Expressionist Movement in Germany. There, it seems, that movement was influenced by enthusiasm for the Great War, followed by confusion and guilt, as shown at an exhibition of Otto Dix on Paper; the Dresden Collection on display at the Scottish National Gallery of Modern Art (Spring 1992). Interest was prompted by the exhibits and by the accompanying written captions (by Keith Hartley, assistant keeper of the Gallery) — revealing different minds at work. The captions said things about Dix's form of expression changing during different periods of his life, and about the content of his works. The following pages include extracts from these captions, which refer to Dix's works shown in the accompanying figures.[1]

Painting is a form of expression which can be effective in placing us in the experience of the painter; not in the external circumstances which the painter experiences, but in experience felt within the painter. You see Dix in the paintings, more than you see events in Germany. This is unlike written commentary; such writing is usually regarded as more attached to the subject matter, and detached from the writer. We tend to think that the written form can be more objective, even when it deals with emotive subject matter.

The captions to the exhibits illustrate this difference, and show that the difference is fragile. The writing clearly is about the exhibits and the painter, and we are not meant to feel the presence of the writer. However, I became conscious of the writer and myself as a third party, as I read the captions, and found the writing contradicting my understanding of Dix's works. Then the writer came alive. I became aware of the mind of the writer, containing much more than appears in the written words, and I found myself arguing.

---

[1] Figures p.1–5 reproduced with permission from the Dresden State Art Collections.

Figure p.1: *Self portrait as soldier, 1915*

"...head is strongly modelled with extensive use of contrasts of light and shade and the tentative imposition of a Cubist linear structure."

The references to head and contrasts of light and shade sit comfortably with the way you look at the picture; it is quite simply and literally a head, and heads are seen with light and shade. The picture shows a face, awakening human sensitivities in me.

But then the reference to imposition of Cubist structure makes it no longer a head. It becomes some other thing, an object, a Cubist painting. What makes it a Cubist object; what is it then? This is not just a matter of style, of how the brush strokes and colours are arranged. There was style and life in the picture before I read it was Cubist. The style reached through to me and, of course, the life was stirred in me. Perhaps by knowing it was tentatively Cubist, I was meant to have something to hang my feelings on, to put them away.

This reference to the painting being Cubist draws the viewer into the studied language of art, into an orderly appreciation of art forms unconnected with what paintings are about, what they do in people.

Figure p.2: *Bautzen, 1915*

"View from the Schützenplatz across the Gerberstrasse to the Ruins of the Church of St Nicholas: ...shows Cubist influences in the way the buildings are dematerialised and their forms twisted to fit in with the overall design."

Now, again, something is put between me and the painter. In this Cubist thing, what is dematerialised? Clearly it is not the buildings that are depicted, nor is it the buildings as thought about by Dix (or at least we cannot know that). Is it the presumed view of how buildings should look in a painting, to 'normal' viewers? On what could such a presumption be based? If the depiction evokes buildings in viewers, then surely something has materialised.

Moreover, what is the overall design...? The picture stirs feelings, differently in separate viewers, perhaps. This effect is not dependent upon correct selection and presentation of content. The form of presentation is evocative, touching us in ways not dependent on recognition of actual buildings. The painting then is a language expression coming from within Dix, now still effective in stimulating interaction.

Figure p.3: *Destroyed position, c.1917*

"...At first the work seems abstract, but gradually, as in Kandinsky's pre-war paintings, figures (bottom right) and exploding shells (top right) can be made out."

Here we have a hint of apology for the work being abstract, with reassurance that some actual things can after all be recognised. This caption points to the familiar dichotomy in art between abstract expression and realistic representation (a dichotomy not so evident in writing and music).

If we accept painting as a form of language expression (with many variations), then all paintings must be expressions of abstractions and not the same as (or not resembling) other real things we find in our world. To make a painting look like something, remains a realisation from some abstraction.

When we say of any painting that it looks like something else, we can mean only that we can easily match it with our own abstractions. Effectiveness then depends on what abstractions are invoked in us, and not on other things that might be depicted.

All paintings are abstract (just as writing and music is abstract), and effective paintings should stretch our abstractions, expand our truths, to remind us we are alive.

Figure p.4: *Two tree stumps attacked by fungus, 1935*

"After Dix's dismissal from Dresden Academy in 1933 he moved to the countryside near Lake Constance. He could no longer paint or draw the sort of subjects for which he had become famous in the 1920s. He therefore turned to nature and landscape. Dix invests such intensity in the minute details of these two tree stumps and of the fungi that are slowly eating them away, that the image takes on symbolic overtones. On a general level the symbolism refers to the eternal cycle of life and death; more specifically it may refer to the way the Nazis were destroying Germany."

Here we have a reminder of the force of art; so threatening to some people that they feel they must disable the artist, and they show their response in very practical and material ways. This can be viewed as a case of violent interaction in language.

That symbolism should arise from minute detail seems a little odd. The detail might be used to mask the symbolism. Of course this work is open to different interpretations, and the symbolism might be more self-centred; it might refer to Dix and his wife having been driven out of Dresden and wasting away in the countryside.

That this drawing is intended to be symbolic is indicated by Dix placing a monogram of his name prominently over the centre of the composition. The monogram is in the form of the German cross, set into the date.

Notice the change in style of drawing; no more reference to Cubist influence. The style is detailed but no longer challenging, no longer seeking to reach into and awaken other people. Dix has given up on the Expressionist Movement.

Fig▪re p.5: *Fir tree (detail), c.1938*

"Dix was not afraid to show his attachment to the German tradition, especially during the Nazi era. It was a constant reminder that Germany and German art had a great and proud history that could not be easily destroyed by the new barbarity. This great fir tree has withstood the test of time and now towers over the forest. In the same way Altdorfer, the German Renaissance Master on whom Dix patently models his style for this drawing, is still felt by Dix to be a living force in German art."

This is a complex comment. Of whom might Dix feel afraid? Of other contemporary artists and art critics, or the Nazis? Repeating the style of a Renaissance Master might have been welcomed by the Nazis. Using that style as a reminder of a great tradition which predates the Nazis, as reassurance that the tradition will overcome current barbarity, seems too subtle.

An alternative interpretation is that the style of the drawing reflects a more personal retreat into values far from the (then) present, away from the conflict over contemporary styles, and away from a confusion over responsibility of art in current politics.

The quality of line used in this drawing is the same as one might expect in a 17th Century drawing, and so consistently that this must be deliberate. Yet there seems to be no intention to make the drawing appear old. Dix is using a form of expression from the past, which can still be easily read today; the parallel in written language would be someone writing today in Shakespearean English. Why Dix chooses an old style (to shut out something from the present?), and why we might object to such displaced use of style (because it shuts out something of the present?), raises puzzling questions about language.

Mixing minds

Some observers might protest that all these deliberations are irrelevant. After all, these just are pictures, and you can like them or not. There seem to be two strong reasons why these deliberations deserve some attention. First, Dix placed himself at the forefront of the Expressionists; he wanted to be important, and wanted to be recognised as such. That is why the position he found himself in, during his later period, was so damaging to himself (however much justified by circumstances). To look at his work as just pictures is to disregard the person, and history, ...and is to deny a bit of oneself. Secondly, these pictures were taken seriously by people who saw them as threatening, and who killed other people they did not approve of. To look at these objects now as just pictures is to deny their part in a bloody conflict, and to belittle lives that were lost.

This does not mean that we owe reverence to the work of Dix, or any other painter. What is being said here is we ought to enter into the language their work expresses, to keep alive critical faculties in us not touched by other forms of expression, so as to be responsible whole persons. Again, this does not mean responsible 'good' and 'nice' persons, but whole in the sense that the whole of our being can participate in all we know and do.

We can note that the writer of the captions is considering Dix's work as drawings and paintings, embracing issues of style. He is also considering Dix as a person in a social and historical context. Moreover, he is aware of writing for readers who may have little knowledge about style in art, and who may have greater familiarity with, and criticisms of, the social and historical context. He is aware that this is likely to bias their assessment of Dix. He wishes to counter this bias, to present Dix as a good person, as someone who is acceptable to us, so as to make us more open to accepting Dix's work. In this way, although the writing may be regarded as a more objective form of expression, it also reveals the writer.

I also am writing on these pages, about the writer of the captions and about the painter. You, the reader, are a fourth party reading my writing. Perhaps you are finding my writing contradicts your experience of the captions and the exhibits, and you might find yourself arguing with me. We then have a four-way interaction, employing different language expressions to reach into each other.

Now we can make an interesting general observation. This interaction between yourself, myself, the writer of the captions, and Dix, can be understood as us dealing in reality, with each of us being in it. This refers to a piece of reality in which each of us is engaged. It matters little that our interactions are not equal, directionally and in time, between the four of us. Nor does it matter that one of the parties is dead. Moreover, we can accept this piece of reality despite its not being known in the same way in each of us, and it is real even if we change what we know tomorrow.

We do not know what this reality is (as anything separate from ourselves), nor do we know how we are in it (our existence in reality). We can, however, know reality and feel our inner sensitivities being stimulated by expressions about it. We commonly have experience of different forms of expression being effective. We can feel drawings and paintings stimulating our inner sensitivities, and their effectiveness becomes evident in our further actions. My writing these notes is an example of effectiveness; in this case, the effectiveness of the exhibition of Dix's work in me.

5 Understanding technology

- *A way forward*
- *Heidegger's everyday practices*
- *Expressionism to Post-Modernism*
- *What we can do*
- *What computers can do*
- *'One-reality' paradigm*

A way forward

Chapter 4 has sketched out a somewhat abstract philosophy which is suggestive of new strategies for future information technology. This might be viewed as a version of holistic philosophy, and it is informed by experience in Japan described in Chapter 2. Now we will consider some examples of similar approaches to philosophy and to practical activities in the west. We will do so in order to reassure ourselves that radically different strategies for developing and using computers can be based on already established western practices.

Alternatives to the orthodox philosophical view of science as dealing in objective truths, and providing logically determinate representations of other things as they are in themselves, have percolated through our history. These alternatives are not anti-science, but they tend to embrace a broader and less determinate view of how people know and do things. They seem to be more readily found in the philosophical traditions of continental Europe than in the analytical traditions of Britain and the US.

Around the early years of this century people engaged in radical re-appraisals of philosophical thought, and in new explorations of aesthetic forms of expression. These efforts coincided with the formative period of modern science, accommodating indeterminacy and uncertainty [Capra '83]. In the arts (and not only the arts) they became evident, as in the Avant-Garde and Expressionist movement. This chapter will present some observations on developments in Europe during this period. We will start with a brief review of a philosopher whose work was contemporaneous with the early Avant-Garde, imbued with the spirit of that movement. He is chosen because of his focus on ordinary everyday activities of people.

We will then briefly review how this thinking led on to the Modern Movement and Post-Modernism, and summarise what all this tells us about ourselves and our involvement in technology. The purpose of these deliberations is to prepare the ground for what will be introduced as a radical 'one-reality' paradigm for new developments in information technology.

Heidegger's everyday practices

Martin Heidegger, who did his formative work in Germany in the 1920s, presents us with a philosophy which I think can be regarded as Expressionist. His philosophy challenges the reductionist analytical tradition and makes room for human feeling and emotion. It focuses on our involved 'being-in-the-world', and investigates our kind of being (Dasein) through interpretations of everyday practices. His notion of everyday practices is in some respects similar to the notion of interaction through expressions (discussed throughout this book); in both cases actions are regarded as rooted in the being that is persons, and not determined by objective (impersonal) knowledge of separate other things. As human individuals, we show (and hide) ourselves in our everyday practices, in our expressions and interactions.

Because of the strong connection he sees between our being and our expressions in everyday practices, Heidegger found it necessary to develop his own language in order to write about our being. This makes him difficult to understand. Most of what I know of Heidegger I have gained from Dreyfus ['91] or, more precisely, I have interpreted from what I have seen in his writing. Dreyfus gives a full commentary on Heidegger's 'Being and Time' in a way which is rather easier to grasp, and which we can use to further our own purpose. Among my other readings on Heidegger are included Steiner ['78], Winograd and Flores ['86] and, in the context of architecture, Coyne and Snodgrass ['93]. Dreyfus is quoted in the following text.

Heidegger, of course, develops his philosophy far more thoroughly than appears in my brief references to it. He presents radical challenges to the traditions of philosophy from Plato onwards, and to orthodox understanding of the way we use knowledge. Dreyfus notes two important qualifications early in his commentary.

Heidegger acknowledges that "an explication of our understanding of being can never be complete because we dwell in it" [Dreyfus '91 p. 22], and that "he can only *point out* the background practices and how they work to people who already share them — who, as he would say, dwell in them. He cannot *spell out* these practices in so definite and context-free a way that they could be communicated to any rational being or represented in a computer" [ibid p. 4]. Note that the term, understanding, is used here to refer to something other than explicit knowledge. Understanding refers to our awareness of being-in-the-world, our existence, and this awareness is in our being. It does not depend on our being taught to know the world, and does not refer to a formal and logically consistent accumulation of learned knowledge.

The implication here is that he (and we) can communicate our understanding only among like beings. This is reminiscent of the position on similarity commonly found in Japan, discussed in Chapter 2.

Kind of being

A central point in Heidegger's philosophy is that human-being, as distinct from other kinds of being, rests on our kind of understanding of being, which, in turn, is founded on the kind of 'thing' we are. This understanding does not start with us assembling knowledge about other things in the world; it is not founded on a knowing relationship between subject and object (though that relationship is subsequently given a place in human-being). Human-being starts with what we are, the way of our existence, which has an in-built sense of being amidst things. Our being develops to include (among other things) manifestations of language expressions to indicate our presence. To illustrate this point, Dreyfus gives the following example:

> "...it is a fact that like any other animal, *Homo sapiens* is either male or female. This fact, however, is transformed into a social interpretation of human beings as either *masculine* or *feminine*. In Heidegger's terminology, we can say that *Homo sapiens* can be characterised by *factuality* (e.g. male or female), like any object, but that, because human beings "exist", have Dasein in them, they must be understood in their *facticity* as a gendered way of behaving, e.g., as masculine or feminine.

> ...The most a Dasein can do is "raise its consciousness", that is, clarify the interpretation in the culture. For example, feminists try to become conscious of what it means to be feminine in our culture in order to modify our practices. Heidegger would be sympathetic to, and indeed provides the appropriate ontology for, those who are trying to get clear about what being feminine means. Heidegger would disagree, however, with people ...who think we should get clear about our sex roles and thus get over them and simply be persons." (p. 24)

So, as a reader of Dreyfus and relating this to myself, what I see here are marks on paper which I recognise as language expressions that I interpret as an indication of us being. This indication of the way of human-being is very rich.

It accommodates the presence of sensory facts and distinguishes between facts of ourselves and other things. It sees our being in the facts which thereby get transformed. Our living the facts, our facticity, means that we cannot expose the facts separately from ourselves, from being human. We cannot expose the facts of what we are so as to lay ourselves bare as simply basic persons. This appreciation of what it is to be human leads on to questions about how we exist amidst other things in the world.

Being and knowing

Heidegger argues against the mind as something distinct and self-sufficient, containing intentionality (and mental models). He argues against the mind as containing representations of detached other things constituting a separate world; representations are not seen as a necessary precursor to action (or expression, and interaction). He also argues that action is not a precursor to mental intentionality. Here Heidegger is challenging orthodox views on the mind making connections between any supposed being within and any supposed separate being outwith. He is posing deep questions about how separate things can enter into a mind, and how things transcend out of a mind. Something must be prior to intentionality. In Heidegger's view, human-being, our existence, is a being-amidst other beings. Our being is structured on the presence of other things, without our having consciously to know them. Our being is being-in-the-world and understanding (feeling, rather than explicitly knowing) that we exist in this way.

In ordinary everyday practices we do exercise intentionality in our involvement with each other, our behaviour. We do so without conscious intentionality in mind before or after the event. Other things are *available* in the world, in our being, without our knowing them as things separate from ourselves. We live the facts of these things, being absorbed in transparent coping. We do not see what is obviously available to us (and do not question the obvious).

When things, actions, situations, are extraordinary (characterised by Heidegger as 'breakdown'), then they do become apparent to us, indicating something *unavailable* in us. They appear as separate unavailable things and we try to raise our consciousness in order to deal with them. Then the subject/object relationship comes into play, and what we think of as knowledge becomes active in our being. However, in Heidegger's view, this awakening of consciousness can happen only as something based on our unconscious being or facticity, our being in or living the facts.

We can then try to decontextualise objects and their context-free properties, and reconstitute them in formal models and scientific theories. These decontextualised things become *occurrent* objects which are meaningless (lose significance), in so far as they are detached from our facticity. This detachment is, however, limited by the involved skills of scientists as human beings; the everyday practices of scientists are not detached from Dasein (as claimed in more orthodox accounts of science).

Our kind of being then includes the presence of other things, and includes our ways of understanding that we exist amidst them. This might be taken to mean that human-being has in-built ability to understand we are in the world, and this ability is structurally determined within us. This is not quite what Heidegger says. He claims our being is made up of our interactions with all things, mediated by whatever each of us, in our collective being, is — our social interaction leads to our being in our facticity:

I think this notion of facticity can be illuminated by a loose analogy with the more familiar notion of city as defining urban being. Many of us live in cities, being in the fabric and equipment of cities. If we think of things that are constitutive of cities as being things independently from us, we might then expect to remove and add these things without altering our existence — and that is the position which Heidegger says is not plausible.

We can try to think of the things of cities as not only affecting our being; they are us. So if I step outside my house, walk along the pavement, step onto a bus, smell rain-wet clothes, hang on as the bus lurches in traffic, brace myself when it lurches to a stop, then mingle in the crowds outside shops — all such encounters have significance in me, and us (our referential whole), in our everyday coping. They cannot be removed from us without removing our existence as urban beings.

The city is constitutive of us, including our grumblings about lurching busses. In time traffic density might increase, leading to more of us being on busses. Our grumblings become louder. We articulate a 'breakdown'.

Some rather special people might then try to isolate a bus, look into the facts of its mechanics, in order to establish what causes it to lurch. That bus then loses significance; I cannot step onto it. Action taken by engineers to modify the bus then moves into the facticity of mechanics, 'distant' in my city (remote but still within the reach of my facticity). If the result of action taken by engineers is busses no longer lurch, that then regains significance as a modification of the city, of our urban being.

The point which Heidegger makes is that our being and coping is inseparable, and even when we go beyond everyday coping, that still rests upon our facticity. In specialised practices we still employ interpretations that rest on our unconscious being-in-the-world. He then sees us as self-interpreting beings, not dependent upon prior knowledge of any world outside ourselves.

Knowing the extraordinary

When we try to explain some extraordinary encounter, we do so only because it seems extraordinary, and we can do so only in terms of our current facticity, our current social interpretation of being. Our current facticity includes all that is obvious and ordinary (unseen and unquestioned). We do not, and cannot, start from fundamental knowledge (detached theory) of a world outside ourselves. We cannot knowingly build upon such knowledge so as to account for extraordinary events existing outside ourselves. When we say that certain things do appear to be outside ourselves, that is to be taken as an indication of extraordinariness (something unavailable or occurrent) in our being, which we show in our expressions.

Heidegger's purpose is to develop an account of the kind of existence which is ordinary human-being, and this enterprise is something extraordinary. It entails putting yourself outside human-being in order to investigate it, and Heidegger accepts that his investigation is subject to the conditions of being human. He proposes a kind of hermeneutic-phenomenology which consists of successive interpretations of everyday social practices to make the obvious visible. Dreyfus reports this position:

> ""...the term 'hermeneutics' is used ..." to mean "the attempt first of all to define the nature of interpretation." Heidegger thus claims to be doing a sort of hermeneutics that lays the basis for all other hermeneutics by showing that human beings *are* a set of meaningful social practices and how these practices give rise to intelligibility and themselves can be made intelligible. Moreover, Heidegger sees that this claim is itself an interpretation. He says that "hermeneutics, used as an adjunct word to 'phenomenology', does not have the usual meaning, methodology of interpretation, but means the interpretation itself."

> "Hermeneutic phenomenology, then, is an interpretation of human beings as essentially self-interpreting, thereby showing that interpretation is the proper method for studying human beings." (p. 34)

Here it may be appropriate to recall that Heidegger is not trying to establish what human beings are, but to identify the way of human-being: certain necessary conditions for being human. This enterprise remains relevant to our interests today; our interest in knowledge processing machines, technology, science and art.

Knowing reality

Heidegger addresses the traditional philosophical problems concerning the possibility of knowing an independent reality, and denies scepticism. He seeks to reformulate and thereby dissolve these problems. Dreyfus reports:

> "Heidegger wants to use his analysis of being-in-the-world to avoid traditional problems while saving what is phenomenologically defensible in common sense and in the philosophical tradition". (p. 246)

Dreyfus continues:

> "It is only when we reflect philosophically on the structure of deliberative, representational intentionality that we get scepticism; coping practices, on the contrary, do not represent and so cannot misrepresent. ...what cannot fail is the background coping that makes the success or failure of all levels of specific coping possible. Once we understand Dasein [human-being] as "being the world existingly", and the world as an organised pattern of practices and equipment that forms the background on the basis of which all activity and thought makes sense, we see that the world must be disclosed along with Dasein". (p. 249, my brackets)

He then quotes Heidegger:

> "The question of whether there is a world at all and whether its being can be proved, makes no sense if it is raised by *Dasein* as being-in-the-world; and who else would raise it?". (p. 249)

Here we have a denial of representation which applies to all fields of human endeavour, including science. Heidegger accepts that science, and its treatment of decontextualised *occurrent* objects, makes a special (authentic?) contribution to human-being, but he argues that it is necessarily a limited contribution in the referential whole (has little significance) in this being. Science then does not have priority over our facticity, and does not have priority over art.

Reality as something extending beyond us, can now be accepted as that in which we exist, but we cannot contain it in what we know. Reality is evident in us, inseparable from our being-in-the-world. This theme will be developed later (under 'one-reality...').

Ourselves here and now

Heidegger's importance does not depend on all of us believing he 'has got it right'. Instead, importance is to be found in his pointing to our kind of being-in-the-world, and the possibility of different ways of knowing the world — including his account of sharing without representation, among similar beings. His account is useful in stimulating our awareness of ordinary and extraordinary things today, and leaves us free to contemplate strange questions. How, then, does the boundary between ordinary and extraordinary occur, which invokes mental knowing about things that seem to be outside our being? More fundamentally, how can we distinguish between factual and factical being, when it is human beings making the distinction?

Heidegger sees four ways that other things can be encountered by human-being, which are summarised by Dreyfus [ibid p. 84]: *availableness, unavailableness, occurrentness,* and *pure occurrentness*. The last refers to disinterested attention (staring) revealing isolated entities, and is the focus of criticism against traditional ontology. The third category, occurrentness, accommodates the rationale (the equipment) of science. My question is how can *we* distinguish between these four categories? The first two appear to be central to Heidegger's argument and amenable to his hermeneutic-phenomenology — peeling away layers of facticity in order to get closer to the facts of unavailable things, but always remaining within some facticity. It is not clear how science can be something separate. Indeed, it is not clear how any set of factics can be distinct from other sets so as to define the third and fourth categories.

The distinction between facts and factics is discussed by Heidegger. He says we do not address the things that are facts themselves, as detached objects, but imply them from factics in human-being. Facts might be pictured as holes (or gaps) in our knowing, which become apparent in extraordinary encounters, surrounded by our ordinary being. A hole indicates something factual must be there, which we might get to know about, but we do not grasp the thing that is the fact itself. The hole, and the fact it implies, then gets covered over, assimilated into our being. Thus we get a blurring across physics and metaphysics.

We cannot distinguish between instances of facts and factics, but we can accept that facts (or real other things that we see as facts) exist separately from human-being. The picture which is now developing is similar to what I found in Japan: knowing about other things, within ourselves, but not containing the actuality of those things existing outside ourselves. It seems that we have here an interesting convergence between western and eastern thought.

Can we associate a more meaningful role with the terms, knowing and knowledge, if we do not regard them as referring to things distinctly mental, letting them embrace unconscious structure and feeling? In my Chapter 4 (and Figs 1.6–11) I have used these terms in this broader sense, without being clear on all the implications of doing so. Knowing can be thought of as sensing existence. I have also used the term, concept, without commitment to any explanation of instances; they remain linguistic things hidden in human-being. Language then is apparent as manifestations of interactions between unseen (not explicitly known) individuals.

From an Expressionist point of view (as we will begin to see in the next section), Heidegger's strong contribution is his bracketing of rationality. We have the rationality of expressions founded on social interactions, and not on detached objective knowledge of other things. Expressions in everyday practices are accepted and acted upon in our involved kind of being, invoking unseen interpretations. Expressions evoked by extraordinary encounters become evident as different, separate, not part of our ordinary being. They might provoke discomfort, joy, and other kinds of awakening, leading to their being accepted into fresh interpretations in ourselves. In time they may come to be assimilated into our ordinary being, no longer seen.

This progression from extraordinary to ordinary does not follow from expressions being objectively and self-evidently true, and depends instead on the receptiveness of a socially determined state of being (built upon similarity, as understood in Japan). With some adjustment to our intuitions, we might recognise these conditions occurring in science. More usually, we can recognise these conditions occurring in more ordinary forms of communication, and especially so in art. In art we typically find expressions which challenge, with no declared separate basis in knowledge, and which subsequently become accepted in our being.

Expressionism to Post-Modernism

Expressionism, as in painting, music and literature (and in philosophy and mathematics), in the early part of this century, echoed Heidegger's fundamental relationship between what we express and what we are. This is illustrated by the words of Nikolai Tarabukin, a Russian philosopher of art, in 1916 (quoted in Duval ['81 p. 29]):

"While old art, from naturalism to early Cubism, is a 'representational' art characterised by the connection between the pictorial forms and those of the real outside world, the new art breaks off this connection, this dependent relationship, in order to create autonomous objects. And while the art of the past was opposed to the real world..., the new art is in a sense immanent to the world of reality; it creates objects, and no longer pictorial copies (naturalism) or arbitrary compositions (Cubism).... Pictorial art is not a 'vision'; this would enormously restrict the artist's work and limit its pictorial and philosophical meaning in the extreme. Just as music is not an art of imitating real sounds, so the art of painting is not 'knowledge', for the domain of knowledge lies chiefly in science. Art is 'fabrication' and action... before all else a voluntary function, for it establishes the primacy of creation.... Painting is not called upon to 'represent' the things of the outside world, but to fashion, make and create objects. It is not a 'representational' art but a 'constructive' art. It is a voluntary impulse... valuing intuition in the highest degree."

The Expressionists recognised that things we show, our realised expressions, are not representational. They do not represent and are not determined by other things 'out there', but reflect what we are — and this can be accepted as true more generally for all things we show in everyday practices. These things reflect the wholeness of our being, beyond calculation, and they indicate what we understand ourselves to be.

The Expressionist movement can be seen as distinct from the more orthodox movements of that time. The latter drew on past values, the aesthetic order of classicism expressed in different ways, and produced works that soothe and reassure, and are delightful. The Expressionists, by contrast, might be seen as primitive northern barbarians challenging the old order — and this, of course, would be a prejudiced view with some truth. The reverse prejudice would be indicated by saying the Expressionists challenged bourgeois sentiments. They felt themselves at war, battling to establish a new direct (non-explicit and, in that sense, non-rational) relationship between expressions and meanings within persons. Emotion erupted in their works, with a harsh directness which was intended to sweep away the old world. They focused on human-being, much as Heidegger did, and rejected the niceties of nature (Impressionism). Their art was deeply provocative.

In Russia Expressionist art was overtly and challengingly abstract (Fig. 1.13, and [Duval '81]), for a short period. Art forms were visibly unlike other ready-to-hand things one might try to associate with them. They might be looked upon as examples of Heidegger's 'breakdown'; evidence of consciousness of things unavailable in our being, in which we become absorbed. Survival of our appreciation of these forms, as art forms in themselves, then is not the issue. The part these forms may have played in the development of human-being, through the Russian Revolution and its repercussions on us, is where we should look for effectiveness. We might then consider this Russian art as fundamentally involved in our awakening to our present modern era.

In Germany Expressionist art was less abstract, and artists sought to reflect what they felt was inside their subjects, often other persons [Whitford '87]. Their language was openly emotive; showing what they felt, and using form to invoke similar feelings in other persons. They used form aggressively and sensitively, to stir up responses, searching for a new awakening of truths in a new time.

Modern Movement

Expressionism broadened into what later came to be known as the international Modern Movement. This became evident in the development of sophisticated abstractions used in expressions, in industrial design and architecture, which were intended to serve human aesthetic and social sensitivities. The search was for vigorous new forms to reflect what people had become, in a modern industrial and technological society. The vitality of this movement reached its peak first in de Stijl in the Netherlands [Jaffé '55], and then in the Bauhaus in Germany [Whitford '84].

The direct forcefulness of the Expressionists faded. Smoothly disciplined, constructed, and geometrically regularised art forms appeared. The emphasis on reaching into people was maintained, but was accompanied by a belief in the possibility of knowing intrinsic relationships between art forms, artefacts, and people. Notions of purity and truth were applied to materials and constructions, which, if correctly applied, would be complementary to truths in persons. These notions could be talked about, thought of as knowledge, and could be taught (as in Klee's *Pedagogical Sketchbook* ['25]); leading to the establishment of the Bauhaus as a modern school.

A driving force of the Bauhaus in the 1920s and early 1930s was the notion that formal abstractions can be realised, that they can be recognised as being pure or corrupt, and that they are deeply involved in the well-being of people. The people of this school were searching for essential and durable truths that could be expressed in the forms of designed objects, looking for truths without explanation or any calculus for justification. Forms had to be known in persons, and could be described by examples (experience) presented to students. But persons who painted or did architecture (or designed furniture, or other artefacts...) had to call on resources within themselves, unexplained, to use forms effectively.

The Expressionists' urge to break with tradition, to deny past conventions, was maintained. The Bauhaus strove for unity in technique (technology) and art, drawing on the achievements of science. It sought to absorb the products of new technologies into a new rational aesthetics; a rationality founded on unspoken reason. Now the search was for new and pure forms emerging from properties of materials, and from functions served by constructions. In architecture this was reflected in the slogan: form follows function.

The notion of form following function was complex. It was recognised that form has to be realised in material, and proper use of material properties was seen as a function of form. Effectiveness of form was recognised as being dependent on connections with sensitivities within persons, and such connections were seen as a function of form. Lastly, it was recognised that form has to do things, when formal objects have to satisfy requirements specified by persons (overtly described, but not necessarily explained), and that also was seen as a function of form. This composite set of functions could not (and now still cannot) be satisfied by artefactual and autonomous formal systems.

The vigour of the early Modern Movement came from the people who were actively initiating it. Their commitment went beyond their descriptions of what they were doing. They were highly involved, functioning fully as persons, effectively stimulating other people. Their written (formal) descriptions of what they were doing, which have been passed down to us, now ought to be understood as incomplete post-hoc rationalisations of all that was going on.

Decline

The early Modern Movement was interrupted by the build-up to the second world war. Following that war, the climate for that movement changed. The germ of degeneration which eventually marred the movement might be found in the earlier quotation from Tarabukin: in his reference to knowledge being in the separate domain of science. This separation of knowledge from art, and the post-war ascendance of detached objective knowledge, became more acute as the movement became increasingly involved in technology. Artists came under attack for expressing mere subjective and emotive whim. Architecture became depersonalised, relying instead on pseudo-scientific rationality as objective justification for actions. We have the consequences in post-war buildings, and planning, from the late 1940s onwards.

The old Bauhaus enthusiasm for technology did not foresee the possibility of technologies being used to impose regularising conditions on social behaviour, and the consequent disengagement of people from responsibilities towards each other. Post-war architecture had to be justified by explanations which had to follow recognised rules. The rules were devised by persons far removed from people designing, constructing, and using buildings, and were based on supposedly matter-of-fact requirements which buildings had to satisfy. These rules had to be overtly rational, to be administered by uninvolved clerks.

The old Bauhaus (and earlier) notion of form following function degenerated into form following rules. Further rationalisations from the

Bauhaus (and associated Avant-Garde influences) were used to formulate rules that were thought to ensure modern (rational and good) post-war building programmes.

Degeneration of the Modern Movement became evident when post-war buildings were prematurely and dramatically demolished, as a consequence of spontaneous and aggressive rejection by people in and close to them. This kind of destructive action (not motivated by a will to do something better) can be viewed as officially sanctioned vandalism, not so far removed from common vandalism. What it indicates is failure somewhere deep in society; social fragmentation.

The Modern Movement eventually failed not because the Bauhaus was wrong, but because it was used as a substitute for new thinking, new involvement, during the following decades. The mistake was to take the words from that time as being the people behind the works we admired, and to reuse the words in place of ourselves, to construct pseudo-scientific rationales for subsequent actions. Thus we denied our involvement as persons among people, in subsequent decades of building.

Post-Modernism

This discussion of the decline of the Modern Movement has relevance to other developments, outside art and architecture. It provides pointers to the effects of depersonalised practices regulated by impersonal rules, in a general context of declining human responsibility. These pointers may be appreciated as bearing on all things we do, including everyday business practices.

This discussion also points to the roots of Post-Modernism. That emerged as a movement around the 1970s, and it grew out of disillusionment with rational determinism. Post-Modernism rejects the idea that any substance beneath surface appearances can be known definitely, and rejects the idea that privileged access to such substance can be exercised for the good of people. Instead, the desire is for something post-rational, with emphasis on interplay of surface appearances involving people. The intellectual grounding of this movement goes back to hermeneutic philosophies around the turn of this century, including Heidegger.

Here we have a movement truly in opposition to modernity. Very briefly, being in opposition, placing emphasis on difference, engaging in dialectic deconstruction, is what Post-Modernism is about. The intention is to use evocative difference to uncover hidden prejudice and privilege, and so, perhaps, reveal similarity. Through such involved engagement, people may uncover interpretations of their actions which bring them closer together.

In architecture this movement is evident in references to language, the use of vocabularies (without grammars), and quotes and jokes [Papadakis *et al.* '89]. Elements of buildings are composed and juxtaposed provocatively, including bits freely taken out of context from past styles or traditions. By this means architects engage other people, playing on their emotions, with nothing of substance (no deep meaning) to determine what must be.

Post-Modernism is opposed to the Modern Movement, but it is a reaction to manifestations from the latter movement's period of decline; the dominance of pseudo-scientific rationales embedded in impersonal rules. Its emphasis on itself being in opposition masks its similarity with the early Avant-Garde. More seriously, its denial of substance denies existence beyond surface appearances. We have a disturbing denial of knowing within persons (not disconnected 'knowledge'), as something to be known about. The consequent emphasis on interplay of surface expressions (as things disconnected from persons) then can have the unintended effect of disengaging persons, and feeding the political ideology of 'free-market' forces (Fig. 1.1).

The successor to the Modern Movement and Post-Modernism will not flow from superficial tinkering with style and fashion, and will not flow from newly constructed rational (reductionist) explanations of the essences of things. Instead, all this now awaits a radical re-examination of what *we* are, our being-in-the-world, as before in the time of the early Avant-Garde. Like then, now we will have to consider breaking with tradition, rejecting past conventions. This time the target is likely to be past self-imposed demarcations between science, technology, and art, and our encapsulation of demarcations in rules. Without diminishing any of these ways of knowing and doing, we need to find a new integration, a newly sustainable unity. We have yet to show that we are engaged in such a deep and broad ranging reassessment.

What we can do

Technology is deeply enmeshed in our being, and this is not new. Our understanding of technology can change, and that can make a difference in any new future which we shape for ourselves.

As a broad and rough generalisation, we can say technology is persons making artefacts which they let loose on other people, so that the artefacts do things other people supposedly want. We also know that technological artefacts, machines, do things according to defined rules; the rules are necessary for them to continue being machines. But we do not want these rules to dictate our existence.

We know ourselves as able to break rules, able to function outside rules (our inner unexplained feeling and knowing); and breaking rules is necessary to our continuing being. The task before us then is to define technology so as to accommodate other people answering back, to question assumptions of the makers of artefacts — and so lose the distinction between makers and users of tools.

Much in the way Heidegger saw facticity coming from all people's involvement in everyday practices, and in the way that Expressionists sought direct engagement with persons, so we now can think of new technology as emerging out of the practices of people at large. Only in this way can we hope to arrive at new information technology which will accommodate whole-person involvement; the space between *yes* and *no,* discussed in Chapter 3. Only in this way will we accommodate the ways of science, and art, and the 'ordinary' everyday practices of people in commerce and industry.

We can do this, and by understanding that we can do this we will be opening the way to a new modernity.

Generally, we can acknowledge that technology has to fit with whatever else goes on within persons. This fitting cannot be explained objectively, scientifically, because we cannot explain ourselves. So making useful new technology is not exclusively within the scope of scientists. Making useful technology also is not within the scope of technologists, or of artists, or any other separate specialisation. More plausibly, we can consider the emergence of a new technology as the outcome from unexplained interactions across differently specialised persons. It is likely to emerge more like ordinary language does, and as the realisations which come to be recognised as language expressions do; and we ought to take heed of the way many people (including those who do not articulate their specialisations) are involved in the emergence and evolution of languages. Usefulness of technology then can be viewed like the usefulness of language expressions, helping people to realise concerted actions to preserve their place amidst all else in reality.

From earlier chapters we have some clues to the way we might move towards such a useful new technology. These clues refer to forms and formalisms employed in the course of human interactions. We are able to employ forms and formalisms to show outward expressions seen as plain prose and evocative poetry, technical diagrams and expressionist paintings, the roar of a motor cycle and the sound of music. Now we will recall how this is possible.

Form

We make expressions and we have different forms of expression. Some differences between forms are readily apparent in expressions, as between writing and drawing. Other differences are less obvious, as between prose and poetry. Even those differences which generally appear obvious do not always appear obvious in particular instances of expression, as when writing is used graphically to indicate something other than words. We can find similar difficulty in establishing demarcations between painting as decoration and painting as art, and between noise (even pleasing noise) and music.

The problem here is that we have ideas for forms of expression (or ideas linked to forms), and we cannot explain these ideas. They cannot be detached from ourselves so as to determine the presence of particular forms.

We then find that we do not need explanations of forms as a precondition on our ability to make expressions. We just go ahead and make expressions. Expressions evoke responses from each other, similar others, other persons. Regularities in expressions become accepted as effective in our interactions, and we can learn them, and use them repeatedly. Forms become recognisable in us. We get to know what forms are, and use the differences between forms of expression to reach into different ideas in us, to evoke desired responses.

We can exploit forms of expression without having definitive explanations of what they are, because the forms are in our being, in us, and it is us using them. Sometimes our use of forms may be deliberate, done in a manner which can be accompanied by indications of purpose. More often our use is spontaneous (even unconscious), employing 'equipment' in us to process expressions, rather like digesting a good meal.

We can, and commonly do, break the rules apparent in the regularities of forms, in order to change and extend the effectiveness of expressions. We can do this because we do not know the limits of equipment within us for processing expressions, and we are not bound by externally imposed rules.

We should recall here that the regularities in expressions have no meaning 'out there' — the expressions themselves do not contain what they are about. The form of expressions is independent of meanings we intend for instances of expression, within ourselves. Certain of these regularities (such as string formation in writing) remain unchanged, and are necessary to our recognition of instances of expression. It is the further regularities found in instances (spelling and grammars or rules) which are connected with language in us, and it is those regularities which quite properly get changed in the course of person-to-person interactions.

Formalisms

Often we think of our use of forms of expression as being deliberate. This means that expressions are associated with some declared purpose, and are formulated so as to invoke functionality in a recipient, to satisfy the purpose. When we do this formally, overtly, the link between expressions and functionality has to be known in the sense of being shown overtly, in further expressions. The link has to be explained in terms acceptable to the functions presumed to be present in a person (or in some artefact, a computer). Expressions formulated to be consistent and complete in this way are often called formalisms.

An orthodox western view of these formalisms is to see them as having an autonomous presence with an ability to do things — and this is accepted as the basis for building autonomous computer systems. The implication is that formalisms can be detached from us and do things in themselves, to be computable formalisms. For reasons already discussed in Chapter 4, this notion that formalisms have this independence and are true in themselves is precarious. There might conceivably be other things unlike ourselves which might use symbols included in our formalisms like we do, but we could not make them do so. Later we will consider what we *can* make other things (such as computers) do.

In ourselves we know we have and can exploit formalisms. We know that we are able to exploit apparent regularities of forms of expression in order to make instances that remain true-to-form — and we do this in all forms of expression, whether or not a form is thought to correspond to some logical calculus. The ability in us to treat expressions in this way, to make distinct and meaningful expressions that are effective in language, points to the presence of formalisms within ourselves (variants of logic applied to realisable forms).

These formalisms can be known to be necessary to our ability to show anything in an expression, to make anything appear formally in some tangible form. They can be known to be present in us, by specialised persons who think deeply about how they can work in us — awakening the idea of language.

Ordinarily, without knowing what these formalisms in us are, people are able to employ them. In the course of ordinary everyday interactions among persons, we commonly make expressions that remain true-to-form. We need to do so for our expressions to be recognised as expressions. Our doing so is evident in the effectiveness of expressions evoking responses, and in the continuity of such interactions. Our use of formalisms is effective in touching inner functions for knowing, in like persons.

We are able to exploit formalisms without knowing what they mean. We can accept that they have no meaning with respect to particulars of other things our expressions are about. There is no such meaning in arithmetic, for example, to determine use of arithmetic in interactions between persons (Ch. 4 p. 149). Effective formalisms are those which apply to the constituent parts and structures of expressions, without determining what instances of expression must be. Arithmetic satisfies this condition; a number, produced by applying arithmetic functions to other numbers, becomes a meaningful expression only if it is associated with something else determined outside arithmetic.

We are able to use formalisms to make expressions that are meaningful in our inner functions for knowing. Meaning becomes evident only as patterns of human interaction, transient in the dynamics of interactions, and cannot be explained outside these interactions. The patterns are evident as instances of language expression, as realisations of forms of expressions. We want formalisms to be meaningless so as to allow unlimited potential for meaning in expressions.

Media-technology

For expressions to be apparent (those that are separated from ourselves) they have to be realised in something, some material substance we are able to sense. Spoken words are generated within us and conveyed as variations in sound. Music is generated on instruments and similarly conveyed as variations in sound. Writing is produced as marks on paper and conveyed as variations in light. Similarly, drawings are produced as lines on paper, and paintings as brush strokes, conveyed as variations in light. There are cases of sculpture produced as 3-dimensional objects intended to be sensed by touch (by blind persons, in Japan). Food can serve communicative intent, stimulating sensations of sight as well as taste, and also smell, touch, and sound (notably so in Japan).

Expressions have to be tangible expressive objects made out of something, materials that are themselves not expressions. We form materials into expressions which serve communicative intent among persons. The materials are media in which we form expressions. The possibilities in media, and tools by which we shape them, then have an influence on what forms of expression can be, and on formalisms for keeping instances true-to-form.

We know (perhaps spontaneously rather than deliberately) that we use media in order to realise expressive objects, and we do not need to know explicitly what the various media we use are in order to do so. We are able to use marks on paper, without knowing what they are as things in themselves.

We know we use tools to shape media, and do not need to know explicitly what the various tools are in order to do so. We are able to use a pencil, without knowing what that is as anything in itself. We become absorbed in media and tools in the course of realising expressions that are effective in language in us.

We are able to use the possibilities we know are present in media, and these possibilities influence what our expressions can be. We do not know all possibilities; that would presuppose knowledge and control of reality in media, which would require super-real powers in us. The possibilities we do know, and know differently over time, influence what our expressive objects can be. We cannot be definite about causal relationships between media and forms of expression, but we can be reasonably certain that we would not have our present-day forms if we did not already have the media in which we currently realise our expressions.

We are able to make expressions by shaping media, by using tools that are effective on media. We are able to do this without the media and tools knowing what we intend our expressions to be, and without them knowing what our expressions are about. We use media and tools for our own purposes, and when we do that we are engaging in technology. Tools applied to media to produce apparent manifestations of expressions we intend to be meaningful in language and knowledge in us, are constitutive of information technology.

So drawing lines in sand, chiselling characters in stone, putting ink to paper, and employing printing presses, all are included in the evolution of information technology. Through time, the tools of this technology have become more elaborate, including mechanical and electronic functions for shaping media into expressions. Our purpose in encapsulating increasingly sophisticated functions in these tools is to make the making and spreading about of expressions easier, to enrich contact among persons, and so share knowledge.

Simultaneously, the influence of increasingly sophisticated tools on what expressive objects can be, as things which stimulate responses among persons, has increased. Complex technology can have the effect of keeping persons apart. We have a tension between expressions that express what individual persons know, expressing people's engagement among themselves, and expressions that express possibilities in the technology, or the media:

We have in the politics of unemployment — "people must be trained to have the skills *required by technology...*, and be retrained as the *needs of technology change*." (BBC TV Ch 2 Newsnight, 16 Feb '94; my italics)

We ought to expect a continuing development of new media-technology, accompanied by new and as yet unforeseen forms of expression. To do otherwise would presume we now have reached the end of human evolution.

However, we can try to be more positive in making technology more available and controllable by people at large, enabling them to use technology to reach into each other in any way they choose. The politics of unemployment, or disengagement, needs to be turned round and in trying to do so we will find ourselves engaged in the politics of technology.

Things we cannot do

Before going on to consider what computers can do, here are a few words restating what we cannot do, or impossibilities. In saying there are things we cannot do I am referring to things we might know about but cannot explain in any definite overt way. If it comes about that these things are explained, we will then have changed ourselves into something that we now would say is 'someone else's machine'.

What we cannot do has a bearing on what we can make machines do. To proceed, we will start with the mind.

Replicate minds: In many western traditions we think of the mind as being something in itself, autonomous, self-sufficient, associated with the brain and operating rationally upon received experience. This leads some of us to believe we can replicate the role of the mind in computers. Those of us who hold that cognition in the mind is prior to all knowledge in each of us, about ourselves and all other things in our world, attach great importance to modelling our cognition in computers.

Opposing views are also found in the west, as in the earlier example from Heidegger, and Dreyfus ['79]. They argue against the notion of cognition in a self-sufficient mind as a precondition of knowledge. Instead, they hold that we come into being with in-built understanding of being-in-the-world, shown in our everyday practices. They claim that cognition is secondary, resting on that already-present understanding. The mind then is inseparable from our whole being, and we cannot replicate its role separately in computers.

These different views are reflected in distinctions commonly made between kinds of knowing, as between science and art. People will generally agree that art is not subject to rational knowledge, but might claim that art comes from minds within autonomous individuals. We then face the problem of explaining demarcations, as between science and art, if we intend to replicate any part of the role of the mind in computers. According to Heidegger and others (even Plato), such explanation is not forthcoming. It would have to draw on aspects of our being which we cannot explain.

We can accept the term, mind, as referring to a concept in us, pointing to something connected with our ability to know and do things. We can accept this without commitment to the mind being a distinct thing, and certainly without commitment to its being self-sufficient. Mind functions might be motivated from anywhere in our being, and might be dependent upon aspects of our being not normally associated with the mind.

We are led to conclude that we cannot explain and replicate the mind in something else. *We cannot replicate a mind in a computer.*

Replicate ideas: As things in mind, we have ideas. They shape our understanding of ourselves and place us in the world. The kind of ideas which are contemplated here are the transcendentals of Plato, and many others that have followed, including the ideas formulated by Heidegger as ways of being-in-the-world. These are *in* our being and are awakened as concepts through which we realise our language expressions: we talk *about* our ideas.

Ideas deal with our understanding of being, as matter for philosophers; and so we have the influence of Plato and Aristotle on western traditions, and Buddhism and Confucianism on different traditions in the east. In more ordinary everyday practices, ideas influence the ways we make things *be* in the world. We do not need to know whether any one philosopher's exposition of ideas is 'correct', before exercising ideas in everyday practices. We just go ahead and *do* things, and experience effectiveness through responses in the continuity of our interactions.

When we talk about ideas, our utterances express ideas but they do not contain or represent them. The ideas are not in the utterances. We can have the idea of 'chair', for example, but we cannot put that idea into some form detached from ourselves so that the externalisation will determine what can be chairs, from among the totality of all things. We might point at something and agree that it is a chair (it is an instance of chair), but that will not reveal what it has to be in order to be an instance of chair. The idea of 'chairness' remains in us and is exercised in us whenever we behave towards something so that we understand it to be a chair.

We can accept the term, ideas, as referring to a concept which points to the nature of our kind of being, closely associated with mind. We can accept this without explaining what any idea actually is.

We are led to conclude that we cannot explain and replicate ideas in something else. *We cannot replicate ideas in a computer.*

Replicate knowledge: Associated with ideas, we have knowledge. This tells us what we can do, where, and when, and tells us the probable consequences of doing things. In our western traditions we often think of knowledge being rational, subject to overt logical explanation. Some of us believe we can explain knowledge to computers, so that our knowledge is captured within them; building mind-functions into computers. By giving them our knowledge, it is thought computers can be made to behave intelligently and usefully on our behalf.

Opposing views of knowledge claim that it is fundamentally not rational, or that its rationality is not logically explainable. Our knowledge is a consequence of whatever it is we are, our ideas already-present in our being. It rests on our in-built understanding of being-in-the-world. Knowledge therefore cannot be explained so as to be complete independently of ourselves, and cannot be put into computers.

These different views are reflected in the distinction ordinarily made between knowing and knowledge, as when we say we know we want something, but cannot explain why we want it. We accept that much of our knowing occurs in this way, and we do not contain such knowing in overt expressions from knowledge. Once more we face the problem of explaining demarcations, this time between kinds of knowledge that we can and cannot externalise. Again, such explanation is not forthcoming; the demarcation indicated here rests on aspects of our being which we cannot explain.

We can accept the term, knowledge, as referring to a concept which points to our ability to know. We can do so without commitment to knowledge being anything in itself, and certainly without commitment to overt expressions of any kind being knowledge. We dwell in the practices our knowledge enables us to perform, which satisfy us.

We are led to conclude that we cannot explain and replicate knowledge in something else. *We cannot replicate knowledge in a computer.*

Replicate facts: Associated with knowledge, we have facts. In the west we see facts as appearances of things we accept into knowledge, which we think correspond to other things as-they-actually-are. We regard them as being grounded in the reality of other things. They are available to separate persons (similar selves), confirmed by their having similar experience of the same other things. Facts then contribute to knowledge within ourselves, and by means of language we are able to communicate what we know to each other.

All this can be accepted as true in the sense that it may be internally consistent within our knowledge, in our being. This view can be true for us, even if we cannot establish that facts are actually grounded in the reality of separate other things. Without contradiction, we might say that facts are grounded within ourselves (as Heidegger's factics), and are about other things within our being, confirmed by our everyday practices. We then communicate by stimulating already-present facts in each other, and stimulating new awareness of facts, rather than by conveying facts overtly to each other. This is the understanding of facts which appears to be accepted in everyday practices in Japan.

Both ways of viewing facts carry the implication that facts cannot be explained. We can form expressions which we call facts, but they are expressions about facts within ourselves, and are not themselves facts. We can use expressions as though they are facts, repeatedly, until they are refuted by other expressed facts; and the act of refuting them reminds us that facts are within our being. We cannot formulate them so as to be facts for anything other than ourselves.

We can accept the term, facts, as referring to a concept which points to our ability to hold bits of knowledge about our being-in-the-world. We can do this without commitment to facts being things explained.

So now we have the last in this list of things we cannot do. We cannot explain and replicate facts in something else. *We cannot replicate facts in a computer.*

In this discussion stress has been put on *us* not being able to do certain things, rather than computers not being able to do them. To put the stress the other way, on computers, would presume too much about computers. That would imply they exist in their own right as a kind of being separate from ourselves, and we might be tempted to consider how we can work with them as autonomous but dissimilar things. That results in much confusion. When we talk about computers we are talking about things we put into our world, which are within our unexplained being.

All that has been said here about what we can and cannot do is summarised in Figure 5.1. Ideas, knowledge, and facts are present in ourselves. Forms, formalisms, and expressions are implied in our outward behaviour. Media-technology (matter and functionality in other things) influences what forms and instances of expressions can be. Expressions show meaning in responses they evoke, in patterns of interactions among ourselves and in our further actions towards other things. Our way of being includes all these things, all present in one reality. With this picture of ourselves in mind, we now are ready to consider what we want from computers, and the possible strategies for getting what we want.

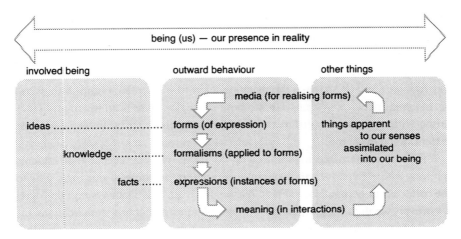

Figure 5.1: *Tentative map of our being*

What computers can do

In the Heideggerian sense, and in keeping with the early Avant-Garde, we can know computers as machines, but not as separately wilful autonomous things. They are things we make, as some kind of expression from ourselves. They reflect aspects of what we are, and we assimilate them into our being. The behaviour we make them show reaches into ourselves, not determined by things 'out there'. We can know machines as materially (physically) distinct, and that implies limitations on what we can make them do. The full implications of all these observations remain obscure. We do not know just what it is we are (despite efforts by philosophers), nor exactly how computers are different, which is why we ought to be cautious about the kind of role we give to them.

Computers are machines built out of micro-electronic technology. For purposes of this discussion we do not need to know what the functions of electronic components within computers are. It is enough to know that the behaviour of computers is determined by mechanistic logic (Ch. 4) which we see as variations of classical logic. This is necessary to keep computers functioning as machines. Again the full implications of this observation are obscure. It does not follow that we can know exactly what mechanistic logic is, nor can we know all it can do.

Strategies for computer systems vary in their treatment of logic, as discussed in Chapter 1 (Figs 1.20–27) and Chapter 3. Some make operations of the machine visible to users, leaving underlying logic invisible, as in programming languages for procedural operations on data. Some try to make logic visible, leaving the associated machine operations invisible, as in logic programming. Others hide both the machine's logic and its operations, and provide users with familiar metaphors for things in the machine, as in object oriented programming. Yet others also hide the machine's logic and its operations, and aim to make the machine learn from its interactions with users, as in neural network systems. In all these strategies there is an assumption that logic within users and (different) logic in a machine can be known (to some extent) to be the same.

This is a plausible assumption in so far as we can accept that logic is present within ourselves and we make computers, so some of our logic gets to be reflected in computers. This is reasonable even if we cannot explain logic. However, we then come up against the problem of explaining demarcations (as we did in the earlier discussion about mind and knowledge). Now our problem is two fold; we cannot explain the demarcation between logic within us and logic we can externalise, and we cannot explain the demarcation between such overt logic and the further informal logic (the real structure and functionality) of material constituents of computers. Such explanations would have to draw on aspects of reality we cannot explain.

In defining a role for computers, we can accept that computers are logical devices and that their logic is linked to logic within us, but we cannot explain the link. We cannot explain any part of computational logic as being the same as any part of our logic. Nor can we explain how our logic might be related to logic in computers. From previous discussions on similarity, in Chapters 1 and 2, we ought to expect their mechanistic logic to be very different from our logic. So we have to define a role for computers in which this lack of explanation does not matter.

As already suggested, we can view computers as media-technology with embedded functionality. We have a long tradition in using media to realise forms of expression, and our use of media influences what our forms can be. We accept that forms made evident in media are meaningless with respect to anything our expressions might be about, and any functionality embedded in media needs to be meaningless in order to allow unlimited potential for meaningful expressions. This qualification is necessary in order to accommodate our lack of explanation for structural and functional relationships between things that are constitutive of media, and ourselves. When we use computers as media, this qualification is necessary to protect us from meanings imposed by unseen persons who program computers.

Computers as machines

Computers are artefacts, machines, which we make to be information technology. As machines, we cannot make them feel and know like us; they cannot know what we mean. We can make them be symbol processors, but cannot make them know they are processing symbols. We can make them show things we see as forms and instances of expressions, but cannot make them know what expressions mean. They are a technology that does not know what information is. These are familiar qualifications to all information technology, going back in time.

Now we have no good reason to think of computers being a fundamentally different kind of technology; they remain information technology in the sense of a realised media-technology. They are machines we use for making and modifying expressions, offering functions which ought not to impinge upon intended meanings in persons. The following examples illustrate some familiar and successful uses of computers as media-technology. None of these presume that computers are more than machines; they do not presume the presence of artificial knowledge or intelligence.

Arithmetic calculators: these first appeared as electronic calculators, and later became generally available in computers. We can note that we have formalisms for arithmetic, which we have represented in machines so that they show numbers changing in accordance with arithmetic. But the machines do not actually have our formalisms for arithmetic; they are given something else so arranged as to show behaviour of arithmetic.

This qualification does not matter as long as patterns of numbers shown by machines continue to conform to arithmetic. We can be reasonably confident that this condition can be met, because we have isolated arithmetic from anything else and made it meaningless. We do not shout numbers into empty space, and expect them to evoke meaningful responses. We use numbers in conjunction with other things, to describe other things, for meaningful interaction among ourselves. So we can use numbers from machines in conjunction with other things outside machines, to stimulate responses from each other.

Text processors: these also first appeared as dedicated machines, as a development of electronic typewriters, and later became generally available in computers. Here the machines deal with a form of expression, ensuring instances remain character-strings. Their functionality helps us to do such things as add or delete characters, insert discontinuities in the form of line and paragraph breaks, and find and overpaste parts of text. We can recall that these things and the operations upon them are parts-of-writing contributing to the form of writing, independently from whatever we might want instances to express. This form, on its own, is meaningless. Therefore we are able to make machines maintain the form without them impinging upon any meaning we intend for expressions.

When text processors include spelling and grammar checkers they begin to infringe the boundary we are trying to set for machines. Spelling checkers are undoubtedly useful, but that would not be the case if the machines were to enforce their spelling on users, and still less so if the machines were to do so unknown to users. What makes spelling checkers useful is that users can see them working, can overrule them, and can make up their own dictionaries in the course of using them. For these machines to be useful, users must have some idea of what spelling is about, and must recognise spelling on the face of the machine.

Grammar checkers are more problematic. That task is more closely linked with language and knowledge within ourselves, and impinges more on the meaningfulness of expressions. Visibility of machines performing checks, and knowing what to do with results, is more difficult. If these checkers become widely used, their effect would be to standardise language; and that effect would not be motivated from within users.

When text processors are upgraded to so-called desk top publishing systems, then extensive further considerations come into play. The emphasis moves to graphical compositions of large bodies of text. This entails formatting pages of text, headings, indents, and footnotes, through to such details as spacing characters within strings, and arranging text irregularly around diagrams and pictures. If you believe the graphical appearance of text contributes to its meaning, its effectiveness in reaching into persons, then you are likely to find yourself arguing with functions embedded (programmed) in the machine.

Drawing machines: these provide another familiar example of mechanised systems which process forms of expression. These systems include formalisms for geometry, to maintain instances in drawings as true to the functionality of a machine. Provided users are familiar with the geometry programmed into the machine, and with the operations it is able to execute on instances, users can use it to construct drawings. The resulting drawings might satisfy users, and editing facilities (as with text processors) are generally provided to enable drawings to be modified. The test of satisfaction then does not take place just between a user and a system, but occurs when the user passes a drawing to other persons; when it becomes an expression in the arena of person-to-person interaction.

Drawing systems pose an awkward difficulty, as compared to text processors. Drawings in general do not show such strong regularities in their form of expression, and variations in instances usually are intended to be rich in meaning. Regularities imposed by a system are likely to be read as meaningful irregularities in terms of expectations and intentions in users; this problem increases as more drawing operations are bundled together and hidden within a system. Those users who depend on drawings as a primary form of expression for interaction with other persons, require fine control over visible machine operations. This is why drawing systems are less widely used than text processors.

All these forms of expression, and media-technology for their realisation, were already present before the arrival of computers. We had mechanical calculators for numbers, typewriters for text, and machines for drawing. These devices came into being not because some particular specialists knew what they had to be. They became mature artefacts in our being, through the efforts of many differently specialised people who became involved in their use in person-to-person interactions. What is noteworthy then is the persistence of these forms of expression throughout past technological developments. This persistence adds credibility to the speculation that counting, writing, and drawing are rooted deeply in ideas within us, not motivated by technology.

With new technology we have the prospect of newly available ways to relate things that appear in expressions, employing computers to maintain logical coherence. We have yet to see whether this will result in radically new and widely used computable forms of expression.

New computable forms

Considering computers as media-technology, what functionality do they offer which might lead to new forms of expression? They offer mechanistic (or computational) logic which we know as a subset of classical two-valued logic, and which enables them to execute logically determinate sequences of operations. Their logic is made available as arrangements of bits and conditions on electronic states which can be programmed, and reprogrammed, without altering their physical mechanics. Computers then can be programmed to show behaviour which is apparent to us as changes to visible things. They can be made to show changing states of numbers, texts, and drawings.

How can this logic be made to extend our already familiar forms of expression? The answer, quite simply, lies in the ability of computers to execute sequences of operations and thereby show dynamic behaviour.

Dynamics can be apparent as distinct steps in making or modifying expressions, and as animation made visible in rapidly changing expressions. Changes to images in space and time can give the appearance of movement, and other transformations can make images appear unlike what they were.

The capacity of computers to hold very many 'memory bits', and to perform operations on them very fast, enables them to show complex behaviour. They can be made to show impressive images which we can see as arrangements of numbers, texts, and drawings, and as other things which lie outside these forms — an example being 'realistic' TV images. By using computers to imitate photo-realism, we have computer graphics and what now is called virtual reality. But now we have a media-technology which also can be used for realistic deception; what separates something we say is deceptive from something true?

Virtual reality: or VR, is heralded as a new form of expression made possible by our use of computers. This is claimed to show things as they really are, or nearly so, and to show imaginary things as though they are real. VR technology invites persons to enter into images, and see and feel and hear them. Earlier (Fig. 1.27) we questioned this realism by asking what is the thing that is a virtual image virtually like? How might we know that the imagery is like the reality of other things 'out there'? Alternatively, should we look upon the imagery like Expressionist paintings, and if not, how do we know that?

The orthodox answer is to say that virtual imagery depicts things 'out there' realistically, so that the images give us the same experience as we would otherwise get from other proposed or already real things — helping us to decide appropriate actions in awkward real situations. This answer indicates strong use of the *real-world* assumption, claiming correspondence between images and depicted things. Acceptance of a separate real reality, and acceptance of specialised (superior?) persons preparing virtual realities for naive users, places most of this work in the orthodox tradition of prescriptive computer systems. And now we have an added twist to prescriptiveness: if virtual reality will do in place of real reality in people's experience, then there will be no need for people to engage in anything real.

As a further qualification, we can add that if VR is a form of expression it is not a form of language expression. At best, orthodox VR presents us with things our language expressions might be about, in place of other real things about which we might interact. Language expressions, however, ordinarily do not embrace what they are about, and by being effective just within ourselves we can use them to talk about anything.

What the idea of VR has done for us is bring to the fore some ancient and really awkward questions about reality, now made urgent by new technology. We also have some old answers which may now gain new currency. An alternative to the real-world assumption has already been outlined in previous chapters. We might say that virtual images reflect reality that is within persons, and images are used by persons to describe what they know to each other. This answer implies a relationship between expressions and the reality of things-of-knowledge within persons, shared across people. Something being virtually real then refers to an expression from reality within persons, about something else; without implying visual semblance, but serving to stimulate responsive behaviour. Virtual imagery understood in this way always is abstract, and nothing tangible is added by calling this imagery realistic. The imagery itself is real and is derived by persons from abstractions they may have for other real things. Here we are moving closer to virtual imagery being like Expressionist paintings.

Now considering the question of deception, or realistic deception, we can call on the notion of complementary truth (Fig. 1.12 and Ch. 5 p. 150). Virtual images being true depends on images being accepted by people already engaged among themselves and further things in reality. It is this already present engagement outside the images which makes them true, or sees them as deceptive. If we are to hold onto truth in this way, in the continually changing circumstances of our collective survival, then we do not want any persons to be immersed just in some prepared virtual reality.

Consistent with what has been said before, the images in virtual reality can be regarded as expressions from within us, and cannot be knowledge. They cannot contain knowledge. The images may reflect knowledge, just as any other expressions do. We might come to look upon virtual imagery just as we look upon the imagery of already familiar forms of expression. The importance of the technology then will not be in its knowing what the images are about, but in its being useful to us when we make images we feel are effective in each other. In any use of information technology, its enabling us to make and modify expressions has value only in interactions among ourselves, not with the technology.

This view of virtual reality presupposes nonsensical functionality in computers, which people can know as making things happen in images, so that these things happening can be used meaningfully in person-to-person interactions. It presupposes some understanding of dynamic multi-dimensional geometry, beyond what most people know today, as well as further as yet unknown logical treatments of images. These treatments would need to become

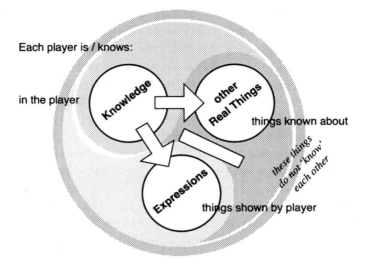

Each player is / knows:

in the player

Knowledge

other Real Things

things known about

these things do not 'know' each other

Expressions

things shown by player

Figure 5.2: *'One-reality' paradigm*

accepted into formalisms by which we (deliberately or spontaneously) show forms of expressions. These formalisms would have to be widely known (without explanation), to be included in language in us. In this way VR might come to be known in us as a form of language expression. How all this might come about remains uncertain, but this kind of evolution is normal in us.

'One-reality' paradigm

All that has been said about making and using computers can now be restated (and summarised) in terms of a *one-reality* paradigm. This paradigm says that all things we know, the world which that constitutes, and the universe beyond, all are equally real — they all exist in a single reality — and this is intuitively quite acceptable. We can acknowledge such existence without committing ourselves to anything else, like how things come to be, why they exist, and what they actually are. We can start by saying that they just are, and that is a sufficient foundation for a firm reality.

We are in the same reality, including our knowledge about ourselves and further things. We know things through our senses, and by means of our inner functionality which we apply to our sensations. We are able to know a lot. But we cannot know all there is to know. If we were other beings with different sensations and inner functionality, we would know other things. Such other things would also be part of the same reality which we now know.

We can know things without explanation. If we think we can explain overtly, in expressions from our knowledge, then our explanations do not have to be overtly logical. The reality in which we exist coheres in one reality, but we do not need to know how it does so, and logical consistency cannot tell us. Logically coherent expressions might reflect part of our ability to know, but only a small and undefined part, and, detached from ourselves, logic cannot touch any reality outside itself.

We can touch reality outside ourselves. Our senses allow us to do so. We can touch and change other real things. There seems little point in denying that when we do so we are in contact with reality. Contention arises over what we can know when we do so, and whether or not whatever it is that separate persons know can be determined to be the same. This contention fundamentally undermines the real-world assumption.

Broadly, we can accept that what we know is conditioned by what we are, our place in reality. The assumption of similarity across persons then tells us that what we know is similar in separate persons. This similarity accommodates differences, but not the fundamental differences that would be present if we were different kinds of beings.

This assumption of similarity supports the notion that we can communicate with each other, and do so effectively, without our having to know explicitly what it is each other knows, and without our having to know any separate actuality of other real things our language expressions are about. It is this notion of knowing similarly but not explicitly which offers us a way out of the real-world assumption.

We use expressions to feel our way into each other's knowledge, without knowing what knowledge is. Sometimes our use of language expressions follows certain rules, to help persons recognise structure in expressions. More often expressions are used evocatively, to stimulate states of mind and evoke responses. Such use draws on sensitivities outside rules, beyond formal logic. Our language expressions make evident our sharing of knowledge, an effective but fragile sharing which depends on continuity of interaction.

The one-reality paradigm sees ourselves as players engaged with each other and further things, Figure 5.2. We can imagine each player as consisting of three parts: things-of-knowledge, expressions, and other real things (and, indeed, other players). The other real things (those unlike us) are presumed not to know what our things-of-knowledge and expressions are. Knowledge (within a player) is sensitive to other real things, and it can touch and change but cannot contain them. Expressions (realised by a player) of their own volition can neither touch nor contain other real things.

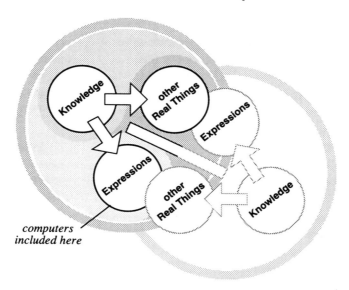

Figure 5.3: *Interaction among players*

Knowledge (deploying a player's sensations and inner functions) can be affected by, and can modify, other things. Expressions reflect knowledge, and refer back to the same or similar knowledge, but cannot modify other things. The game then is for separate players, each with their own knowledge and using their own expressions, to evoke responses from each other so as to satisfy themselves that they are talking about the same real things.

Playing in reality

The one-reality paradigm takes as its key premise a holistic absolute reality; perhaps we can argue about whether it really is absolute, but that would make no difference to this paradigm.

It draws a pragmatic distinction between things within ourselves, our inner reality, and things that appear outside ourselves, the rest of reality — and this distinction does not require an explained and fixed demarcation. Our inner reality is accepted as a sub-set of all reality, equated with our knowledge, and its purpose is to make us show behaviour with high survival value in the rest of reality. We cannot know definitely the boundary of our sub-set of reality, nor can we know definitely any relationship between our sub-set and any further reality. We know these things only as indicated by our senses and included in our knowledge. These conditions apply separately but similarly in each of us.

Our language expressions emanate from things in our inner reality and require interpretation back into such things, so as to access functions within ourselves. They are used to perturb and stimulate knowledge, and evoke responses from within ourselves, to make us exercise beneficial behaviour in touching and changing other things 'out there'.

There are no preordained rules and no external arbiter of the correctness of things we do. Beneficial behaviour becomes evident in the way we continue to exist — our continuing interaction among ourselves and our actions on further real things. Failure is indicated if competition among ourselves and with other things results in destruction of parts of reality, in a manner which threatens to upset the holistic interdependence of all things.

The one-reality paradigm then is a game in which players construct and modify expressions that they find meaningful within themselves, Figure 5.3. This game is played within the players; each sees expressions as real things coming from other players, and tries to make them fit what he or she already knows of other things. It is a game with no start and end states, and no ultimate winners. The object is for players to remain in play. We all are involved in this game.

Imagining that we are looking at these players from 'outside', we can say knowledge is hidden in the players, expressions appear on the surface or as separate things associated with the players, and further real things may be observed separately from the players. These are considered as interlinked elements of the game, which are integral to the existence of the players. The paradigm then says that these elements also exist separately and differently; each does not 'know' what any other might know of him- her- or itself.

Separate players making their own and modifying each others expressions is the way this game is played. Expressions can be anything made by players from other real things they choose to use as expressive media. They make expressions to satisfy themselves, reflecting knowledge currently active in themselves, stimulated by their current engagement with other players and further real things. They then observe responses which their expressions evoke, which appear as further expressions from the players, or as behaviour shown by other things.

Players can recognise this happening by observing each other's expressions and interpreting what they see in terms of what they know and feel in themselves. What this paradigm now tells us is that expressions, irrespective of their form, can be expressions only if they are realised and interpreted through knowledge. Expressions cannot separately touch or be verified by other things outside knowledge. Moreover, they are expressions from and to knowledge

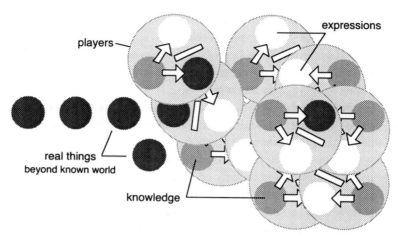

players

expressions

real things
beyond known world

knowledge

Figure 5.4: *Players constituting a world in reality*

which remains hidden in the players. The players we are concerned with here
are persons who have similar knowledge.

Correspondences between expressions and anything else can be known
only within players. Other relationships which may exist in reality can be
known only through players. This condition applies in the same way in all
players, irrespective of their being scientists or artists, industrialists or business
persons.

Staying in play

As the game proceeds, involving many players over a long period of time, it can
be expected that there will emerge a large and fairly stable corpus of
expressions. This corpus can be presumed to reflect current knowledge in and
across the players, with local variations reflecting differences in knowledge in
particular groups and individuals. The stability of the corpus then indicates the
presence of a known world shared by the players, and local variations may
indicate emergent changes in the evolution of this world.

As interactions between players continue, it can be expected that
satisfactory responses will stimulate repeated use of certain expressions. Within
the known bounds of chosen expressive media, regularities will become
established. Forms of expressions will be recognised. Formal equipment for
constructing expressions will be assimilated into the everyday practices of the
players.

Nothing outside these players determines what expressions, their forms,
and associated formal equipment must be. Without knowing explicitly what is

going on in their own knowledge, the players use this game to evolve expressions which satisfy what is called language within them. Their expressions might then reflect feelings and ideas in players about their being-in-the-world, their place in reality.

A corpus of expressions reflects a current state of involvement among players, as known in themselves; it does not represent their knowledge to anyone else outside their involvement. The corpus links the players together, separately satisfying knowledge in each of them. The players can then be considered as sharing knowledge; without anyone else having to verify that separate players have the same actual knowledge.

This shared knowledge effectively constitutes the players' world, including all other things which they have taken into their world (which they know about), Figure 5.4. This knowledge does not need to include what other things actually are, and it accommodates the possibility of further things not known about, in reality.

Expressions which are produced by the players and survive, become other things as seen by the players. They become the focus for subsequent player-to-player interactions. Any corpus of expressions players generate continues to be subject to unforeseen changes.

For their world to be coherent across all players, the expressions appearing in their interactions must be available to all (or most) of the players. These expressions have to appear in a form which players can interpret into their knowledge, and which allows players to show their continuing involvement. Players have to know form, including nonsensical functionality of formal equipment, so as to be involved.

The goal in this paradigm is not properly a goal in the sense of a defined end state. It is for players to satisfy themselves as to the acceptability of what they see before them, as felt within each of them. Their involvement calls on judgement rather than calculation. Consensus then depends on interactions employing expressions to nudge states of knowledge within themselves. They might choose any forms of expression which they think will reach deeply into each other. Their motivation for doing so is to stay in play.

A virtue of this one-reality paradigm is that it leaves the way open for the games of science and of art. It points to a unified understanding of how we know and do things, which accommodates the different ways things are done in science and art, and in material commerce or spiritual religion. This paradigm does not say what ought to be known and done, but says that whatever is known and done is subject to the same functions exercised within ourselves, the same truths.

Evolving technology

The one-reality paradigm gives us a way of looking at any game of interaction among persons, in which things are realised as expressions, including technological artefacts. Things that get realised are possibilities that players uncover in reality, which they show to each other and which shape our world. The particular game we are focusing on here is one in which we devise and use computers as formal equipment for informing ourselves.

In developing computer-technology, we seem to have two distinct ways of looking at what we are about. One way is to focus on the inner functions of computers; uncovering already-present possibilities in the reality of things out of which technologists make computers. Imaginative technologists seek to make as yet unknown functions apparent and controllable, so that they can be seen by other people as computer-behaviour, and thus be realised in our world.

The other way is to look at computer-behaviour in terms of its acceptability and usefulness in persons. In more abstract terms, this implies looking at computational logic as something acceptable to informal logic in persons. This interest is more theoretical and philosophical, prompting diverse responses from variously specialised people. Responses from certain theoreticians seem distinctly odd: insisting that people in general are motivated only by computable logic, waiting to be explained.

The one-reality paradigm accepts specialisations, and sets no limit on what specialisations can be (Fig. 1.5). But specialisations are not things in themselves; nor can specialisations alone know other different specialisations. All specialisation are developed on mind-muscles that are present similarly in ordinary persons, all people. They rest on this similarity. Different specialisations, as in technologist and non-technical people, can reach into each other only by stimulating that which is already similar in separate persons, by touching unspoken similarity.

In the one-reality game no single specialisation can justify a privileged position for itself over others. New developments in the world of all players cannot be prepared by certain specialists (super-humans) working in isolation.

In this game we can expect the evolution of computer-technology to come about just as any technology in our world. The one-reality game includes players who are specialised in their knowledge about computers, but who are otherwise like other players. They use much the same forms and formalisms in language for expressing anything from their knowledge, drawing on similar inner functions for knowing and showing. The game includes other players who may know little about computers, and who are differently specialised in their ways of reaching into reality. These other players are candidate users of new technology, who will determine whether or not it will come to be accepted into their world.

The players who are computer-specialists are specialised in seeing possibilities already-present in the reality of things constitutive of computer-technology. They have their ways of reaching into that reality to make computer-functions apparent to themselves, which they find acceptable within themselves. Making these functions apparent to other players requires computer-specialists to show the effectiveness of what they know, outside their specialisation. They have to engage with other players in interactions outside computing, which draw on their unspoken similarity.

This similarity is what makes it plausible that functions which satisfy these specialists will also come to be recognised by other players. Such wider recognition then depends on how the game continues; with computer-specialists engaging other players in computer-technology, and with other players engaging computer-specialists in their own various other ventures into reality.

Development of new technology occurs through use, and involves all kinds of players. Players who see themselves as makers and those who see themselves as users have to engage in interaction to clarify their shared understanding of computer-technology, or else find reason to reshape the technology. Users, including so called naive users, should want to be involved in determining what new technology has to be, for it to be included in their world.

All players ought to see themselves as engaged in reaching a shared and continuously evolving understanding of computer-functions, and of combinations of functions which they may take to be computational logic. All players can and should be involved in shaping computer-functions into forms and instances of things that come to be recognised as computational forms of expression. This means that all players will have to know enough to enable them to modify the regularities in their use of computers, without endangering the continuing being of computers as operational machines.

We can generalise this position. In the course of using computers we make them do things for us, to make things we recognise as expressions. But in making them do things, users have to retain the ability to undo and redo. Players have to retain the ability to get into computers, to make them do differently. This condition is common to all information technology, pointing to the need for people to be literate in their use of technology to express themselves.

Evolved in this way, new computer-technology may come to be accepted in the world of all players. This can happen without any preconditions on what bits of technology must be, and without preconditions set just by technologists. No technologist can tell us, objectively and definitely, what a computer is. Only through the collective efforts of all players can we expect to develop a notion of what computers can be, and in time computers will become something other than what they presently seem to be.

We now have what might seem to be a formidable picture of a familiar game. The game is familiar in its parallels with ordinary developments of logic and language in us, undertaken spontaneously by us. Familiar developments employ functions in us which we use unknowingly. They are subject to spontaneous self-correcting behaviour among ourselves, prompted by experience. If we were to try to describe how all this works, that description also would be formidable. Yet playing the game is easy.

Summary

This chapter has brought together a number of western perspectives on how we know and do things, leading to a one-reality paradigm for new information technology. We started with Heidegger's philosophy. He gives an account of our involved being-in-the-world based on already-present understanding, manifest in our everyday practices. He argues against knowledge as something separate, self-sufficient, and representational, and sees no need to establish expressions as independently (objectively) true. Science is included in this account, dealing with things not (yet) assimilated into our being. Without undermining the effectiveness of science, Heidegger's philosophy is strongly suggestive of human practices bridging across science and art

We then saw how this philosophy is echoed by the Expressionists. They attached great importance to human involvement, showing themselves in direct and provocative expressions that reached into other people. The Modern Movement which followed became more sophisticated and more rationally articulate, but still saw its actions as emanating from unexplained human involvement. This involvement degenerated in the post-war enthusiasm for pseudo-science, and reliance on depersonalised rules. Post-Modernism then reacted by denying rationality and denying any substance to anything, leading to superficial (tired) aesthetic expressions (transient fashions). These developments all reflect changing attitudes to the central question of how we know things, and how we express what we know.

The discussion moved on to technology seen as persons making artefacts intended for use by other people. Information technology reflects our use of forms and formalisms, and has to be realised in physical matter or media. In developing such technology we have to be aware of things we cannot do, referring to things we might know but cannot explain. Here it was argued we cannot replicate a mind, ideas, knowledge, and facts in a computer. Given these limitations, computers still can be useful and their use can lead to new computable forms of expression.

A *one-reality* paradigm for all human interaction has been introduced, which is suggestive of how we can develop and use computer-technology. This paradigm rests on a holistic understanding of ourselves in our world, amidst all other things in reality — with no one outside telling us what we must know and do. We are the players, we make the rules of the game, and remake rules as the game proceeds. We show our involvement in the game by seeing possibilities in other things, and realising possibilities in our world — realising expressions from our knowledge. Realising expressions entails the use of technology, and devising technology is part of the game.

Consistent with this paradigm, the things we want computers to do are not the same as what is in persons. All people can be involved in identifying functions that are useful to the task of realising expressions; functions which do not pre-empt what expressions must be. The goal for new information technology then ought to be nonsensical functionality that enriches meaningful human interaction.

Holding onto our marbles

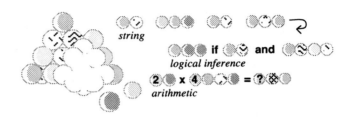

string

logical inference

arithmetic

Being

Let many variegated marbles
be things in ourselves,
our things-of-knowledge
about other things out there.

We then come into being
marbles in already-present patterns,
similarly and separately
in each of us.

We have patterns of understanding,
Plato's ideas:

being...	in reality
unity...	one reality
truth...	in us
good...	well-being
beauty...	awakening.

Ideas in us are real
measuring other real things
bringing them into our world,
our kind of being.

Knowing

We come into being
inwardly knowing,
senses and inner functions
already-present.

Senses deliver sensations
stimulated by other things,
touching our patterns of marbles
in ourselves.

Functions on patterns,
logic in us:

matching...	sameness
quantification...	all/some
inference...	if/then
and more...	*unexplained*

hidden in our being.

Other things are true
if functions fit received sensations
to already-present patterns,
stimulating knowledge.

Showing

We come into being
outwardly apparent,
our mechanisms of behaviour
already-present.

Our behaviour
sensed as other things,
known as patterns of marbles
in each other's knowledge.

Behaviour made visible,
outward actions:
    complementary..   to each other
    touching...   our marbles
    awakening...   patterns
    evoking...   responses
affirming our kind of being.

We show what is true
by behaviour towards others
meaningful in ourselves,
from knowledge in us.

Explanation

Our variegated marbles
do not appear outside ourselves,
these things-of-knowledge
remain hidden in our being.

We cannot show marbles
in our expressions,
we cannot explain
what they are about.

Patterns of ideas,
how we are:
    our being...   reality in us
    our unity...   like beings
    our truth...   knowing
    our good...   continuing to be
    our beauty...   awakening ideas.

We dwell in our ideas
sustained by expressions
maintaining our togetherness,
without explanation.

Expressions

Apparent as outward behaviour
reaching into each other,
realised as things motivated
from within ourselves.

We refine expressions
through use,
develop their effectiveness
in evoking responses.

Expressions formalised,
realised:
    things...   out there
    semblance...   unlike other things
    about...   things-of-knowledge
    coherence...   in ourselves
being true-to-form.

We make expressions
out of media-matter out there
true to form within us,
to do things in ourselves.

Machines

Like other expressions
with inner functionality,
exploited by our inner logic
to do whatever we want.

Possibilities in other things
made available in us,
not knowing what we know
not solving our problems.

Artefactual machines,
a computer:
    sensing...   our expressions
    knowing...   its inner logic
    doing...   our imposed logic
    behaviour... its expressions
serving person-to-person interaction.

To hold onto our marbles
entails being literate
in our use of machines,
to express ourselves.

Conclusions

- *Knowledge*
- *Technology*
- *Information processing*
- *One reality*

Knowledge

At the outset of these deliberations, the words *self* and *ourselves* were used to suggest the idea of a collective *us*, including *our knowledge*. This us includes all that is constitutive of our kind of being, including equipment within ourselves by which we are able to know. This equipment gives us our ability to sense, and to take abstractions from sensations that are acceptable to our further functions for knowing. In this way we are able to take abstractions into knowledge.

We show our equipment being active in our everyday interactions among ourselves, evident in expressions about further things found in our experience. We express our knowledge about other real things, and so know ourselves as being in reality.

This is a human self-centred picture of knowledge resting on equipment which remains within us, unexplained. This is a 'realist' picture in the sense that it accepts the *reality* of things, and it is 'idealist' in the sense that it accepts our knowledge is founded on abilities in us by which we know *about* real things. Knowing about things is not the same as the things known about, but is effective in enabling us to maintain our presence in one coherent reality.

The further notion of there being different realities, and of things being not real, is denied. What can it mean to say something is 'not real'? Some may argue that certain utterances may be not true, implying something said is not resolvable to knowledge in a recipient, and in many people, so that it does not fit their world. However, in the past chapters I have been expounding a view of all peoples' worlds connected in one world in reality, giving us the world of human being. This world includes local worlds known by certain people, with

208

indistinct soft boundaries separating them, and the possibility of differences and conflicts. Saying something said by someone else is not true then becomes a political assertion.

We now have a picture of knowledge which accepts the different ways we imagine we use different kinds of knowledge, as in science, in art, and in more practical everyday commercial and social activities. This picture accepts these kinds as different but without fixed demarcations separating them, and without absolute truths associated with them. So in science we have the reality of knowledge which was expressed in the distant past as the 'flat-earth' model of the physical world, and the reality of knowledge which now is expressed as 'cosmic' models of the universe. We have experienced an evolution of knowledge by which the former was displaced by the latter — with the possibility of future yet unknown displacements.

This is a self-centred picture in which all knowledge is derived from all we are able to know and feel, not limited by logical explanation. Knowledge subjected to formal disciplines is not determined by, nor contained in, such disciplines. Formality cannot tell us 'what is' in other things, other objects, objectively and separately from ourselves. Claims for objectivity in science, expressed as '*it* is...' or '*it* will be...', are not necessary to science. Exploratory formal expressions of the kind 'what happens *if*...', regulated by rigorous formality, can be accepted as the proper stuff of science. That can also be beneficial outside science, with the caution that knowing any 'it' to be anything is subject to ordinary informal feeling and knowing within scientists, just as in non-scientists.

Our dependence on already-present functions for knowing, conditioned by whatever it is we are, opens up the possibility of our sharing knowledge. We share through our use of expressions from knowledge, giving them meaning within ourselves, as in literature, music, and paintings. We give meaning without explanation, and do not (need not, and cannot) externalise what we know. Shared knowledge likewise cannot be shown, but is affirmed and evolves through the continuity of expressions and responses among us.

Dependence of different kinds of knowledge, specialisations, on non-specialised functions for knowing is unavoidable and is beneficial. This is what makes it possible for specialists to interact and share understanding with other different specialists, other individual persons. This is what makes it possible for scientists and artists and other people to know they are in the same world, and recognise each other's contributions to their continuing presence in one reality.

Technology

Technology includes all those things we see as possibilities in other real things 'out there'. We reshape such possibilities into practical things in our world. As well as the more commonly recognised cases of technology, as in engineering and architecture, we include all forms of expressions that are realised apart from ourselves, apart from our direct bodily behaviour (talking, smiling, hitting...). Technology, in this broad sense, includes the texts of literature, copied and reproduced through time, and includes the realisations of music and paintings.

A narrower definition might focus on materials and processes for realising expressions; treating structures and functions separately from content. But finding possibilities in materials, and defining processes, are acts of expression, without fixed demarcations to separate them from further expressions. As acts of expression about possibilities for further expressions, finding materials and defining processes are actions motivated in ourselves, in unexplained ways, like the texts of literature, and like music and paintings.

A further attempt at a narrower definition might focus on determinate mechanistic functions within other things, as in machines. But such functions also are expressions of what we think we can make other things do, imposed on whatever those things really are able to do. We do not know the reality of things we see as machines, as things-in-themselves, but know them as expressions from knowledge in ourselves, like literature and music and paintings.

The temptation to see technology as being governed by laws that are independent from ourselves is deceptive. All technological artefacts are motivated from within us, even when we employ what we think are physical or natural laws. They all serve interactions among ourselves and serve our further actions towards other 'naturally occurring' things. They are artefacts serving as expressions that touch unexplained knowledge in us, and they are effective if we can use them to help us maintain our presence amidst all else. To suggest that technology can do anything else, can know what we know, is to be irresponsible.

For technology to be effective in human interactions it has to be apparent, not hidden from users. This means that technological artefacts have to be available to our senses and must stimulate abstractions in us which we find acceptable and useful in our knowledge. They have to be acceptable to our functions for knowing, not limited by other people's anticipations of what our knowledge must be, or what it must be about. These artefacts have to be apparent as things which are visible and graspable (physically and mentally), to provide a means by which we can touch and interact with each other.

Technology being apparent is necessary because we cannot explain the connection between knowledge in us, and our outward expressions. Attempts to infer knowledge from expressive behaviour, and explain outcomes in logical patterns (in further expressions), reflect specialised knowledge in the observer rather than in those who are observed. We therefore cannot rely on specialised technologists to determine what knowledge is, and build knowledge into technology. Technologists hiding what they think is knowledge from users, and revealing only outcomes they think are true in supposed user-worlds, becomes a strange kind of exploitation without clear winners.

We have here a number of conditions which bear on technology, and we cannot know explicitly whether these conditions are being met. However, we can feel and know inwardly, informally, when they seem to be met, or when they are not met. We feel if the apparent functions of a technology are useful in us, and that feeling should leave us free to use the functions in any way we find effective — a freedom conditioned only by our experience of use.

We commonly engage in technology without explanation; that now is the kind of being we are. Our appreciation of technology comes from feelings that reach deeply into us, more in the way we sense and judge things of art than the way we determine things of science. Technology then impinges on all that is constitutive of our being, and our technological well-being depends on engagement of all people.

We ought willingly to open ourselves to wide-ranging questions and exercise responsibility as we engage in new technological developments. We want artefacts that enhance our world, feel right, are beautiful, and stimulate our sense of being alive.

Information processing

Information technology is not new. We have noted that, throughout our history, people have engaged in technology to inform ourselves and each other — informing informally, inwardly, from things formed outwardly. Informing is something that happens in ourselves, employing our inner functions for feeling and knowing, similarly in similar selves. Things formed outwardly include all technology used to inform ourselves, to impress information on us; such outward things as typewriters and computers in our present time.

The present vogue of new technology sees information not as abstractions in knowledge in ourselves, but as something externalised in technological artefacts, in books and in computers. This vogue is confusing and misleading. We cannot explain information in us, and cannot put it in other things that are not us. We cannot put information into computers:

We can put certain things in computers, by instructing things into them; but that is not information. Data and instructions are expressions from whatever someone knows a computer can be made to do.

We can instruct computers to do things so that they evoke regular responses from many people, invoking similar information in separate persons; but that also is not putting information into computers. This association of artefactual functions with information in us is like any association between mechanical artefacts and us.

We can make computers perform operations on things we call abstractions, as in the case of operations on numbers or symbols; but when computers do that, they do so without information. They do not know what our symbols are about. The things computers operate upon are not our abstractions, but are realised things that appear in our expressions.

Any artefactual functionality can be used to make or do things we find meaningful in ourselves, to stimulate information in us, and so inform our knowledge. What distinguishes computers from other artefacts is not that they can possess and process information. Instead, the distinction comes in the way we are able to make computers show different mechanistic behaviours. Once realised as physical artefacts, we are able to remake them by programming (instead of more physical interventions). This is rather like remaking machines by putting words to them, to tell them what behaviour we want them to show. The same artefact, a computer, might appear to be a text-processor or an arithmetic calculator. This way of controlling machine-behaviour is what marks the emergence of new technology.

The change brought about by programming is not quite so radical as enthusiasts for computers suggest. The task of programming remains obscurely technical, uncertain, and highly specialised. This is because the words and word-combinations used to instruct computers work unlike ordinary language. They have to be prepared with predefined interpretations acceptable to known machine-functions (down successive and invisible layers of programs), and they have to be used consistently, with no connection to anything the words might be about outside a computer. The words used in programming computers are more like buttons for activating mechanical functions (defined by system-programmers), than words used in ordinary human interactions.

The conditions for successful and widely useful technology become more difficult to satisfy. The mechanisms of computers (their micro-electronic components), and the obscure formality of programming, make the functionality of computers less accessible to users. It is difficult to feel and know them.

Many computer-specialists, in order to exploit more of the potential of computers, believe they can model information processes to match or be acceptable to whatever goes on in users (employing the *real-world* assumption). They feel they have to believe this, in order to make more ambitious and useful virtual machines. So we find ourselves engulfed in an ideological move which insists that information can be externalised in artefacts, in books and computers. This ideology insists that artefactual information processors can be made equivalent to our functions for knowing (or behaviourally so), with consequent advantages from 'error-free' consistency, accuracy, and speed-efficiency.

The people who advocate this move are critical of what they describe as yet-to-be-explained and unreliable functions in ourselves, and their ideology threatens to take responsibility out of persons. Their belief is that ordinary human responsibility can be represented correctly and reliably in standards built into formal functions in computers (a mechanised form of bureaucracy). The serious danger we then face is that new technology established through faulty ideology will depersonalise information, and so threaten the further evolution of our kind of being.

There has to be some other way of making new technology useful, which leaves information within ourselves, and which uses computers to support human interaction. This way has to place importance on the functions offered by computers being apparent to users. Being apparent is necessary to enable users to make these machines do, undo, and redo whatever they want, and still keep them functioning as operational machines. This condition is crucial in the case of computers because (unlike most other machines) they are not tools identified with regular and well-understood tasks performed on visible material things. They are intended to be a means for interacting with unseen abstractions in the minds of persons.

One reality

To find this other way, we have to return to basics. Earlier we said that things-of-knowledge we have in mind, things that are expressions from our knowledge, and things our expressions are about all are present in one reality. This reality is elusive, but we show intelligent behaviour as though we know what it is. We reach into reality to uncover possibilities that we make apparent and shape into our world. These possibilities have to be made apparent and acceptable to already-present knowledge in us; that is what possibilities are.

Possibilities have to come from within us and be interpretable by us, connecting with our experience of reality. We can think of possibilities being limited by functions in us, and limited by what can be in reality, but we cannot know what these limits are — because we dwell in our functions, in reality.

We build our world on currently realised possibilities, including such things as motor cars and space vehicles (expressions of spatial mobility). New possibilities make things different from what they were, making past things old, and sometimes that is called progress. Alternatively, we can view our uncovering of new possibilities just as what we have to do to stay in reality; that is our way of showing we are alive.

We can think of aspects of our world being durable, persisting as all else in it changes. But we cannot know what must be durable. We cannot define aspects of our being that are necessary to our continuing presence in reality, separated from other things that are transient. The notion of a world continuing into the future, continuing in time, rests on the notion of us continuing to be us, continuing to play in reality.

The coherence of this world depends on our recognising interdependence among all individuals, all playing in the same reality. Differently specialised individuals have to make their possibilities accessible to other people. All individuals have to call on their unspoken similarity with others, to be in touch, in order to stay in play.

All these conditions apply to information technology, just as to all else we do. To help us ensure these conditions apply to new information technology, we have the *one-reality* paradigm. In this paradigm we accept that the world we know is determined by functions in us, and is sustained by our interactions. It is sustained just by us, all of us, with no one standing apart (no super-human) telling us what must be.

Computers as realised expressions, machines (different other things), coming from technically specialised persons, can be known as realisations of formal equipment for making further expressions. They offer formal functionality which is nonsensical, but which may be assimilated into language in people and used by us to shape expressions from ourselves, to each other. Such formal functionality then will be given meaning in use, in ourselves.

Computers have to be known in this way, not containing human knowledge, for them to be included in our world. Users have to know their functionality, by recognising machine behaviour which implies the presence of mechanistic logic. Users have to know how to employ that logic in their own further expressions, and may come to know it as computational logic. This logic is not yet well understood, but it may in time be accepted just like logic in other realised equipment that is widely used for shaping expressions.

Using computers, getting people to accept them into language within themselves, will not come about as a result of claims that computers offer superior knowledge processes, and artificial intelligence. This development also will not come about as a result of computers doing useful practical things, if such doing presupposes what is real and disengages other persons.

The way forward needs to be much more adventurous and speculative. It needs to accept the legitimacy of unforeseen contributions from any responsibly involved persons; not limited by some supposed fixed base-line for knowledge, or by supposed correspondences to objectively real things. The way forward needs to engage all kinds of people in making nonsensical computational logic acceptable to undefined meaningful logic within themselves, and involve them in making computers show anything from whatever they know.

This engagement of all kinds of people has to be self-motivated, driven by diverse interests in how all things come together — not by a survival-of-the-fittest competition in a crude 'free-market'. Speculations must be encouraged, and allowed to fade gracefully, more in the old Enlightenment tradition of linked science and art. Now we need a new generation of adventurers, a new enlightenment. Just as was done before when people sailed beyond the edge of the known 'flat-earth', we now want to encourage people to venture beyond the edge of the so-called *real-world*.

References and Bibliography

Ben-Dasan I., 1972, *The Japanese and the Jews,* translated by Gage R.L., Weatherhill.

Bernstein J., 1973, *Einstein,* Fontana/Collins.

Bijl A., 1989, Computer Discipline and Design Practice - Shaping Our Future, Edinburgh University Press.

— — 1990, 'Formality in Design: Logic and What Else?', in proc. *Int. Symposium on AI in Engineering,* pp 17-24, as part of the *Pacific Rim Int. Conference on AI'90,* Nagoya, Japan.

— — 1991a, 'Relations, Functions & Constraints Without Prescriptions', in *Intelligent CAD, III – proc. 3rd IFIP 5.2 Workshop* (Osaka, Japan 1989), pp 79-97, Yoshikawa H. and Arbab F. (eds), North-Holland.

— — 1991b, 'On Knowing, Feeling, and Expression', in *CAAD futures '91,* pp 157-176, Schmitt G. (ed), Vieweg.

— — 1993, 'Information Technology: Using Computers', in *Journal of Design Sciences and Technology,* vol 2 no 2 pp 191-257, Zreik K. (ed), Hermes, Paris.

— — 1994, 'What's in a Concept? – Thoughts on Formal Techniques and Usefulness', in *Information Modelling and Knowledge Bases V: Principles and formal techniques,* pp 34-49, Jaakkola H. *et al.* (eds), IOS Press, Amsterdam.

Bijl A., Stone D. and Rosenthal D.S.H., 1979, *Integrated CAAD Systems,* UK Department of the Environment published report.

Björk B-C., 1991, 'Intelligent Front-Ends and Product Models', in *Artificial Intelligence in Engineering,* vol 6 no 1 pp 46-56.

Boden M.A. (ed), 1990, *The Philosophy of Artificial Intelligence,* Oxford University Press.

Brachman R.J., 1979, 'On the Epistemological Status of Semantic Networks', in *Associative Networks: Representation and Use of Knowledge by Computers,* pp 3-50, Findler N.V. (ed), Academic Press.

Capra F., 1983, *The Tao of Physics,* Fontana/Flamingo.

Churchland P.M., 1984, *Matter and Consciousness; A Contemporary Introduction to the Philosophy of Mind,* Bradford Books, MIT.

Codd E.F., 1970, 'A Relational Model of Data for Large Shared Data Banks', *Comms. ACM,* vol 13 no 6.

Coyne R. and Snodgrass A., 1993, 'Rescuing CAD from rationalism', *Design Studies,* vol 14 no 2 pp 100-123, Butterworth-Heinemann.

Dawkins R., 1976, *The Selfish Gene,* Oxford University Press, reprinted in Paladin Books 1978.

Dreyfus H.L., 1979, *What Computers Can't Do: The Limits of Artificial Intelligence,* with introduction to revised edition, Harper Colophon Books, NY.

—— 1991, *Being-in-the-World: A Commentary on Heidegger's Being and Time, Division 1,* MIT Press.

Duval J-L., 1981, *Avant-Garde Art 1914-1939,* Skira Macmillan.

Einstein A. and Infeld L., 1938, *The Evolution of Physics,* Simon and Schuster, NY.

Feynman R.P., 1992, *The Character of Physical Law,* Penguin Books.

Friedman T. and Goldsworthy A. (eds), 1991, *Hand to Earth, Andy Goldsworthy Sculpture 1976-1990,* Many & Son, UK.

Frost R.A., 1986, *Introduction to Knowledge Base Systems,* Pan Books.

Hayes P.J., 1979, 'The Naive Physics Manifesto', in *Expert Systems in the Micro-electronic Age,* pp 242-270, Michie, D. (ed), Edinburgh University Press.

Heriot-Watt Seminar on Visions of Knowledge, 1992, Riccarton campus, Edinburgh.

Hussey M., 1972, *Automatic Computing,* Open University Press.

Interalia 1992, *Order, Chaos and Creativity,* Bright R. (ed) proc. Art and Science Conference, Royal Botanic Garden, Edinburgh.

Jaffé H.L.C., c.1955, *de Stijl 1917-1931: the Dutch contribution to modern art,* Alec Tiranti.

JIPDEC, 1981, *Preliminary Report on Study and Research on Fifth-Generation Computers 1979-1980,* Japan Information Processing Development Centre.

Klee P., 1925, *Pedagogical Sketchbook,* introduction and translation by Sibyl Maholy-Nagy, Faber and Faber.

Kowalski R., 1979, *Logic for Problem Solving,* North-Holland.

Levine D.S., 1991, *Introduction to Neural and Cognitive Modelling,* Lawrence Erlbaum Associates, US.

Magee B., 1987, The Great Philosophers: An Introduction to Western Philosophy, BBC Books.

Mandelbrot B.B., 1983, *The Fractal Geometry of Nature,* W.H. Freeman & Co, NY.

Minsky M., 1975, 'A Framework for Representing Knowledge', in *Psychology of Computer Vision,* pp 211-277, Winston P.H. (ed), MacGraw-Hill, NY.

Mitchell W.J., 1990, *The Logic of Architecture,* MIT Press.

Nilsson J.F. and Palomäki J., 1994, 'Category-theoretical Modelling of Concepts', in proc. *4th Japanese - European Seminar on Information Modelling and Knowledge Bases,* Stockholm, Sweden.

Nitobe I., 1905, *Bushido - The Soul of Japan,* Tuttle (22nd printing) 1990.

Oxman R. and Oxman R., 1991, 'Experiences with CAAD in Education and Practice', in proc. *ECAADE Conference,* Pittioni (ed), Technische Universität München, Germany.

Papadakis A., Cooke C. and Benjamin A. (eds), 1989, *Deconstruction Omnibus Volume,* Academy Editions, London.

Pears D., 1985, *Wittgenstein* (with postscript), Fontana.

Putnam H., 1981, *Reason, Truth and History,* Cambridge University Press.

Rheingold H., 1991, *Virtual Reality,* Secker & Warburg.

Russell B., 1912, *The Problems of Philosophy,* Oxford (9th impression 1980).

RWCP, 1992, *The Master Plan for the Real-World Computing Program,* Feasibility Study Committee of [Japan's] Real-World Computing Program.

Searl S.A., 1984, *Minds, Brains and Science,* Reith Lectures, BBC Publication.

Steiner G., 1978, *Heidegger,* Fontana.

Stiny G., 1975, *Pictorial and Formal Aspects of Shape and Shape Grammars,* Birkhauser Verlag.

Stone R.J., 1992, 'Virtual Reality and Cyberspace: From Science Fiction to Science Fact', in proc. *10th Eurographics UK Conference,* pp 23-42, University of Edinburgh.

Sutherland I.E., 1963, 'Sketchpad — A man machine Graphical Communication System', *Spring Joint Computer Conference Documents,* Spartan Books.

Tweed C. and Bijl A., 1989, 'MOLE: A Reasonable Logic for Design?', in *Intelligent CAD Systems II: Implementation Issues — proc. 2nd Eurographics Workshop* (Veldhoven Netherlands), pp 146-167, ten Hagen P.J.W., Tomiyama T. and Akman V. (eds), Springer-Verlag.

Walsh W.H., 1975, *Kant's Criticism of Metaphysics,* Edinburgh University Press.

Weizenbaum J., 1976, *Computer Power and Human Reason,* Freeman, US.

Whitford F., 1984, *Bauhaus,* Thames Hudson.

— — 1987, *Expressionist Portraits,* Thames Hudson.

Winograd T. and Flores F., 1986, *Understanding Computers and Cognition: A New Foundation for Design,* Ablex Publishing Corporation, New Jersey.

Wittgenstein L., 1921, *Tractatus Logico-Philosophicus,* translated by D.F. Pears & B.F. McGuinnes, Routledge & Kegan Paul, 1961.

— — 1953, *Philosophical Investigations,* translated by Anscombe G.E.M., Blackwell (2nd edition with index 1968).

Wolpert L., 1992, *The Unnatural Nature of Science,* Faber & Faber.

Yoshikawa H., 1990, *Competition from Product to Knowledge,* Tokyo University internal paper (preparation for talk in US).

Zeeman E.C., 1977, *Catastrophy Theory: Selected Papers 1972-77,* Addison-Wesley, Massachusetts.

Index

Numbers in bold indicate pages
with corresponding section headings

abstraction 83, 87, 161, 176, 195
aesthetics 4, 44, 46, 140, 151, 176
aggression 57
agreement 55
AI cultures 108
altruism 93
ambiguity 46, 53
anarchy 52
architecture 37, 96, 176
arithmetic 127, 149, 155, 183
arithmetic calculators **191**
art 88, 137, 158, 174, 211
artificial intelligence 101, **107**
associative links 104
Avant-Garde 166

Bauhaus 176
beauty 48, 129, 150
behaviour 49, 53, 67, 100
being 85, **168**
being amidst 86, 151, 168
being together **50**
being-in-the-world 93, 167
beliefs 45, 52, 62, 86, 94, 146, 151, 213
Ben-Dasen 47
Bernstein 138
Björk 35
blasphemy 55
Boden 88, 109
Brachman 29, 103
breakdown 169
Buddhism 43, 52

calligraphy 63
Capra 166
categorisation 131
chaos 34

Christianity 47, 52
Churchland 109
Codd 31
collaboration 35
commerce 64, 73
commitment 64, 69
common good 48, 52, 93, 176, 178
competition 2, 65, **70**, 150, 199
complementariness 144, 148
complementary behaviour **147**, 150
complementary truth 21, **144**, 151, 176, 195
computable concepts 83, 91
computable forms **193**
computational logic 155, 190, 203, 214
computer aided design 111
computer applications **74**
computer interaction 20, 141
computer programmers 110, 149
computer programming 101, 189, 212
computer science **73**
computer scientists 125, 156
computer-functions 156, 202, 213
computing machines **191**
concepts 19, 80, **82**, 125, 138
concepts & language **137**
concepts formal **84**
concepts human **85**
conceptual space **87**
conflict avoidance 51, 54, 67
conformity 60
Confucianism 43, 47
connectionism 87
consciousness 109, 169
consultation 69
context 53, 164

cooperation **65**
coping 169
corporate behaviour **64**
corporate structure **68**
correctness 62
Coyne & Snodgrass 167
creativity 88
Crowley 122

dance 135
data & processes 95
Dawkins 92, 109
de Stijl 176
degeneration **177**
demarcations 59, 85, 96, 101, 179, 185, 190, 198
description 30, 107, 131
design 95, 111, 176
desk top publishing 192
detachment 13, 84, 125, 134, 170, 182
devising new concepts **90**
difference 42, 90, 151, 178
dimensions of knowing 18, 80, 88
disagreement 67
disengagement 81, 177, 185
dissimilar selves 22, 141
dissimilarity 135, 141, 143
distance learning 82
Dix 158
Dix on Paper 158
drawing machines **192**
Dreyfus 9, 14, 85, 109, 167, 185
Drogemuller 121
Duval 27, 174
dwell in 167, 187, 214
dynamic behaviour 193

eastern philosophy 41
eccentricity 51
effectiveness 125, 139, 152, 175, 182
efficiency 71, 213
Einstein 138
Einstein & Infeld 90

email 116
empty space 43, 48, 58
engagement 12, 80, 184, 211, 215
engineers 116
everyday practices 2, 11, 46, 61, 81, 86, 137, 151, 167
evolution 50, 65, 72, **92**, 109
evolving expressions 26, 201
evolving new logic **153**
evolving technology **202**
existence **38**
experience 60, 137, 144
explanation 48, **58**, 68, 82, 85, 94, 131, 181, 190, 197
exploration 95, 166
expression 16, 53, 59, 89, 102, 152, 163, 175
Expressionism 166, **174**
expressions **133**, 195
expressive objects 183
extensional objects 103

facticity 168, 173
facts 145, 150, 169, 173, **187**
facts & rationalty 146
facts & values 146
fantasy 56
feeling 18, 126, 130
feeling & knowing **125**
Feigenbaum 86, 148
Feynman 9, 129
form **181**
form/function 176
formal methods 97
formalisms 16, 24, 87, 127, 140, 145, **182**
formality 24, **40**, 125
fragmentation 3, 50, 71, 84, 113, 178
frames & scripts 30, 107
free-market 3, 7, 71, 179, 215
Friedman & Goldsworthy 88
Froese 116
Frost 105
functionality 22, 49, 99, 182
games 108

gene-machines 92
Goldsworthy 88
grammar checkers 192
grammars 89, 97
gravity 129
grounding 187

Harra 75
Hartley 158
Hayama 75
Hayes 28
Heidegger 14, 85, 93, 146, **167**, 185
Heriot-Watt Seminar 82
hermeneutics 171
hierarchies 105
holism 43, 59, 62, 86, 164, 175, 198
homogeneity 51
honour 69
Hori 43
Hussey 99

ideas 87, **186**
identity 2, 44, 51
ideology 3, 52, 71, 179, 213
imperialism 100
impossibilties **185**
inconsistency 46
indeterminacy 34, 166
individuality 14, 44, 45, 50, 92, 167,
    174
informal 46, 51
information **8**, 90, 211
information processors 2, 89
information technology 2, 10, 12, **39**,
    81, 184, 191, 211
innovation 65, **72**
integration 83, **112**
intelligence 9, 103, 109, 149
intensional objects 103
intentionality 144, 147, 169
interaction 18, 20, 27, 80, 90, 101,
    140, 162, 181
Interalia 88
interdependence 50, 125, 199, 214
interpretation 20, 106, 140, 171, 174

involvement 73, 91, 131, 151, 169,
    174, 177, 180, 201
IRMA Workshop 116
IT Charter **38**

Jaffé 176
Japan **41**, 87, 131, 146, 168, 173,
    183
Japanese Spirit 52
Judaism 47

kanji 53
kinds 105
Klee 176
know-how 71
knowing 15, 43, 46, 126, 130, **169**,
    173, 187, 197
knowledge 45, 48, 59, 94, 108, 110,
    127, 130, 173, **186**, 199, 208
knowledge & explanation **59**
knowledge & language **131**
knowledge processors 2, 28, 81
Kowalski 32

language 53, 77, 83, 100, 134, 137,
    179, 182
language expressions 11, 139, 199
language games 143
language in Japan **53**
learning 33, **62**
leaving room 48
Levine 33, 87
life 93, 214
linguistic acts 143
linguistic things **133**, 137
literacy 26, 203
logic 42, 47, 58, 73, 99, 109, **151**,
    182, 197
logic formal 23, 46, 92, 98, 151
logic in expressions 155
logic in Japan **42**
logic in language 156
logic in west **45**
logic informal 22, 92, 98, 152
logic notation 154

logic orthodox 152
logic-choppers 52
logic-machines 23, 45, 48, **98**, 108, 153
logic-systems 84
logical behaviour 152
logical connectives 84, 154
Lovelace's objection 99

machine behaviour 147, 202
machine functionality 105, **189**
machines 81, 99, 154, 189
Magee 124
making technology **179**
Malevich 27
management 68
Mandelbrot 34
marbles 206
March 97
market ideology **10**
marks on paper 105, 168, 183
materialism 52, 60, 136
mathematics 127, 129, 149
meaning 17, 27, 104, 155, 170, 181, 183, 190
media-technology 74, **183**, 190
memes 93
meta logic 32
metaphysics 109, 173
methodologies 62
mind 101, 126, 169, **185**
mind-muscles 19, 90, 126
Minsky 30, 105
Mitchell 97
modelling 83
Modern Movement **176**
morals & ethics 55
motivation 43, 81, 89, 99, 147, 153, 210
mystery 60, 87, 89

Nagao 74
names 105
names & compositions 137
nemawashi 67

neural networks 33, 73, 105
Nilsson & Palomäki 24
Nitobe 52
nodes & links 29, 30, 103
nodes as concepts 104
noisy dichotomies 42
nonsense 20, 24, 85, 195
not losing face 49, **54**
NSF Workshop 97
numbers 139

objective knowledge 134
objectivity 15, 45, 125, 134, 142, 151, 174, 177
objects **133**
Ohsuga 43, 47
one reality 213
one-reality paradigm **196**, 214
Open University 82
orthodox IT **28**
Oxman 97

paintings 158
Palladio villas 97
Papadakis 179
people **38**
perceptions & definitions 111
philosophy 4, 124, 167
physical laws 129
physics 129
pictures 27, 83, 150, 188
Platonic ideas 18, 93
players 11, 12, 197
players' involvement 203
players' world 201
playing in reality **198**, 214
politics 2, 44, 45, 184
popular AI **110**
position 47, 53, 68
possibilities 88, 184, 202, 210, 213
Post-Modernism **178**
prediction 108, 112, 114
prescriptiveness 28, 81, 107, 194
privilege 178
problem solvers 2, **95**

problems 95, 97
product modelling 35, 90, 116
products 69
properties & dimensions 137
pseudo-science 177
purpose 92, 182
Putnam 9, 136, 146

Queen Ann houses 97

real things 37, 134, 142
real-world assumption 28, **94**, 110,
    194, 197, 213
realistic deception 195
reality 21, 36, 88, 94, 127, 130, 165,
    172, 196
recognition 72, 181, 203
records-and-pointers 106
reductionism 45, 86, 93, 167
reference 45, 55, 58, 67, 85, 86, 124,
    138, 143, 168, 170, 198
regulation 70
relational tables 31
relativism **135**, 146
religion 44, 45, 136, 150
replication 185
representation 27, 97, 136, **140**, 169,
    175
resolution 45, 67, 81, 99, 126, 208
responsibility 1, 55, 68, 86, 97, 110,
    146, 178, 210
Rheingold 36
Rietveld 37
rote learning 62
rule systems 95
rules 88, 97, 108, 177, 179, 199
Russell 84, 92, 139, 152

science 4, 59, 81, 137, 150, 172, 180,
    211
Scottish Special Housing
    Association 111
self 15, **132**, 136, 208
self-consistency 22, 151
self-regulation 6, 52

semantic networks 29, 103
semantics 17, 103, 154
shape grammars **97**
sharing knowledge 19, 49, **124**, 201
Shintoism 52, 55
silence 55, 60, 67
silicon 86
similarity 14, 44, **49**, 53, 87, 101,
    126, 140
slot/filler systems **105**
social cost 70
society 7, 71
solution-paths 96
solution-spaces 96
space & time 138
specialisation 14, 87, 112, 129, 137,
    180, 202, 209
spelling checkers 192
spiritual matters 60, 136
statistical functions 33
statistical probabilities 34
staying in play **200**
Steiner 167
STEP 119
Stiny 97
Stone 36
strong AI 108
structure 22, 49, 53, 86, 151, 170
subject/object 168, 169
substance 178
Sumo wrestling 56
super-human 48, 55, 86, 144, 214
Sutherland 111
symbolic logic 32
symbols 84, 102
system failure 112
system fragmentation 113
system strategies 189
system users 114

talking to machines **100**
Tarabukin 174
technology 26, 73, 94, **166**, 179, 204,
    210
text processors 191

things **132**
things & relationships 131
things available 169, 173
things extraordinary **171**, 173
things occurent 170, 173
things-in-expressions 156
things-in-themselves 142
things-of-knowledge **133**, 144
Tinker Toys 106
togetherness **47**, 50, 64, 72
Tolman 118
tools 1, 82, 110, 183
true-to-form 23, 140, 145, 182
truth 21, 44, 45, **143**
truth-functions 84, 154
Tweed 107

uncertainty 129
understanding 43, 168
universe of things 131
usefulness 1, 25, 94, 131, 134, 155, 180
user-friendly 13
using computers 1, 25

vandalism 51, 178
violence **56**
virtual imagery 194
virtual reality 36, **194**

Walsh 124
way of knowing **15**
Whitford 175, 176
Winograd & Floris 167
Wittgenstein 9, 20, 84, 87, 92, 152
Wolpert 90
work practices 65
Wright houses 97
writing 158

yes & no **80**
Yoshikawa 71

Zeeman 34
Zen 47, 58

3-D constructions 106
5th-Generation' project 73